Biology of Human A

D0427508

The Biology of Human Action

VERNON REYNOLDS

UNIVERSITY OF OXFORD

W. H. Freeman and Company
SAN FRANCISCO

Library of Congress Cataloging in Publication Data

REYNOLDS, VERNON.
  The biology of human action.

  Bibliography: p.
  Includes index.
  1. Psychobiology. 2. Human behavior. I. Title
[DNLM: 1. Behavior. 2. Genetics, Behavioral.
3. Physiology. QH457 R465b]
QP360.R47 1976   155.2'34   76-3459
ISBN 0-7167-0495-1
ISBN 0-7167-0494-3 pbk.

Printed in the United States of America

9 8 7 6 5 4 3 2 1

To Jane and Jake

Preface

AT THE 11th Ethology Conference in Rennes in 1969, Konrad Lorenz delivered a paper on the 'generation gap', looking at it in a highly biological way.† With me at that conference were two sociology students working with Dr. W. M. S. Russell, Martin and Hilary Waterhouse; all three of us were interested in ethology and had done ethological research on primates. We had been very much involved in the whole biology–sociology debate, working inside sociology departments and yet having a biological orientation as students of primate behaviour. I had written two papers, in 1966 and 1968, using a biological frame of reference for the understanding of human behaviour and society. But taken to the extremes to which Lorenz was now taking biological arguments, we felt the time had come to try and define the extent to which inferences could be sensibly drawn about human 'behaviour' (or preferably 'action') on the basis of man's undoubted evolutionary ancestry. We had listened to Lorenz's lecture, and we felt that the 'generation gap' wasn't an ethological or biological problem so much as a historical, social one. But how did the two kinds of explanation connect? This book is about the ideas that are relevant to a meaningful discussion and ultimate resolution of that *kind* of problem.

This book is the work of an anthropologist, albeit one who does not believe in epistomological 'boundaries' in the quest for understanding. I do not apologize for 'trespassing', for I do not accept the idea of that. But I am aware of the fact that others—geneticists, physiologists, psychologists and sociologists among them—all have their special competences. I hope and believe they will take this book in the spirit of synthesis in which it is written and forgive me where I am lacking in their special expertise. To undergraduates and others interested in the human sciences may I express the hope that the book will provide useful material for their needs. They, more than anyone, will be able to judge whether it tackles the central issue— the relation between biology, psychology and sociology—fairly, i.e.

---

†This, or a very similar paper, was subsequently published in Nobel Symposium 14, 1970, and arguments derived from it are present in Lorenz's book, *Civilised Man's Eight Deadly Sins*. The crucial steps in Lorenz's argument are given in quotation form in Appendix 1 (p. 238).

without slanting the arguments in favour of one or the other but presenting all sides of the debate and looking for a synthesis.

What is new in the book? Let me say first what is *not* new—this is not a book of hitherto unpublished research findings. What *is* new, I believe, is the bringing together between one pair of covers of a series of arguments and bodies of data relevant to the description and understanding of human action. At times I have had to set these out simply side by side, but wherever possible they have been contrasted and compared, argued against each other, and hopefully to some extent fitted together. The result is imperfect and readers will be able to judge for themselves just how much question-begging and issue-dodging has gone on. Looking back (for one always writes one's Preface last!) the central pillars of the synthesis here attempted are, first, the physiological 'running' of the individual human organism; second, the coherence of the system of ideas he or she maintains; and third, the surrounding cultural and normative matrix. These three are intimately linked together, but the nature of the links has only just begun to be investigated scientifically. The reader in search of easy answers will be disappointed: the field is baffling in its complexity; as author of the book I promise nothing except, hopefully, a more acute awareness of the issues involved in trying to explain human action, and a series of pointers to the lines of research that seem to be most promising at the present time.

A last word. It has not been possible to encompass an ecological dimension here; it would have been foolish to try. Surrounding all that is in these pages is the wider problem of man's relation to the environmental resources he needs to survive. One cannot do everything, but I stress that I have not looked at human ecology simply because there was so much to do already. It is, however, necessary to hold that perspective in mind because in the ensuing pages man is presented as a creature who has in many ways freed himself from certain internal constraints by coming to inhabit the world of knowledge. I should not like it to be thought that this has enabled him to be free of external constraints; the reverse is the case. The subject of this book, however, limits itself to man's inner dimension, to the explanation of human action, about which very little is truly known.

Oxford 1976   V. R.

Acknowledgements

MANY PEOPLE have helped in the preparation of this book, and I can name but a few of them. Among the unnamed are those undergraduate and graduate students at Bristol and later at Oxford Universities who have patiently heard me out and then argued with me—often an unrewarding process for them but rewarding for me! Among my colleagues and friends at Bristol University I should like to thank Michael Banton, Ian Hamnett, William Watts-Miller, Robert Reiner, Theo Nicholls and all the others for their helpful ideas in early discussions of the relationship between sociology and biology. To Michael Chance I owe my introduction to primate ethology and I must thank him for his patience with an argumentative student. To him also I owe my introduction to W. M. S. Russell, who has never failed, in countless discussions, to jog me out of my accustomed patterns of thought. At Oxford I have an immediate debt to Geoffrey Harrison, Anthony Boyce, Dougal Jeffries, Robert Attenborough, Alan Rosen, Rom Harré, Michael Cullen, Kenneth Kirkwood, Michael Argyle and Rodney Needham, many of whom have read and commented on parts of the book, or in some cases the whole of it. Thanks also to Professor J. M. Tanner for his comments on Chapter 7. In addition I should like to thank Christopher Stringer, Peter Smith, Robert Drewett and John Gillman for many useful suggestions. Last but not least, the typing, most of which was done by Grace Pickford and Sue Perry; my thanks to both of them for their splendid help as also to Gillian Naish for her help with the index.

Grateful acknowledgement is made to the following for permission to use illustrative material: *Scientific American* (Figs. 3.1, 4.4, 7.8, 10.4); Eyre Methuen Ltd. (3.2, 10.1, 10.2, 10.3); Cambridge University Press (4.3); Oxford University Press (6.1); Prentice-Hall, Inc. (6.2, 6.3, 8.1, 8.2); British Museum of Natural History (6.4); Blackwell Scientific Publications Ltd. (7.1, 7.2, 7.3, 7.4, 7.6, 7.9, 7.10, 7.11, 7.12, 7.13, 7.14, 7.15); Taylor and Francis Ltd. (7.5); Plenum Press, Inc. (9.1, 9.2); Pergamon Press Ltd. (9.3, 9.4); Weidenfeld and Nicolson Ltd. (9.5, 9.6, 9.7); *Zeitschrift für experimentelle und angewandte psychologie* (10.5); American Elsevier Publishing Co. Inc. (15.1); Hemisphere Publishing Co. Inc. (15.2).

Grateful acknowledgement is made to the following for permission to use quotations: Hogarth Press Ltd.; Academic Press, Inc. (London) Ltd.; Cambridge University Press; American Association for the Advancement of Science; *New Left Review*; Wiley Interscience; Free Press, Ltd.; Eyre Methuen Ltd.

Contents

Introduction

MAN IS the product of millions of years of slow evolution, and yet at the same time he is a product of the society in which he lives. When we try to understand ourselves ought we to seek for answers in the selection pressures that have slowly moulded us during the 99 per cent of our existence as hunter–gatherers on the plains, or ought we to seek for answers in the history of our particular culture, its dominant values and ideas? If both, how should we relate the two to each other?

If it is a mistake to try and understand man and his society without taking into account his evolutionary past and his relationship with other species, then what does this mean for the view that man's nature is not 'animal' but 'cultural'; that because of his mind, his unique abilities to conceptualize and symbolize, he can and does continually reconstruct both his society and himself? What is the force of the argument that it is not only foolish but wrong and in bad faith to suggest that man is subject to biological constraints, because this just acts as a bit of reactionary ideology, standing against change for the better?

Human nature, according to some writers, is not separate from the social scene but a part of it, interacting with institutions on a two-way feed-back basis, so that our whole personality is as malleable as the social forms themselves. But to others there are limits to the plasticity of the social forms, and these limits are set by the 'wiring' or the 'programme', the behavioural tendencies within the individual, inherited from bygone times.

The first part of this book seeks to show explicitly what it is that is deficient in theories of human social action† that try to account for it in terms derived from the study of animal behaviour. The second part tries to set out a speculative evolutionary perspective that enables us to see the emergence from animal beginnings of a new kind of creature—one who came to construct his social world, himself and therefore his whole way of life and thought. Part III seeks to describe our physical development, drawing from studies in human biology, psychology and physiology. The thesis is de-

† For meaning of the term 'action' see **Box 1** below.

veloped that it is in the study of the *physiological* mechanisms of the body that there exist the clearest links between biological, psychological and sociological processes. Attention is drawn to some of the psychosomatic endocrinological finds of the last few years in which one can discern some newly emerging points of synthesis for a biology of human action. Part IV examines the processes of development from the behaviour of infants to the actions of children and adults. We look at psychological and observational studies that either focus on infants, or take fully into account the structure of knowledge people come to carry in their heads. It is this structure that forms the framework within which and by means of which people interact, and see the world and themselves. The final part of the book draws upon a number of relevant areas in social psychology and sociology in order to place the biological data of earlier sections within the socio-cultural context of our own society.

It is concluded that in the investigation of human action we need to see man as a biological self-constructor whose well-being depends on his personal integration in a world of ideas. This contradicts the view that both man and his society are the products of inner genetic programming, and also to some extent the psychoanalytic view that man is the product of inner psychic forces that are manipulated by the twin processes of repression and liberation. It complements the view of man expressed by authors such as Tinbergen (1972), Harrison (1973), Pringle (1972), Boyden (1970) and others who see modern urbanized man as caught up in an anthropogenic world that is subjecting him to various new stresses and strains. The question they ask is whether man has the adjustability to cope with his new cultural environment—not just with its tangible aspects such as pollution, but with the less tangible but no less real changes in relationships, patterns of child rearing, pressures of formal educational instruction, competitiveness, crowding, anonymity. The question is reducible to three monosyllables: can man cope? In Tinbergen's words: 'are there signs that this new situation imposes demands on "human nature" that exceed the limits of its phenotypic adjustability?'

The re-formulation of this kind of question proposed in this book arises from the fact that, to a great extent, man makes his own nature as he goes along. Perhaps Sartre goes rather far when he denies that there is any such thing as 'human nature'. It is a matter, at least in part, of definition. But it *is* true that man constructs himself as a social being.

The advantage of seeing that man constructs his own society is that if we can establish how the society he has made, and continues to make, affects the mental and physical health of the various sectors of its population, we can put ourselves in a position to do something to improve it. At present we are still very ignorant, very much the victims of forces that, though we have ourselves made them, we are now almost powerless to control. We do not understand the nature of these forces, nor how they affect us. We blindly follow an ideology of 'progress' inherited from the last century, we pin our faith on technology, on 'success', and yet for many people the result is a personal disaster, and even for the conventionally successful, their triumphs come to have a hollow ring. To move forward we need to understand ourselves better in relation to the prevailing forces of our society. Such an understanding would at least put us in a position to think our way towards a better future, to plan, not just for greater national affluence, but also for greater personal well-being.

The questions to which this book addresses itself are thus: what is known of the physical and mental properties of man? How variable are we as individuals? How do we develop as physical and mental beings? What is known of the relation between our physical nature and the prevailing social context? And finally, given what we know already, what directions should future research take in order to improve the quality of human health and well-being?

Box 1

'Behaviour' and *'action'*

The distinction between *behaviour* and *action* is of central importance to the arguments throughout this book, to the distinction between the activities of animals and those of men, and to the understanding of the relationship between biology and sociology.

The distinction was very clearly expressed by Max Weber (1864–1920) in his *Wirtschaft und Gesellschaft* (Weber 1947).

The main terms at stake are 'Verhalten' (behaviour), 'Handeln' (action) and 'Sinn' (meaning). If we describe what people or animals do, without inquiring into their subjective reasons for doing it, we are talking about their *behaviour*. If we study the subjective aspects of what they do, the reasons and ideas underlying and guiding it, then we are concerned with the world of *meaning*. If we concern ourselves both with what people are, overtly and objectively, seen to do (or not do) and their reasons for so doing (or not doing) which relate to the world of meaning and understanding, we then describe *action*. The reader is referred to Appendix 2 (p. 242) for a series of quotations exemplifying Weber's use of these terms.

An excellent discussion of the concepts and problems involved is to be found in the first chapter of R. Harré and P. F. Secord's *The Explanation of Social Behaviour* (Blackwell, Oxford, 1972).

PART I

Biological determinism
and human action

Introduction to Part I

In this part of the book an effort has been made not to summarize but to pick out the main threads of the arguments of a number of writers who, over the last fifteen years, have made systematic attempts to derive an understanding of human life, human behaviour, and what it is to be human, from the study of human evolution, non-human species, and other biological perspectives. In all cases the authors discussed have accepted a pre-eminence of biological factors as causal agents underlying cultural patterns. This position is examined critically.

This part of the book is not intended to be wholly negative but on the contrary to lay a basis of detailed thought about all sorts of possible explanations of the causal connections between evolutionary forces and human action. It is against this background that the further arguments presented in later parts are to be understood.

CHAPTER 1

Society and the neo-biologists

THE 1960s SAW an upsurge of biological thinking about man and his social life, in the work of a number of ethologists, notably Konrad Lorenz. There was, we were told, a basic biological individual, man; he was compounded of the same sort of ingredients as other forms of life: drives, behavioural tendencies and so on. Mind was essentially a 'rationalizing' organ, giving meaning (in Weber's sense) to what was essentially a meaningless biological existence. Society and its institutions were not so much the cause of as the outcome of interactions between individuals. Sociology had made the mistake of putting the cart before the horse: we should not look, as for example, Marx, Weber or Durkheim did, to the history of our ideas and institutions for explanation of the here and now, but to sex, aggression, territoriality, pair bonding or other evolved social bonds for the real mainsprings of human action.

Such explanations are very much post-Freudian, even though Freud's conception of the structure of the individual in terms of id, ego and super-ego is generally rejected by ethologists in favour of their own formulations based on empirical research with animals. What is post-Freudian is the very conception of the human individual as a biological entity, as opposed to a wholly cultural one. While Weber was telling us that the tendency to save money, to hoard capital, was an outcome of Protestant asceticism, Freud said it was an outcome of faeces retention during infancy; the two views cannot be easily reconciled!

In this chapter I want to look at the work of the three authors of the sixties who can, without reservation, be called 'neo-biologists' of man: Ardrey, Lorenz and Morris. They stand at a point in the history of ideas which seems to me to represent something of an extreme biological watershed. Before them come writers such as Julian Huxley (1943), C. H. Waddington (1960) and Teilhard de Chardin (1959), with their preoccupations with the utility of biological thinking in the quest for an ethic. All argued in their various ways that biology can and does provide an ethic, in terms of a definition of good based on the enhancement of the quality of life for individuals. But in the sixties the word 'ethic' had an antiquarian ring about it. Instead of focusing on what *ought* to happen, we gave up the struggle and decided instead to concentrate on what actually *did* happen. Ardrey, Lorenz and Morris concentrate their attention on the here and now, to explain the situation that exists to find a theory that can do this; and the theory they find is orthodox Darwinism.†

Robert Ardrey's first book, *African Genesis* (1961), subtitled 'A personal investigation into the animal origins and nature of man', marked a new departure in the literature on human life; it walked like a biological ogre through the little world of man, crushing whole cities of metaphysical and theological theory, unheeding of any storms of sociological or philosophical opposition, unregarding of literature, art, music, humour, conversation, religious commitment, political commitment and ideology. The book was concerned with demonstrating, or perhaps one should say preaching, that man's view of himself in previous centuries had lacked a sure foundation, and that the foundations had now, in the twentieth century, been laid. There were two foundation stones in Ardrey's scheme— first, the facts of human evolution, by now (in Ardrey's view) well documented with fossil evidence, and secondly, comparative ethology, which also possesses a good many studies of the social life of non-human species.

Man the killer

What fascinated Ardrey most about human evolution was the stage immediately preceding *Homo*, when the ancestral form *Australopithecus* was living as the first hunting primate on the plains of eastern and southern Africa. We know that *Australopithecus* was a predator, that he scavenged and probably killed baboons and a number of other species of game for food, and that he used weapons to do so. Whether he killed members of his own species is an open question. But it seems quite probable that he *was* a killer, perhaps only occasionally, and perhaps concentrating on the younger and more helpless members of other species, and on small animals (Isaac 1970).

†The kind of theories I am discussing in this part of the book are sometimes called 'strong' theories in human ethology. Such theories can be criticized because (a) they extrapolate too readily from one species to another, (b) they use functional analogies as though they were homologies, (c) they stress biological rather than ideational factors as determinants of action. What may be called 'weak' theories, by contrast, stress (a) the probabilistic nature of human responses, and (b) the inevitable conjunction of response tendencies and learned components. 'Weak' theories, which have far more to commend them than 'strong' ones, are discussed in Part IV.

From the idea that this, our immediate ancestor, may have been selected for his killing prowess over several million years, Ardrey deduced that there had come into existence, in man, a 'killing imperative'. This, for Ardrey, was the one central fact about human nature: it embodied an obsession with weapons, a definite instinctive ability and even a necessity to kill. This instinct in due course was overlaid, when the hominid brain expanded to more than twice its Australopithecine size, by cognitive control mechanisms, but 'we cannot expect too much from the human capacity to reason, since its most elaborate energy is channelled as a rule into self-delusion'.

As for developments other than reason that went with larger brains, the only one Ardrey stresses is what he calls 'conscience', which is 'an essentially antirational power'. This is in part the case because conscience is always harnessed to the maintenance and survival of the group; it thus becomes an act of conscience to prevent any harm coming to members of one's own group but to hate and if need be to kill members of other groups. Conscience, in Ardrey's view, is an outcome of territoriality, which forms the subject of his second book (Ardrey 1966). His evidence for the development of territoriality in evolving hunting man is derived largely from Carpenter's studies of the behaviour of gibbons (Carpenter 1940), and gibbons are indeed, as a recent re-study by Ellefson (1968) has shown, territorial in the strict sense of the word. Gibbons live in small groups which defend an area of forest against all other gibbon groups, by ritualized vocal 'battles' and by actual fighting at times. But in this they are, as we know from a large number of field studies of various primate species, very unusual, for most primates recognize 'ranges' but do not defend 'territories'; they often share some or all of their foraging grounds with other groups of the same species, and may meet with and mix with members of other groups from time to time without hostility.

If we now examine Ardrey's thesis in the light of the available evidence, his view of our ancestors, evolving as killer-apes in tight-knit, closed groups, cannot be upheld. They were predators, but it does not follow that they killed their own kind and there is *no* evidence to indicate *conclusively* that this ever happened (for a full discussion see Roper (1969)). At the present time, chimpanzees are known to predate occasionally on a variety of other species in some areas of their range, but cases of 'cannibalism' are extremely rare (Teleki 1973). As for their group size and territorial habits, the available comparative evidence from our 'nearest relatives', the chimpanzees and gorillas, indicates that our earliest ancestors before the Australopithecine stage may have been largely non-territorial and perhaps did not live in closed groups (although this is necessarily a speculative matter and alternative arguments exist, in particular those that stress ecological factors in the determination of social organization and base their speculations on baboons and macaques). Some kind of 'open group' adaptation would seem, however, to have many advantages, not possessed by a gibbon- or baboon-like closed system, for a large primate subsisting on a hunting and gathering economy, in particular the advantage of greater flexibility in times of crisis. Arguably, *Australopithecus* lived in this sort of way and never was in closed, mutually antagonistic groups, so that his predatory way of life was not linked to territoriality and built-in out-group antagonisms and he rarely, while a hunter–gatherer, needed to be hostile to his neighbours. Frequent hostility between groups is much more likely to be a recent cultural innovation, resulting from the settled economy of agriculture, from pastoralism, and from property ownership, which made defence of territory more necessary than ever before. (For a fuller exposition of the arguments see Reynolds (1966).)

Human aggression

Much the same can be said of Konrad Lorenz's *On Aggression* (1966), for Lorenz uses a model of our ancestors strikingly similar to Ardrey's, displaying an amazing unawareness of the findings of palaeontology and social anthropology. Lorenz is, *par excellence*, a biologist of animal behaviour and is recognized as one of the founding fathers of ethology. He is strongest on fish and birds, weaker on mammals, and, it seems, weakest of all on man.

Lorenz begins his analysis in the sea, with a study of fish living on a coral reef near the Florida coastline. Here he finds that some brightly coloured fish are highly aggressive to other members of their own species, and demonstrates how this leads to a spacing out of members of the species so that the food supply is not exhausted. Aggression is thus seen to be 'good' for species: it keeps them alive, and without it they would quickly eat themselves into extinction. This aggressive force, or drive, or instinct, is Lorenz's starting point for the analysis of behaviour, which he argues is spontaneous, not the outcome of environmental stimulation. An individual male of a given species will begin to show aggressive behaviour and to direct it against appropriate objects at a certain point in his maturation. Man is such a species.

In claiming spontaneity for the aggressive drive, Lorenz meets much opposition, especially from some ethologists such as Hinde (1972) and from one school of psychologists who argue that aggres-

sion is the outcome of frustration, an argument which has been integrated into a human biological framework by the Russells (1968).

A further interesting part of Lorenz's analysis is his treatment of
the relation between aggression and love. Ardrey saw love or amity
between fellows as the inevitable concomitant of out-group hostility;
Lorenz takes a more intimate view, probing into the motivational
structure of individual relationships on the basis of his studies of
birds, in particular geese. He suggests that aggression is not just an
out-group phenomenon but is a feature of every relationship within
the group, for all relationships start on an aggressive basis. The
aggression leads to appeasement which becomes ritualized, and this
is the basis of the love bond. He argues that there cannot be love
without hostility because love is constructed out of the forces of hostility.

Whether this view of human relations can really be upheld is
highly debatable. One wishes that Lorenz's knowledge about primates were greater. In those species of monkeys and apes for which
we have enough data, we know that one of the primary forms of
positive attachment is mother–infant attachment, which in the wild
lacks aggressive elements. Besides this there is brother–sister
attachment and other kinds of kinship attachment, and also there
is male–youngster attachment, attachment between adult males and
other adult males, and between one mother and another. Finally,
there is the heterosexual attachment between adults. In chimpanzees, to take but one example, there seems no evidence to indicate
that any of these bonds is based on appeased aggression. Indeed,
one of the main problems encountered by 'bird-and-fish' ethologists
when they come to the study of the higher mammals is that their
own traditional body of theory is barely adequate for the task. This
is true for the study of many mammalian species and especially for
primates. It seems there may be a much more complex neural network underlying behaviour in mammals than there is in birds and
fish, so that even without taking into account those peculiarities such
as self-awareness that are unique to man, one still has problems in
accounting for mammalian behaviour on an ethological model with
clear-cut 'drives', 'ritualized appeasements', and so on. For Lorenz
to jump from goose to man thus seems wholly unacceptable; it would
not have worked if he had jumped only from goose to monkey. In
any event, the whole business of extrapolating from one species to
another is highly speculative. Comparison is one thing; extrapola-
tion another.

On the place of reason in the human schema, Lorenz agrees with
Ardrey. He writes that 'human social behaviour, far from being de-

termined by reason and cultural tradition alone, is still subject to all the laws prevailing in all phylogenetically adapted instinctive behaviour'. That is, he accepts that humans have the faculty of reason but also accepts that they behave unreasonably. As for morality, like Ardrey he sees it as a naturally developed social instinct underlying the cohesion of the in-group, and committed to vilifying all enemies and strangers.

Regarding human warfare, Lorenz has two main points. The first is that it is easy for politicians to work up the aggressiveness of human populations, especially among young people, because the young, particularly during adolescence, have a surplus of aggressive energy and they will harness this energy to a cause. 'If [writes Lorenz] the clever demagogue gets hold of young people at the susceptible age, he finds it easy to guide their object-fixation in a direction subservient to his political aims.' Here he seems to be thinking back to the Hitler youth movement, but he recently gave the lecture referred to in the Preface deploring the languid idleness of contemporary adolescents, so it looks as if instincts are not so strong in modern Germany as they were a generation ago.

Lorenz's second point about war is that modern techniques and weapons have made killing a non-emotional affair, in the sense that there is no emotional commitment involved in pressing a button inside an aeroplane, or shooting a shell fifteen miles from the target, or even of shooting a man who is half a mile away. We cannot see the effects of our actions and so the natural inhibitions that prevent other species from harming their own kind, and that would prevent man too, cannot operate. This has led to the situation where without emotional involvement, a handful of men have the power to destroy most or all of humanity, and 'only thus can it be explained that perfectly good-natured men, who would not even smack a naughty child, proved to be perfectly able to release rockets or to lay carpets of incendiary bombs on sleeping cities, thereby committing hundreds and thousands of children to a horrible death in the flames'. He offers no solution to this problem of non-involvement, but we need to ask whether his assertion that men could not act this way if they could observe the results is acceptable. Events in Vietnam (e.g. at My Lai), and the activities of the Nazis, as well as systematic purges and ravages in bygone times such as those of the Viking Norsemen under King Harald, seem to indicate that human cultures or sub-cultures can become obsessed with violence which becomes normatively sanctioned and spares not a thought for the sex and age of the victims, only for the social category they fall into. Such events make it seem improbable that any natural inhibition on face-to-face killing that may exist cannot be overlaid by cultural exhortations, in other words that the latter are stronger than the former, which is what Lorenz seeks to deny.

The human animal

Some years passed before another book appeared in the biological vein, and then the world was amused, intrigued, and not a little shocked by the revelations about our inmost selves made to us by Desmond Morris in his first book about man, *The Naked Ape* (1967), subtitled 'A zoologist's study of the human animal'. This book seems to me to suffer from far fewer defects than the two discussed above. Being 'a zoologist's study', it sheds what light zoology can on human activity without regarding alternative explanations as necessarily wrong.

Morris begins his analysis by asserting that 'in becoming so erudite, *Homo sapiens* has remained a naked ape nevertheless; in acquiring lofty new motives, he has lost none of the old earthy ones'. These 'old earthy' motives are systematically treated in the following chapters: sex, rearing, exploration, fighting, feeding and comfort. We are presented with a view of a certain kind of animal, with certain kinds of attributes, physiological and behavioural. The 'lofty new motives' are, by and large, not discussed, and one is left assuming that they are not susceptible to valid zoological analysis, which I believe is indeed the case.

Most people will be familiar with the general contents of the book, but I will mention some of the main points and some of the anomalies. One anomaly comes right at the start, when the reader is almost thrown off his chair by Morris's assertion that his book will be concerned with people in advanced Western societies only, because these are the 'successful' ones, primitive peoples having been, in one way or another, side-tracked into blind alleys. This amazing statement could easily have come straight out of nineteenth-century social evolutionary thought and is best forgotten; in fact Morris himself demolishes it when he later writes how Western man may, one day, blow himself to bits, leaving the few remaining primitive tribes to carry along the torch of human enlightenment.

With regard to human origins, Morris has a much more sophisticated view than Lorenz of the ecological context early man had to face on the savannas, and a less killing-oriented view than Ardrey's. He introduces the concept of neoteny, or prolonged infancy, seeing as a behavioural correlate of this that man has remained an exploratory creature right into adult life. He also emphasizes the 'pair bond'—the tendency for a human male and a human female to form an emotionally intense relationship with a greater or lesser degree of permanence—as a new feature in human evolution. This idea has caused widespread argument and confusion, and is perhaps best left alone until our knowledge of human development is much more complete than at present.

Morris's chapter on sex is perhaps one of the more widely read pieces of writing on the subject the sixties produced. Based on North American data, it does nothing more than describe human hetero-sexual activity, about which, it seems, people were inordinately curious as late as 1967, despite having lived in the 'permissive society' for a number of years. Perhaps what they had been deprived of was an evolutionary dimension to their activities. Morris attributes to many features of sexual behaviour a function back in our evolu-tionary past. Our nakedness and our heightened sensuality, our ear-lobes and mucous lips, breasts, buttocks and scented armpits, are all seen as evolutionary developments geared to the development of the pair bond and the need for long-lasting mateships to ensure the adequate rearing of our increasingly neotenous offspring during the Pleistocene epoch.

For the rest, Morris's book is pleasantly informative or speculative. His chapter on fighting offers more detail on physiology than Lorenz or Ardrey gave, but it tends to resemble Lorenz's analysis despite points of difference. Fundamentally man is seen as living in a hier-archical social system in which he defends, or loses, his own status, his family's territory, and his group's territory. I doubt whether our social systems are or ever were as strictly hierarchical as Morris makes out, and the territory issue is very debatable. We can best look at this debate in connection with Ardrey's second book, which appeared just before Morris's *The Naked Ape*.

Territoriality

Robert Ardrey's *The Territorial Imperative* (1966) takes up a theme already explicit in *African Genesis*: that man is territorial in the strict animal sense of the word, i.e. that he is a creature programmed to threaten and if need be to fight in defence of a particular piece of ground which we can call his 'territory'. In *African Genesis* he argued that human territoriality had evolved out on the plains when man, or proto-man, became a hunter–gatherer. *The Territorial Imperative* looks at the phenomenon of territoriality in a large number of non-human species and finally at the master species itself. This is, he agrees, rather a case of isolating one particular aspect of human be-haviour from its general context, but no matter. By the middle of the book the reader is either convinced that territoriality is man's most basic drive or he has stopped reading. We have only reached page 5 when we are told that the territorial instinct is as potent a force as the sexual and maternal impulses; indeed it is more potent than sex, says Ardrey, justifying this by the illogical if factually correct assertion that more men have died for their country than for a woman (pp. 6–7).

The territorial instinct is as basic to Ardrey as the aggressive instinct was to Lorenz.† In fact, the two authors reverse the relations between the two instincts. Lorenz sees aggression as basic, and territorial defence as arising out of it, whereas Ardrey claims that territoriality is basic and aggression is one of its expressions. Whereas for Lorenz it is our innate aggressiveness that threatens our survival, for Ardrey the true threat comes from the territorial urge.

The crux of Ardrey's argument hangs on whether the human phenomena that are generally thought of as territorial behaviour, such as defence of property against thieves or marauders, fence-building, and international aggression and war, have a biological base similar to the territorial relations of other species, such as for instance the fighting response of cock robins to intruders on their breeding grounds or the group antagonism to intruders of howler monkeys or gibbons. It could just as well or even better be argued that the panoply of human cultures shows that, at the individual or family level, property often does not exist or, if it does, is not defended. And at the group level aggression is most often an outcome of prolonged failure of negotiation. There are times when war is little more than invasion and response to trespass, as in the medieval wars between the European and Scandinavian states or in the Middle East today. But in these cases, we see quite clearly the emergence of a war ethic and a set of arguments that legitimates aggression for the invaders. It becomes a convention that in given circumstances you invade, pitch your forces for battle, rape and destroy; it is a convention that, if invaded, you fight back sooner or later, or if the enemy wins, that you temporarily surrender everything. The animal who loses a territorial combat also surrenders and flees, but not within the framework of a system of rules and conventions; it is an analogous not a homologous process. Ardrey's claim, backed by quotations from Hediger, Harrison Matthews, Burt and Heape, that human and non-human territoriality are basically one and the same

---

†I refer here to Lorenz's ideas as expressed in *On Aggression*. Recently he seems to have done a complete *volte face*, judging from an interview published by the *Sunday Times Magazine*, 1 December 1974. In that interview he both denies that he ever said that aggression was basic (p. 41, column 2) and states an entirely new position (for him): namely that aggression in man is a result of the development of agriculture (p. 85, column 1).

process remains an unproven speculation and one that I think is probably wrong.

Overcrowding and stress

The next book to appear that I want to consider in this chapter is Desmond Morris's *The Human Zoo* (1969). This book has its intellectual roots firmly in the hypothesis used by the Russells (1968), that overcrowding causes stress that leads to distortions of behaviour. Morris's analysis focuses directly on the twentieth-century urban situation as the context (analogous to the zoo) in which overcrowding and behaviour distortions take place. He is concerned with explaining the breakdown of peaceful cooperation into destructive competition and the diversification of reproductive and 'pair-bond' sex into other kinds of sex such as self-rewarding sex, occupational sex, tranquillizing sex, commercial sex and status sex, all of which have analogues or homologues in the behaviour aberrations seen in animals, especially monkeys, living out their lives in zoo cages.

The trouble with this book is that, unlike *The Naked Ape*, it attempts to explain too much—the whole of urban life and more besides—within a single frame of reference, that of the diagnostician of animal behaviour pathology. This will not suffice. To understand urban man and his admittedly bizarre ways we need to take account of *economic* forces as determinants of human behaviour, not just the preoccupations with exploration or status-seeking. Also we must consider as central the loss of communication between individuals and sub-groups in the city—the failure of individuals to comprehend the projects and values of those around them—in the explanation of some other characteristics of urbanites: their indifference to others in the anonymous crowd or 'super-tribe' as Morris calls it.

Worse, Morris is at pains in this second book to show that the human intellect and all our thoughts and ideas are of no practical consequence in the organization of our behaviour. Revolution under tyranny, he says, is not intellectual but biological altruism, the co-operative urge reasserting itself. To Morris this urge is the basic thing and ideas are used to give it meaning and comprehensibility. Can this view of one-way determinism be upheld? Cannot ideas have the power to move? Do all men feel the urge to revolt at the same moment? Do not a few lead the way, feeding their followers with a diet of verbal, even if emotively verbal, messages and stimulating them with the prospect of a new and better order of things to feel a sense of unity and meaning? And who is to say that even the first few are altruistic and not just self-seekers as Machiavelli held? Revolutions against tyrants most often arise out of long-cherished or newly coined *ideas* about personal freedom, and these *non-biological* ideas are the primary units underlying revolutions.

Hierarchies

The next book to appear in the neo-biologistic tradition was yet another opus by Robert Ardrey. It might be thought there was nothing left to say, but the book is longer than either of his previous two. *The Social Contract* (1970) is an effort to analyse and understand 'hierarchies' in human society by reference to (suitably selected) animal societies. As before, the same fundamentally unsound premise underlies the whole argument: that processes which give the appearance of similarity in animals and man are in fact causally homologous. Hierarchies certainly do exist in some animal societies. Some members of a group are able to dominate others when they compete for scarce resources. The details differ from one species to another, but the mechanism is always the same and there is no conceptual thought involved. Ardrey argues that man is caught up in just the same kind of competitive struggle as a group of chickens or baboons, but man is too much of a conceptual animal for his argument to succeed, and unfortunately the ensuing thesis is highly doctrinaire and unpalatable—far more so than in his earlier books.

Having established that man is by nature a hierarchical species, Ardrey goes on to argue that social equality is an unnatural state of society and that we should not regard it as some kind of an ideal to strive towards. A society in which all are equal, says Ardrey, must lack coherence. Evolution has produced social order out of inequality: it is the differences between individuals that make up the viable whole. We must have inequality. Ardrey's title *The Social Contract* was chosen precisely because he saw his book as a direct refutation of Rousseau's book of the same title, published in 1762. Rousseau had argued in favour of equality and the brotherhood of man; Ardrey regards this not only as Utopian but as unnatural and therefore endangering our survival.

I have discussed elsewhere some of the grosser mistakes and misconceptions in Ardrey's thesis (Reynolds 1970). For present purposes what is of interest is his direct participation in political theory on the basis of biological theory. In this he has gone further than Lorenz or Morris. Ardrey has a political message: 'Form hierarchical societies or die!' He gives the green light to domination of man over man. Certainly societies built on oppression can be very strong. There are plenty of examples in the world today, and always have been. But social order that is built on constraint alone is only half as flexible and lively as it can be. Consensus is the other face of politics, just as cooperation is the alternative face of competition in personal relations. Where conditions permit, man can be friendly enough; where they do not he may well become hostile.

But even that is only half the story. In our social lives we are very much preoccupied with what we think others will think of us if we do such-and-such. We work it out; we don't just behave, we act. Every action is informed with meaning, and meaning is part of our personal integration with our society and its culture. States can emphasize consensus rather than constraint. I think that is the essence of what Rousseau was after. Ardrey wants instead to worship at the shrine of social inequality. He isn't after the good life for all, but the good life for a few and survival for all. His philosophy, if accepted, leads to a denial of the goal of equality and thus to a lifting of the pricks of conscience most of us feel if we are hard to our fellow men. Ardrey, like Lorenz, Morris, Adler, Machiavelli and others too no doubt, sees the 'inner man' as a thrusting, questing, status-seeking thing and he wants to give him the go-ahead. I think we have to check or even stop him. Freud argued that we develop our 'super-ego' to do just this. Huxley and Waddington have argued likewise that there is that *within* us which can and does evaluate our behaviour in terms of good and bad, right and wrong. Others such as Mead would locate the source of our moral nature *outside* ourselves in society and see each of us as an embodiment of this extrinsic force. Perhaps there is no internal 'mechanism' of the kind Freud, Huxley and Waddington have suggested; is there, in fact, anything internal at all? How far is the organic construction of our bodies and brains causally responsible for our eventual actions? Let us look next at some more recent writings on this topic.

CHAPTER 2

'Preprogrammed Man'?

THE TITLE OF this chapter is a translation of Eibl-Eibesfeldt's book *Der Vorprogrammierte Mensch* (1973) (which at the time of writing is available only in German), except that I have included a question mark. The question mark isn't there to express doubt about *whether* man is preprogrammed: all forms of life are preprogrammed by their genetic make-up. It is there to express doubt about how far this pre-programming controls action.

Eibl-Eibesfeldt's first book on this subject, *Love and Hate* (1971), was an extension, or rather a sophistication, of essentially the same paradigm as that of the authors whose works we examined in the last chapter. Man is seen as an 'organism', having 'drives' and 'innate learning dispositions', and social interaction is understood in terms of 'aggression', 'fear', 'threat' and 'appeasement'. As with Lorenz, the analysis takes place in a wider framework, in which the main problem facing mankind in general and the author in particular is: how can we avoid destroying ourselves; how can we survive? Man is seen by both Lorenz and Eibl-Eibesfeldt as having one and only one way out of his dilemma—the use of his higher faculties to understand his true biological nature, how he 'ticks', how the black box with its evolved capacity for destruction can be harnessed by the intellect and brought to heel. Once we understand ourselves, we are home and dry. Demagogues will no longer be able to control their peoples by threats and displays of dominance, because the people will know what they are up to. Politicians who put on leadership displays—firm, confident gestures, padded shoulders, and the fixed stare of the threatening adult male—will invite ridicule, for all will be known.

Innate love

But there is another side to man's evolved capacities, and this is where Eibl-Eibesfeldt makes his own contribution to the debate. He is concerned with showing that in man and all other species, evolution has led to strong associative, or friendly, or loving tendencies, as well as to aggression. Thus, it is not a case of reason, alone and unaided, having to face the aggressive forces within us; our actions are founded as much on an innate altruistic tendency as on self-interest and hate. The evidence for this is found in the universal existence in man of gestures and facial expressions that express positive feelings towards others. There is the eyebrow flash of greeting, the smile, and a variety of ways of touching one another. Man, like other species, is funda-mentally a friendly and co-operative beast. Where Lorenz saw aggression as the basic life force, from which, in the course of evolu-tion, positive bonds (or love) have been derived, Eibl-Eibesfeldt wants to put more emphasis on the basic nature of love—that is, of all positive forms of social bonding including sexual, infantile and maternal feelings.

One thing we must ask is whether this whole paradigm, the whole frame of reference in which the argument takes place, is adequate to the questions asked. Can ethology, the study of *animal* behaviour, be anything more than a contributory strand of thought when it comes to the understanding of human action? What other strands must be taken into account?

Lorenz and Eibl-Eibesfeldt hold the view that man, like other ani-mal species, has innate learning potentials, gestures, expressions and drives. The opposition, as they see it, comes from the 'blank-sheet' school of learning psychologists, who claim that every aspect of human activity except for muscular reflexes (such as blinking or swallowing) is learned during the course of growing up. Certainly that view is wrong. One thing ethology can do supremely well is to show that 'blank-sheet' learning psychology is nonsense. But when it comes to man and his activities, the demonstration that there are innate predispositions underlying behaviour is not, unfortunately, enough to explain more than a fraction of what we *do*, it has very little to contribute to an understanding of what we *say*, and it doesn't begin to touch on what we *think*. Thus ethologists of man are forced to rely heavily on non-verbal behaviour in their analyses, and to put words and thoughts aside. This is a very good exercise, a refreshing one, and writers like Desmond Morris have given us many new in-sights into our non-verbal communication system. Eibl-Eibesfeldt now adds more, and in addition does a valuable job of putting the whole thing in a comparative framework, for he looks at people living not just in Europe or the U.S.A., as had been the case in previous books on the subject, but all over the world—in Bali, in Papua, in France, in the South American rain forest and in Africa. He draws on data collected on film, made by Hans Hass and himself on their journeys around the world, filming with a sideways-pointing lens which enabled them to get candid shots of people who didn't know they were being filmed. The resulting material is the best we have for a thorough comparative documentation of human non-verbal expression and communication. It does seem to support the view that there *is* a set of culture-free signals that all peoples everywhere make and understand. So, at this basic level, all people can communicate with one another.

This point alone needs to be made and made again. It has considerable significance at a time when people are shooting and bombing each other, and when many of us are still riddled with false notions about the strange and rather unpleasant ways of those in other lands. If we are ever to get out of the web of pejorative social categories and labels in which we are enmeshed at the present time, we need to stress what all men have in common. But the demonstration of this common system of communication and the proof that neo-learning psychology is untenable does not, on its own, enable one to explain human hostility or to put forward a balanced programme for the improvement of mankind, a strategy for survival. The reason is that the neglected areas of thought, ideas and verbal communication are of crucial relevance to any understanding of the human predicament. It is not just by means of manipulating people's drives, by 'fixating' their aggression, that the 'demagogues' referred to by Lorenz and again by Eibl-Eibesfeldt succeed in mobilizing their armies and citizens to hatred and war. It is much more a case of manipulating their minds by the careful selection of words and images transmitted by the mass media in the form of propaganda. Certainly there *is* such a thing as hatred to be aroused, and certainly it has its characteristic external expressions. Ethology can help us to define these. But it is wrong to think that the mechanisms by which these feelings and their expressions are aroused are non-ideational, non-intellectual, non-verbal; they are not. The mechanisms by which people are brought into action involve the transmission of socially sanctioned ways of thought. We prefer the company of those who think like ourselves; we try to adjust our thinking to theirs, they do likewise. But if it emerges that we are poles apart in our thinking, then we separate and drift apart or, worse, argue and fight. This separateness of minds cannot be overcome by non-verbal posturing and gesturing. Even touching and caressing, the essence of love, become abhorrent when administered by someone we distrust. In the last analysis, it is what we *think* that counts, and to deny this is to deny the unique feature of human evolution, the conceptual mind, which sets us apart from other species.

So Eibl-Eibesfeldt's books present us with something of a paradox.

On the one hand, he pushes forward the frontiers of knowledge about man. There is much to be learned in his pages about ourselves—about how we greet one another and court one another and attempt to impress one another; how in different cultures the diverse ways of expressing friendship or respect or threat are modelled on basic patterns of movement that resemble the movement patterns found in the social behaviour of other primates. For example, the padded shoulders of their jackets tend to give men a more imposing appearance. Why? Eibl-Eibesfeldt shows that emphasis on shoulders is a characteristic of the dress and ornaments of men who are trying to make an impression or cut a dash in a great many cultures. The Waika Indians use feathers, Kabuki actors use specially shaped clothes, generals use epaulettes. Again, why? The answer given is that our hairy ancestors, when threatening, raised the hair on their shoulders, and the flow of hair on our bodies today supports this. With the advent of clothing, the signal value of hair erection was lost, but the response to big shoulders remained and has been put to use in different cultures in different ways.

Let us look at some further examples of Eibl-Eibesfeldt's line of thought. Some of his most interesting data concern greeting rituals and the kinds of behaviour that characterize friendly interactions between people. These he relates back to the more primitive responses of mothers and offspring, and to behaviour patterns characteristic of our primate relatives such as chimpanzees. For instance, he gives a long description of the way visitors are greeted by the Waika Indians—by 'embracing, kissing, fingering and patting, rubbing noses, rubbing lips and nibbling'. What does he have to say about all this? First, he takes the initiating of contact by rubbing with the forehead. This he has seen also in a film of chimpanzees and he feels that 'one root of this behaviour lies here'—i.e., in our primate heritage. Secondly, he notes that Waika greeting ritual involves rhythmical side-to-side movements of the head, rubbing the mouth against the partner's cheek. Of this he writes, 'I consider this behaviour to be ritualized searching for the breast'—and adds 'the same head movements are also made by people who bury their faces in another person's chest to be comforted'. In both cases, he says, 'it is a case of recourse to childish behaviour, a "borrowing" from the childish repertoire, designed to elicit the cherishing behaviour of a parent'. Kissing is subjected to a similar analysis, its roots being found in feeding movements, especially mouth-to-mouth feeding by mothers to their children, which is found in both humans in various parts of the world and in anthropoid apes.

These are just a few examples. Kissing, holding or shaking hands, smiling and scowling, grooming, comforting and many other of the ways we interact are shown to relate back to biological origins. In all these respects, the insights offered by ethology are valuable in so far as they help to answer the question *why* we do the things we do.

But the paradox is that the more Eibl-Eibesfeldt involves himself in this sort of interpretation, the further he finds himself from answering the very questions he has set out to answer. Like Lorenz, he is strangely stuck with his biological concepts, and there is not a scrap of sociological awareness in the whole book. Nor is there even any awareness of the kind of social psychology of G. H. Mead (1934), with its emphasis on man's development of a self-concept by and through which he relates to others in the social world. I think we need these perspectives as well, not to replace but to counterbalance the ethological one. Just as ethology can enrich and partly replace blank-sheet learning psychology, so social psychology and the sociology of writers like Erving Goffman (1956) can enrich and to some extent replace naïve observational interpretations of human action. It is odd that Eibl-Eibesfeldt's book lacks discussion of the conceptual nature of human interaction, but the fact is that his thinking is almost wholly biological; he regards biology as the key to the understanding of man's problems. I do not entirely share his opinion. May it not be that biology can bring us in some measure nearer to an *objective* understanding of ourselves, but that social relations are very largely composed of people's *subjective* interpretations of themselves and their social situations? Then the struggle to achieve objectivity might fail if it did not take adequate account of these subjective elements.

The 'biogrammar' of society

A rather different tack from the straightforwardly biological one, and yet one that seeks to build up social theory on the basis of biology, is to be found in the writings of Lionel Tiger and Robin Fox, a sociologist and a social anthropologist respectively.

Tiger's book *Men in Groups* (1969) is a discussion of the biology and sociology of a particular type of institution—that in which men alone participate and women are not allowed. Borrowing a term from primate ethology, Tiger calls such associations 'all-male groups' and asks: why do we form them, what do we do in them, and what are they for? The hypothesis underlying his analysis is 'that the behaviour of men in groups in part reflects an underlying biologically transmitted "propensity" with roots in human evolutionary history (or phylogeny)' (p. *xi*). The argument is clearly stated: 'I will argue ... that male bonding as a biological propensity is not only a phenomenon unto itself, but that in part it is the very cause of the formation of those various male groups observable around us' (p. xv). Male bonding is 'both biologically transmitted *and* socially learned'. Tiger accepts that he cannot *test* his hypothesis, an unfortunate but inevitable fact. There are other sciences in which hypotheses cannot be rigorously tested. But it is rather more unfortunate that neither can predictions be made on the basis of the dual causation offered, for since neither the extent of biological transmission nor of social learning can be measured (the latter could in principle be measured, but how would one do it in fact?) it is always open to Tiger to select those cases where all-male groups do exist and are exclusive as 'typical' in terms of biological causation, while those groups that accept a few women, or, as time goes by, drop their exclusiveness more and more, can be argued to be cases where the social-learning component is great.

Initially, Tiger claims that the big differences that have been said to exist between animal and human society do not exist, that studies of primate social structures and of non-human cultures, as well as those showing that there are innate bases to human behaviour, force us into a common framework for both. In a well-written chapter he looks at much of the material relating to this topic, including writings by sociologists, biologists, psychologists and others. But there is a problem that remains. In the search for biological origins and biological aspects of social behaviour there is always a half-hidden philosophical question of whether one is simply reinterpreting the old in a new paradigm, i.e. making an analogy, or whether one is actually discovering hitherto hidden but very real causal elements. Tiger is very aware of the existence of these paradigmatic problems, but his arguments at times seem to shift from biological reinterpretation to the 'discovery' of hidden biological ingredients, and back again.

A further problem not clearly expounded, but which is crucial to the enterprise, is the question of whether and how data from one paradigm can be incorporated into another. For instance, Tiger writes: 'Presumably the traditional view of man as a relatively un-programmed, relatively "un-animal" creature cannot be sustained in face of the various kinds of evidence from other sciences. For example, it would seem a matter of urgency for political scientists to try to determine whether man is intrinsically hierarchical, or not, or what' (p. 15).

But the difficulty is this: whereas for Tiger himself the evidence pertaining to man's animal nature, deriving from other sciences, is germane or even essential to the study of politics, from the point of view of political theory the question is: 'into what section of political theory should ideas that man is an animal with behavioural tendencies rooted in his evolutionary past be put?'† What is 'evidence' (evident) to one man may not be so to another who lives in a different conceptual world. Far from being 'a matter of urgency for political scientists to try to determine whether man is intrinsically hierarchical', such a project may not be on the cards, and it is no solution to merely widen the horizons to encompass the new data arising from ethology or primatology, for any amount of widening cannot resolve the question of whether biological data should take precedence over or be subsumed under socio-political ones. Existential man, like a refractory child, declines the offer of a biological reinterpretation of his nature and retorts that his existence precedes his essence.

How much can we infer about the present from a study of the past and of other species of primates alive today? Tiger sees human male bonding as a prehominid ecological adaptation, and finds male bonding in non-human relatives of man, and with all this I agree. But the question is: does it follow from the demonstration of male bonding in chimpanzees and baboons, and its probable occurrence in early hominids, that it still underlies our social arrangements? The strict answer, however attractive the idea and however indicative the evidence of a positive answer, would seem to be 'no, it does not'. But maybe it is likely? Yes, it is likely if and only if the same organizational principles underlie social developments in *Homo sapiens* on the one hand and his fellow primates and ancestral forms on the other. However, we know that the principles behind human social arrangements are unique in that they embody the fruits of much conceptualizing and hypothesizing.

The actual mechanism posited by Tiger for the selection during evolution of those qualities that underlie male bonding and hence male groups is as follows: 'the relationship between male bonding, political organization and sexual difference is possibly a function of human brain development which was based upon a particular breeding and ecological system and which culminated in *Homo sapiens*. This system was characterized by the genetic advantage of those males who could dominate, who were willing and able to bond to dominate and hunt and who could nonetheless maintain "affectionate" if undemocratic relationships with females and young' (p. 52). We should note Tiger's stress on 'brain development'. It is in the brain that we must seek the physiological differences that arise from genetic

---

† A good example of an analysis of biological views of man in terms of their ideological positions is the work of Robert Young (1971). In general he views them as conservative and reactionary.

sex differences. On this topic Tiger writes 'I take the existence of somatic or physical sexual differences to point the way to possible social and social-systematic differences'. He continues:

There are two major and important features of the process linking somatic sexual differences to systemic behavioural differences which I have not treated here in sufficient detail and scope. The first is the genetic variable—the specific manner in which the encoded information of one generation is fertile or sterile in terms of the succeeding generation. Now it is the case that male and female body cells differ, and that the very DNA molecules of males and females look different under the electron microscope. There is also the suggestion that mammalian sex differences may depend upon hormones acting on the brains of the newborn. The knowledge of how these and similar phenomena are reflected in evolution—with particular reference to such a hypothesized pattern as male bonding—must depend on investigation by specialists.

Had Tiger in fact dealt with these molecular and hormonal sex differences 'in sufficient detail and scope', would he have found the clues to sex differences in bonding and grouping that are the basis to the book? We shall look at some aspects of human biology in Part III of this book, and include a consideration of sex differences in genetics and physiology. The current state of knowledge in neurophysiology is such that statements about sex differences that determine 'social and social-systematic differences' in man would seem to be premature. It is just not possible to make the connection between the undoubted differences at the genetic/chromosomal level and those that Tiger wants to explain, namely social-grouping tendencies. In a subsequent chapter we shall look at some of the physiological data bearing on sex differences. And we shall run into a distinction fundamental to the understanding of what Tiger is talking about and yet absent from his pages—the crucial distinction between sex and gender.

Tiger writes only of 'sex' differences, not of 'gender' differences. But what in reality are the differences he is trying to explain? Are they matters of 'maleness' and 'femaleness' as he says or are they matters of 'masculinity' and 'femininity'? Owing to the fact that the human social world and all its institutions are constructed of rights and duties, norms and expectations, the behaviour of men in their clubs and other organizations is necessarily so constructed. If I play football in an all-male team, that is because the rules of the game include a norm about the members of the team being men, or put another way, playing football is a masculine activity, and it is the fact of having a masculine gender that makes me engage in football, or be encouraged or even forced to so engage by others who think that football is part of being a man. Women footballers are an anomaly not because any biological programme is being violated but because a gender rule is. Women are supposed to form netball, lacrosse and hockey teams, not football teams. There is nothing biological about that, surely? Indeed, the game of lacrosse was invented by the Iroquois and it was played exclusively by *men*.

According to Tiger 'it is men who dominate the public and private State Councils of the world' (p. 57) and while in part true, this remains a statement about gender, not sex, because of the traditional manner of construction of State Councils. Therefore the ensuing suggestion that 'females may not release "followership" behaviour', drawn from a non-human primate paradigm, is not a valid explanation, unless it can be shown that sex and gender differences are homologous (which they certainly are not) or that underlying gender differences there are sex differences, which may well be Tiger's unargued assumption. To argue this thoroughly, Tiger would need to explore in detail the relation between those behavioural properties of man and his relatives that are undoubtedly linked to maleness and femaleness, and those qualities or attributes recognized in societies and cultures all over the world, and documented by social anthropologists, as being masculine or feminine. Some work on these lines has been very painstakingly accomplished already, for instance by D'Andrade (1966). This work would undoubtedly clarify the issue of the *universality* of the masculinity of, say, hunting, and the *universality* of the femininity of, say, child care, but such demonstrations of universality would still fall short of a demonstration of underlying biological sex-attributes.

There are other possible explanations of universality across cultures. A powerful argument holds that universality of social patterns indicates strongly that such patterns are essential for the construction or functioning of societies, that they cannot be 'done without'. If all societies were to be found to contain all-male groups, much as they have all been found to contain some form of family, a case could well be made that such groups are an essential component of human societies. It would then remain to be shown whether there was a biological basis for them or whether they were a universally adopted stratagem resulting from conceptual thought and selected by trial and error. The alternative extreme to Tiger's thesis is thus that man thought up all all-male groups; they have arisen as conscious solutions to ever recurrent problems. This would avoid all reference to evolutionary origins or brain-behaviour organic sex differences. An intermediate type of explanation could posit a biosocial evolutionary origin in that our ancestors may have had all-male hunting groups, and some of our relatives among the primates do have them (in actual fact they are found in certain species only), but that our current institutions are linked only very tenuously with these, being subsequent transformations resulting from rethinking and replanning society down the ages. There is no need to posit genetic continuity of behavioural tendencies or tendencies to form bonds, or to look for brain mechanisms or hormone mechanisms.

I have left until last the recent and comprehensive venture into biological thinking about human social behaviour, *The Imperial Animal* by Lionel Tiger and Robin Fox (1972), but I shall not dwell on it. It takes all the arguments with which we are by now familiar and explores their implications further than hitherto. It draws widely on anthropological material, for which one is grateful. The treatment of primate material remains biased to the baboon–macaque group which best illustrates the theme of hierarchy and structure in social organization. It coins the term 'biogrammar' to describe the inborn faculties and potentials that underlie and steer our social interactions, relationships and institutions. It manages to evade a naïve biological determinism by stressing that man is a 'cultural animal', that culture is his particular form of adaptation. But in its insistence that we are all varieties of a common denominator whose essence is to be accounted for by our hunter-gatherer past it continues to miss the central target of the controversy, which pertains to the question of the priority of 'existence' over 'essence'.†

The authors use a computer analogy: the human organism is like a computer that is set up or 'wired' in a particular way, the 'wiring' having got there by natural selection; certain types of life experiences, life styles and societies inevitably follow. But what of the claim that man makes his own social institutions? The appeal to biology, or to science in general, for 'hard' evidence, for the 'facts' on which to build a theory of human society, confuses an ambitious and thoroughly pursued train of thought with a true demonstration of causes and their effects; it argues that matters concerning human minds—ideas and their embodiments in social actions and social institutions—can be accounted for by reference to other fields of data. The presence of much protestation seems to mask the absence of any coherent proof that such is the case.

† See box on next page for the sense in which these terms are used.

Box 2

'Existence' and 'essence'

These words are used in a specific and technical sense, namely according to my interpretation of their use by Sartre. They are, in fact, French words and not English ones. A number of colleagues, reading drafts of the manuscript, commented that some explanation of their use would be helpful to the reader. I have therefore attempted this in what follows. It is a summary and forlorn attempt, since the words relate to an entire philosophy of life. However, I have attempted to offset the problems of this over-simplification in two ways. First, in what I have written I have stressed only those aspects that are relevant to this book. And secondly, I have included a series of relevant quotations from Sartre. These have in fact all been taken from P. Mairet's translation of Sartre's *L'Existentialisme est un Humanisme*. The quotations appear in Appendix 3 (p. 244).

'Essence', as I interpret it, is all the ingredients that go into the making of man or of 'human nature'. Thus where man is conceived of as being a product of the Divine Will, 'essence' relates to the manner of his construction by the Divinity. Where man's mind is conceived of in terms of a 'conscious' and a 'subconscious', or his psyche conceived of as being made up of an 'id', an 'ego' and a 'super-ego', these are aspects of his essence. Of most relevance for the present work, where man is conceived of as a product of evolutionary forces, then those aspects of his body, brain, mind and behaviour that are attributed to genetic and maturational processes are parts of the human 'essence'.

'Existence', by contrast, is all that we make of, or do with, our essence. We are born into a world of forces—historical, sociological, psychological, genetic—and in that world we are free to choose between alternative courses of action: it is the act of choosing and the outcome of our choices that constitutes 'existence'. Thus if we find ourselves in a position in which all the forces of 'essence' are inclining us to a certain course of action, we are nevertheless free to do the opposite. Unlike animals, we are free to choose death rather than life, and in less dramatic ways always to choose to act either in accordance with, or against, any impulses that may be pushing us in a given direction.

In saying that *'l'existence précède l'essence'* Sartre resolutely denies the appeal to any religious, psychic or evolution-based inner programme of inherited tendencies in the explanation of human actions. As I see it, he is not denying the existence or the possible existence of such forces or tendencies, but only the appeal to them as undeniable and inescapable sources of, or controls on, what we think, say and do. To make such an appeal is to act in bad faith. To act in good faith is to acknowledge the primacy of freedom of choice.

Thus, for present purposes, scientific efforts at any form of objective analysis or theorising about human action or behaviour, including an appeal to 'drives', to 'innate behavioural tendencies', to the 'wiring' or the human 'biogram', to past experiences, or to the prevailing social order (including both institutional and linguistic structures) can only shed light on 'essence'. Whatever can be learned from an objective standpoint can never provide more than a background for the explanation of action, the foreground being occupied by the subjective choices of free individuals.

The evolution of human action

Introduction to Part II

In this part of the book an effort is made to find a way forward from what, in Part I, was seen as the 'dead end' of biological determinism without, however, turning into the equally 'dead end' of sociological determinism. The approach adopted is to compare the processes of social life and communication of man with those of selected non-human species. Especial emphasis is placed on the evolution of conceptual thought. The consequent modelling of social institutions, rules of action and ideas of right and wrong out of what went before is seen as the major step in the emergence of humanity. As a result man has come to inhabit a universe perceived in terms of the structures developed during the ancestry of his culture.

This part relates back to Part I in that it puts much greater emphasis on the conceptualization by individuals of their life-situations and ideas of what it is appropriate for them to do than on inner causal mechanisms in the explanation of social action. It leads on, after the necessary considerations in Parts III and IV, to what is hopefully a re-integration of inner causal mechanisms, in Part V.

CHAPTER 3

Animals: society without conceptual awareness

THERE IS CLEARLY some sense in which human action and society are related to animals, for we have a long animal social past, our bodies and minds are the outcome of evolution and we *are* in fact animals, not vegetables or gods.

First and foremost, we need to know something of the processes of animal society, on which the authors so far discussed rely so heavily for their ideas about man. And secondly, we need an evolutionary perspective on ourselves. These issues form the subjects of this chapter and the next.

Animals are the beginning of the problems about man, but unfortunately there is nothing simple about them. In fact the whole of modern science and technology has not yet been able to demonstrate exactly what happens in the nervous system when an animal's paw is touched and the animal responds by withdrawing the paw. Biology has not yet explained how the chemical material in the chromosomes is 'translated' into organs, arms, tonsils, let alone how tendencies to behave in certain ways arise, given certain clues in the environment. Students of life are like ants crawling around the foothills of the Himalayas, mostly seeking to conquer minor obstacles, not even looking towards the invisible summit, not knowing where it is. We do not know how much, one day, will become clear in terms of the brain, or the genes, or the social world. But these three must surely be among the key concepts in an understanding of human action.

Conceptual thought

I want in this chapter to explore the problem of how animals achieve co-ordinated social systems, and yet maintain a flexibility so that their societies can adjust to new conditions. The first point about animal society is an absolutely crucial one. It is that animals (by this I here mean all species other than man) do not think conceptually; they respond to stimuli or configurations of stimuli coming from within their own bodies and from the surrounding environment, but do not conceptualize either themselves, or others, or the external world and its parts, or their social group. The reason is that animals other than man lack symbolic language-systems needed to produce the cognitive constructions that are necessary for symbolic concept formation.

The point at issue here has to be clearly understood. It is not just a question of whether animals do or do not have 'consciousness'— a conscious awareness of themselves, of things and relationships. Undoubtedly they do have some kind of consciousness. But the point we are concerned with goes beyond whether they do or do not 'have consciousness'; it is whether their consciousness is encoded in symbolic forms that really matters. For if animals cannot think in the sense of manipulating conscious symbols, one is forced to explain the events one sees in animal relationships and society in ways that do not involve such thinking. If animals cannot play symbol-games in the mind and act on the basis of these games, then one is forced to find adequate answers to explain their society and behaviour in other terms. It would only be if one were unable to find other answers that one would need to resort to symbolic thinking in explanation of the facts.

The dichotomy proposed above: man, on the one hand, with symbolic language enabling concept formation and conceptual thinking, 'versus' animals on the other hand, with their signalling systems, is presented in a rather extreme fashion and therefore calls for justification (cf. McBride 1968; Holloway 1969). Current work with chimpanzees calls for consideration, as does the work of Lenneberg (1967) and Chomsky (1968), and the debate in comparative psychology concerning the extent to which chimpanzees can be taught to communicate symbolically.

Before discussing this it will be useful to examine briefly the ideas of Gaston Viaud, presented in a little-known book, *Intelligence, its Evolution and Forms* (1960).

In Viaud's scheme, activities can be divided into four levels, as follows: (1) reflexes, (2) instincts, (3) practical intelligence and (4) rational intelligence. Reflexes and instincts are relatively primitive forms of activity. The distinction that interests Viaud and takes up the bulk of his work is between practical and rational intelligence. The dividing line between them is language. Practical intelligence is found in both children and adults, but rational intelligence is fully achieved only after childhood.

To distinguish in this way is necessarily to deform an ongoing process of development from child to adult, but is intended as an heuristic device; the dichotomy, sharply drawn, may be false, but it draws attention to two very real and very different facets of human action—the practical or doing, making aspect, and the logical, conceptual, thinking, rationalizing aspect. In just the same way the dichotomy I have used, between human symbolic communication and animal signalling, is a false dichotomy if over-sharply drawn.

Viaud's ideas can detain us a little longer since he often puts his finger on the heart of the problem. His definition of the 'concept' is as follows: 'A concept is a generalised and abstract symbol; it is the sum of all our knowledge of a particular class of objects' (p. 75).

Further, he contends that

> *our conceptual thought forms an immense network, each strand of which consists of a particular concept* [his italics] ... This, in outline, is the structure of conceptual thought. Its elements—concepts—act first of all as labels for classifying the objects of our concrete experience according to their properties. Secondly, by means of the words which describe them, concepts are consolidated systems of knowledge; finally, and still with the help of language, they form a vast network containing all our knowledge. Conceptual thought is therefore a vast organization of ideas which our verbal habits keep constantly at our beck and call [pp. 78–9].

Such a scheme seems quite adequate for our current purpose in this chapter. It should not, correctly understood, imply that we arrive at our conceptual networks suddenly; on the contrary we build them up and dismantle bits of them all through life. Neither is there a denial of the non-verbal aspects of human communication which are ever present in face-to-face interaction and can have great significance, as the work of Michael Argyle (1967), Ray Birdwhistell (1949), Adolf Scheflen (1965) E. T. Hall (1966) and others has shown (see Chapter 13).

Nor does Viaud deny, though there may appear to be some neglect of, the biological origins and neural–anatomical organization of our communicatory systems stressed by Lenneberg (1967), or the possibility of inborn neural organization enabling human children to master with relative ease the exceedingly complex formations of grammatical word-use, enabling meaningful communication to be achieved, as stressed by Chomsky (1968).

What perhaps niggles the reader most about the approach of Viaud is his attitude towards the method of study and presentation of data. Though he has a long and distinguished career as an animal ethologist whose work has been of the most empirical kind, he more or less abandons empirical research as a basis for his remarks on human (adult) thought and intelligence, preferring to reason the arguments out in an 'armchair' style. Is this scientific? How can anything be proved? How do we test Viaud's statements, which are after all hypotheses, to determine their truth or falsity?

Such questions take us beyond the scope of this chapter or of this book. In defence of Viaud (should he need defending) it can be said that the direct study of conceptual thought along scientific lines is not yet a possibility. We do not yet have the knowledge or techniques to distinguish between conceptual and non-conceptual brain processes at the neuro-physiological level.

The communicative abilities of chimpanzees

Reverting to our theme, it is perhaps the recent work with chimpanzees that is most relevant to the question of conceptual thought and symbolic language use by animals.

In two of the earliest studies, by the Hayes (1952) with the chimpanzee Viki, and the Kelloggs (1933) with the chimpanzee Gua, efforts were made to teach young apes to speak and to see if they would pick up elements of human speech if reared in a sympathetic way in a human family. Little or no success was achieved with speech in those pioneer efforts. (I have examined these cases in more detail in my book *The Apes* (1967).)

More recently a new idea has come to the fore—that of teaching young chimpanzees to use signs made with the hands or other kinds of objects with symbolic functions, i.e. standing for objects in the environment, or for actions by the ape itself or surrounding people, or for abstract notions, or for mere parts of sentence construction.

Initially the Gardners, working with the young chimpanzee Washoe, made a breakthrough when they showed that this ape was able to use signs from Amaslan (American Sign Language, a system of hand signs for the deaf) in the same communicative way as is done by humans. Essentially the technique was to show the young ape the sign in connection with the object or quality or need to which it referred, and reward her when she gave the sign or an approximation to it. Eventually Washoe came to use a very large number of signs, albeit in a rather rapid, offhand, almost blasé way, for all sorts of things—to obtain what she wanted, to comment on things, to refer to others or herself. She combined numbers of signs to form sequences that in many senses could count as sentences. Whereas many of Washoe's signs were taught and learned by trial and error, others she put together herself. And eventually she was able to surprise her tutors with quite unexpected achievements. All this is made clear in the Gardner's publications (e.g. 1969) and even more so in their film. Theirs is indeed a magnificent achievement.

The next major effort to become widely known was that of David

Premack, using the young chimpanzee Sarah (see Premack 1970). Using plastic pieces of diverse colours and shapes he was able to train Sarah to express herself (to those who understood!) with even more detail and complexity than Washoe (see Fig. 3.1).

Most recently, Duane Rumbaugh has, by a process of continual reinforcement, using food rewards, trained the young chimpanzee Lana from a very early age to press signs on a computerized keyboard to communicate with her keeper and to make a large variety of requests or statements (Rumbaugh 1974).

The achievements of Washoe, Sarah and Lana, not to mention

FIG. 3.1. Sarah, after reading the message 'Sarah insert apple pail banana dish' on the magnetic board, performed the appropriate actions—she put the apple into the pail and the banana on to the dish. (From Premack and Premack (1972). Copyright © 1972 by Scientific American, Inc. All rights reserved.)

those of the Gardners, Premack and Rumbaugh, have been sustained, ingenious and extremely impressive. They have given much pause for thought, mainly to psycho-linguists such as Roger Brown (1970) but also to all who have wanted to posit the essentially *unique* nature of language use and symbolic communication by man. Clearly, in perpetuating this distinction, one is taking sides on what is at present a delicate and undecided issue as to the extent to which apes can achieve essentially human levels of conceptual thought and communication.

There are a number of aspects to be considered. One is the fact that a considerable amount of dedicated training, of constant reward in the form of food for correct responses, is always needed in these studies. In this respect the apes seem, though they are young, to be learning language in a way different from that used by human children. Children actively come to the task without constant reward. This is not to say that rewards in the form of maternal delight, smiles, word games and laughter or loving contacts do not play a part in human language learning by young children, for they do. In some of the chimpanzee studies such rewards have also played their part. But there are clear differences in the ways the subjects come to the task of learning the code or sign systems. Human children move, slowly at first but then with increasing rapidity, to the speaking of a hundred or more words, to sentence construction that is at first faulty but corrects itself either by trial and error or instruction or imitation, and by the age of 5 or so years they have an incredibly versatile language ability. Chimpanzees, brilliant though their achievements are, seem to rush their manipulations and at the same time to be offhand about them; their achievements fall far behind those of normal children.

The point at issue, however, is whether or not the existing work can be said to show the existence of conceptual thought in the way defined by, for example, Viaud. We noted that, for Viaud, there are *things* in the external or internal environment (objects, qualities, feelings); these are reciprocated in the form of mental constructs or concepts linked up in rational networks; and language acts as the intermediary between the inner mental world of the cerebral cortex and the world of things.

Is the same true in the case of these carefully trained apes? Are they using language to mediate between the world of concepts and the world of things? The answer must surely be 'yes'. The clearest evidence is that all of them have succeeded relatively early and easily in initiating imperatives, e.g. 'gimme water', in the absence of the thing wanted. This might be thought simply to refer to the feeling of thirst, but not so, for the apes can readily learn signs distinguishing water from, say, milk or coke. If an ape can choose between the signs for water and coke, then it must have the concepts of water and coke in its mind. If, having asked for coke, it is told there is no coke it may then elect for water. There is thus a graded hierarchy of preferences between the concepts. Thus we have the beginnings of Viaud's 'network of concepts' in these highly-trained, humanized chimpanzees.

But, to revert to the opposite tack, we have only the beginnings.

In man alone there is found the enormously ramifying system of concepts, related back and forth with each other in millions of crosscutting connections, that forms the world in which he lives, the rules that govern his actions, his values and prejudices, his attitudes and opinions concerning what others think of him and how he should comport himself in view of the prevailing social definition of his situation and his aims and objectives within it. The writings of Erving Goffman (e.g. 1956), the work of G. H. Mead (1934) or the sociology of Berger and Luckmann (1967) describe an *exclusively* human world.

As is to be expected, it is with man's closest relatives, the chimpanzees, that the closest approximation to human thought and communicative techniques can be *made* to take place. But let us now go back to the basic question to be examined in this chapter: what are the main processes of communication in *natural* animal societies that make for social cohesion—sometimes in highly complex and beautifully adaptable and flexible social systems? And I refer now to naturally occurring situations, or at any rate to situations that are *not the result of special training*. Do such situations incline us to conclude that conceptual thought and symbolic communication are in fact widespread in animals? Or can we find other ways of accounting for the data derived from observations and experiments on animal societies?

Insect communication and society

The first example that presents a number of features relevant to this problem I take from the honey-bees. The problem is to see if we can explain events in the social life of animals without assuming that the animals think. Very few people would argue that honey-bees think. And yet their way of life in the hive presents us with certain events that demand explanation. I am not here referring to the elaborate signalling devices by which bees just back from foraging communicate the whereabouts of flowers to hive-mates. I am thinking instead of a less well-known series of experiments made by von Frisch (1954) when he removed some of the members of a colony and observed the reactions of the remaining inmates whose normal activities were in consequence upset.

In order to understand the significance of what von Frisch did, it is necessary first to know something about the development of worker bees. Von Frisch divided the life of the worker bee into three stages. In the first period (the first to about the tenth day) she is occupied inside the hive as a house bee. At first, she crawls into newly vacated cells and cleans them out, she sits on the brood cells, spends some time idling up and down, and then after a few days she behaves as a nursemaid to two or three larvae. Towards the tenth day she

makes her first flight and then from the tenth to the twentieth day
her behaviour changes. Her feeding gland becomes reduced, her wax
glands increase in size and her behaviour consists of building the
honeycomb, taking over and digesting nectar for the storage cells,
pressing down the pollen baskets, removing hive refuse to the outside
world, and stinging intruders near the hive. Finally, during the third
period, from the twentieth day to death (at about the thirtieth day),
the bee is a forager, flying forth to collect pollen and nectar for the
hive, or, if the weather is bad, idling about in the hive.

Noting the fact that certain changes in bodily organs of the bee
were correlated with the changes in behaviour, von Frisch wondered
if the order of these physiological changes determined the order of
the behaviour, and 'whether this order is irrevocable even under con-

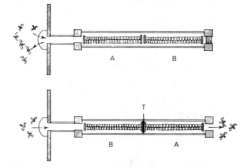

F ig. 3.2. Turntable observation hive with inmates divided into old and young bees
(horizontal section level with entrance hole). *Above:* before turning; the inside is
not divided, only *one* entrance hole is open. *Below:* the hive is turned through 180°,
the inside is divided into two parts by the board T; previously all the bees had
been moved into A and the second hole is opened. The young bees remain in A,
while the old bees fly off to the right; on their return they come in by their usual
entrance to the left of B. (Redrawn from von Frisch (1954).)

ditions that seem to demand its modification in the interest of the
colony'.

To test this he cleverly managed, by rotating through 180° a
special hive (Fig. 3.2) with two entrances and a partition in the
middle, to separate all the foragers from the younger members of
the hive, producing a 'young colony' with no foragers and an 'old
colony' with no brood nurses. Here, in his own words, is what happened:

The 'young colony' lacked foragers; there was nobody there to bring in food.
Their meagre stores were all too soon used up. At the end of the second day we
had to witness the sad spectacle of some bees lying on the ground, starving to death,
while other bees started dragging their own larvae out of their cells to suck them

dry in their need. Then suddenly, on the third day, came the turning point. Contrary to all tradition, young bees only one or two weeks old flew out foraging and returned heavily laden with food. Though their fully developed salivary glands stamped them as foster-mothers it was the need of the colony, and not the state of their bodily development, that determined the behaviour of these bees. Their glands had to follow suit, becoming reduced in size in a few days' time. On the opposite side of the hive, in the 'old colony' there was a shortage of brood nurses. Here, every bee that was still the least bit youthful stepped into the breach, retaining her fully developed salivary glands long after the end of the customary period [p. 48].

Not only did von Frisch get behaviour to speed up or remain static in response to an emergency, but he also found that it could retrogress: 'In another experiment the majority of the builders were removed from their colony by a simple operation. Thereupon this colony was confronted with a situation in which the making of new cells was an urgent necessity. And constructed they were. The building this time was carried out by bees that had long since passed the age of normal builder-bees. Microscopic examination revealed that their wax glands, by now atrophied, had been built up again and had reached an astonishing degree of new development' (p. 49).

Von Frisch's own interpretation of these findings is that a certain degree of flexibility is needed to cope with naturally occurring vagaries of the weather, and so there is always in the hive a number of 'idlers' who can jump in and fill the breach. These idle bees fulfil the hive's needs. 'They investigate all round, put their heads into one cell after another and start working wherever they consider it necessary.' But in fact bees do not 'consider', they respond to particular stimuli in particular ways. Even then, has von Frisch really *explained* what happens, with his 'idle bees'? He has described it beautifully and done a crucial experiment, but he has not really explained anything, least of all how the needs of the hive are related to the activities of individuals.

These experiments seem to me to raise a number of extraordinarily difficult problems which we have to try and answer as best we can, for von Frisch did not answer them. Fundamentally we are faced with the fact that a society of bees is capable of adjusting to a terrible setback in a way which saves it from extinction and enables it to survive. Development can be either 'speeded up' or actually be *reversed*, so that bees regress to an earlier stage, if need be. But as far as we know, no bee is able to conceive of the problems faced by the colony. The queen does not issue symbolic orders, and nor do any of the bees; no bee formulates the problem. To explain, we have to assume that normal development for any one bee takes place in the context of the behaviour of others, more and less developed.

Behaviour of the individual is modified by behaviour of others. It is as though each bee has tendencies to behave in a number of ways, so that, say, a guardian (stage 2) also has weak tendencies to behave like a nursemaid (stage 1) and a forager (stage 3) but the strongest of its tendencies is to be a guardian at that stage, and its tendencies to stage 1 and stage 3 behaviour are inhibited or suppressed because there are other bees physiologically and behaviourally more strongly geared to cleaning and foraging behaviour.

Recent experiments with bees (and termites) have in fact shown with remarkable clarity how one such mechanism works. These experiments focused on the fact that if the queen is removed from the colony, the remaining bees, after a short time, produce a new one. It is essentially the same problem as the one that engaged von Frisch. The explanation is as follows. The queen normally emits a pheromone (or 'smell' substance)—9-oxodecenoic acid. This is transmitted from worker to worker right through the colony as a result of their constant contacts with each other. This pheromone is responsible for inhibiting the sexual maturation of the female bees, which consequently remain as 'neuter' workers. If now the queen is removed the supply of 9-oxodecenoic acid dries up, and developing females begin to achieve sexual maturity, are mated by males and become 'queens'. Too many queens are produced initially, and this situation resolves itself by the elimination of all but one queen as a result of fighting between the queens themselves. By now, production of 9-oxodecenoic acid is normal again and no further queens are produced.

Here we see a beautiful mechanism for the replacement of a keystone in the social structure of the hive. Whether von Frisch's findings can also be explained on the basis of the action of inhibitory pheromones remains to be seen. Certainly we know from a great deal of recent work on the social behaviour of insects that pheromones are the essential signals that co-ordinate social activities. Holldöbler (1971) has even described a form of 'pheromone trick' by which a certain beetle can live parasitically in an ant colony that would normally reject outsiders. The beetle looks quite unlike an ant, but because it emits the correct pheromone it is fed by colony ants just as if it were a member.

Reverting to von Frisch's experiments, we have to explain why, when we take away the forager bees, the society does not just go on without food intake until it starves to death. There must be a feed-back mechanism by which absence of incoming food and the consequent hunger of hive inmates leads to speeded-up development in some bees and speedy replacement of the missing foragers with new. Likewise there must be a feed-back mechanism by which presence of larvae in the hive leads to regression of some forager bees so that the missing brood-nurses are replaced. The important thing is that the finely balanced set of co-ordinated behaviour patterns has this homeostatic property: *le roi est mort; vive le roi*! But in what kind of terms should we describe this process?

Looked at as individuals, bees can be said to pass through successive 'stages' in their life cycle. At each stage a bee exhibits particular behaviour patterns in response to particular stimuli in the environment. Looked at in social terms, bee colonies can be said to have a 'structure' and the structure can be said to have 'positions' ('queen', 'guardian', 'brood nurse', 'forager', 'builder', 'cleaner'). No one would claim the bees are 'aware' of either the structure of their colony or the positions. It is their behaviour which leads us as observers to isolate the structure and positions—they exist in *our* minds, not the bees'. What determines the behaviour of individual bees? Very probably there is a large innate or maturational component and, as the experiments show, this is closely geared to environmental inputs. Some of these inputs are pheromones. But it seems very probable that other inputs are the actual behaviour patterns of bees. Bits of behaviour in one bee stimulate the same or other bits of behaviour in other bees. The whole system, the whole colony of individuals, is a tight-knit and highly elaborate behavioural network with self-repairing properties, a tendency to homeostasis of structure, so that even major upsets do not wipe out the colony, but cause merely a temporary setback.

We can refer to the behaviour patterns characteristic of given positions as 'roles' in animal society. Others have done this before, in particular of monkey society. We could just call them 'position-behaviour', but this seems to confuse two levels of the thing studied, the observer's level ('position') and the bee's level ('behaviour'). The word 'role' is firmly at the level of the observer's analysis; it is the behaviour *he* associates with the positions *he* has isolated within the structure *he* conceives of.

By using the word role in the above sense we gain an advantage: the word has for many years been used in sociology to describe the things people do when they are in a given social position in a social structure. This is where our extreme stand with regard to animals' inability to think conceptually becomes important. Use of the word role to describe animal behaviour would lead to nothing but confusion if we had not made that prior distinction. As it is we can make a useful contrast: animal roles are entities not conceived symbolically in the minds of actors of those roles, nor indeed in the minds of those they interact with. But just because there is this difference it does not seem necessary to stop using a single term; whether roles are conceptualized or not they remain the essential basis of all social organisation.

The fact that we have found a term that seems to fit both human and non-human society may seem small cause for excitement, and indeed it would be if everything ended there. But the opposite is the case: everything starts there. We start not from the individual, but from society, where there is a basic similarity. We start with social events, social organization, social structure. We regard individuals as bits of something bigger, as pieces of a jigsaw. But this is no ordinary jigsaw, for in this case the pieces can change their shape, and the picture changes, either by new kinds of behaviour with or without genetic change (animals and men) or by new ideas (man). Neither people nor animals are simply cogs in a machine; each can adjust when the machine goes wrong in a way cogs cannot. Nor can cogs change the entire organization of the machine, but men and animals can and do bring about changes in the structure of their societies.

Primate societies

Let us move on now from bees to monkeys. If, as seems certain, there is more to bee society than has yet been explained, then how much more baffling can we expect to find the society of the primates— the most advanced group of higher mammals. In monkeys and apes we have to reckon with a much slower development to maturity, with much more of what we can call 'learning' as against behaviour that is largely the outcome of physical maturation. This is bound to make social responses more complex, as a new element of flexibility is introduced into individual behaviour, a finer assessment of the surrounding variables, a more complex conditioning. We would expect to find this reflected in a wider range of individuality among primates. This is what we do find: monkeys are individuals. And finally, each monkey shows a wide range of behaviours which are distributed differentially among its associates: it has individual relationships. In all these ways, monkeys are more like human beings than bees. But, and this is for us the important thing, the actual processes of monkey social organization, the ways in which it works, are much more bee-like than man-like. Monkeys stand between bees and humans in that their development as individuals is progressive, i.e. like that of man; but the organization of their social systems is not man-like for it lacks conceptual thought, just as the bee's does.

It is primarily from field and captivity studies made during the sixties that we know what we do about primate societies. I do not intend to review all that we know; this would by now require some ten volumes of close print. But what are the main findings to have emerged from these studies? First, we know that the same species in roughly the same environment tends to show a certain kind of social organization characteristic of that species. For instance Hamadryas baboons, first studied in London Zoo in the late twenties (Zuckerman 1932), have always, wherever studied, shown a tendency to organize socially into 'one-male groups' or 'harems'; this has been found in captivity in Russia, Switzerland, Germany, as well as England, and also in the wild in Ethiopia. Secondly, we know that when environmental conditions vary either seasonally or from one place to another in a species' habitat, then this is frequently matched by a change in social organization (examples of this are to be found in Jay (1968)). Thirdly, we know something about the way natural social organization becomes distorted when a group is artificially overcrowded in captivity: the amount of aggressive behaviour usually increases, and the society tends to become more hierarchical and more structurally rigid than in the wild (see e.g. Southwick 1967). Fourthly, it is by now clear that there is no single principle underlying the social organization of monkeys. Sex is not the basic principle, as was once thought, and neither is dominance, a power drive, biological altruism or co-operativeness. All these kinds of principles have been suggested as the basic 'glue' holding animals together in society, but all must now be seen as relevant to some species but not others and, even where relevant, as partial explanations, often circular and mostly unsatisfactory.

How then are we to attempt an explanation for primate society? What does hold groups of monkeys together, and bring about the particular forms of their societies? The answer can never be simple. It must always be in terms of the maturation from a genetic basis of individual behavioural tendencies. These tendencies mature always in a three-way environmental matrix in which inputs from other monkeys are one part of the environment, the surrounding physical conditions are another part, and the physiological conditions of the behaving individual himself are the third and final part. The resulting activity is still only individual behaviour, moulded by social interaction.

There remains the question of the integration of one individual's social behaviour with other individuals' social behaviour, which is just as interesting and in some ways more problematic. For you cannot evolve 'leadership' behaviour, whatever its advantages, without at the same time evolving 'followership' behaviour. Male Hamadryas baboon leaders keep their females in close proximity to them by giving them a bite in the nape of the neck when they wander away; this 'herding' behaviour by males could not have evolved apart from the female response of *attraction to* the herding male, even, indeed especially, when he bites.

This is not just something peculiar to monkeys. In all species where social co-ordination occurs we have to think of two or more linked behaviour patterns evolving together, e.g. in the courtship behaviour of flies or fish. But this integration of individuals' social behaviour perhaps reaches its most highly evolved condition in mammalian society, and especially primate society, and for this reason: because only in these forms do individuals have great flexibility, great behavioural resources, a 'hidden repertoire' of behaviour which can be drawn upon as necessary. One and the same individual can maintain a number of quite different relationships with other individuals, and besides this can exhibit quite new and, for him or her, hitherto unobserved activities when there is a change in the composition or organization of the group.

Let us look at some examples. Irwin Bernstein (1966), in describing the social behaviour of capuchin monkeys, noted that while there was no 'hierarchy', one adult male in the group served as 'control animal', 'assuming a position between an external disturbance and the group, attacking whatever appears to be distressing a captured group member, and approaching and terminating most cases of intra-group disturbance'. An important observation of Bernstein's was that 'removal of the control animal resulted in rapid substitution ... this suggests that the functions of the control animal are essential to the society, and failure to fulfil the function will elicit the responses in substitute animals.' He concluded that 'control animal' was a *role* in capuchin society and that such a role could be found in the societies of a number of other primate species as well.

All this is, obviously, exactly what we are talking about, and the use of the word 'role' is wholly in line with the usage described earlier in connection with bees. The problem, however, remains just as acute and unsolved as before: how does a substitute animal come to act the role of control animal when the previous control animal stops? We cannot assume that he 'thinks' about it and arrives at a conclusion: that it is 'up to him now'. While I was observing a group of rhesus monkeys at Whipsnade Zoo† I noticed that whenever the 'dominant male', Henry, went inside the sleeping hut the second-ranking male, Dick, began 'acting up', raising his tail and bouncing up and down. When Henry came out of the hut Dick reverted to his usual quiet submissive state. If Henry had died I think Dick

† A Zoo in Bedfordshire near London.

would have taken on his behaviour patterns rather quickly. It could be said that Dick's natural ebullience or dominance was inhibited by Henry's presence. This, then, might provide some sort of explanation, but it does seem to make one untestable assumption—that there is a striving for dominance or control in males, at any rate in rhesus monkeys—and moreover we know that the same process of role takeover occurs in capuchins, which are non-hierarchical, i.e. all males have the same status.

How does this role takeover happen in capuchins? I think one is forced to assume that in such a species there is a social system which is made up of the co-ordinated activities of a number of monkeys of various ages and sexes and that if a part of the system (one monkey's behavioural input) is lost, then this loss is made good out of the 'hidden repertoires' or behavioural potential of one or more other monkeys. But even that is only a description, not an explanation: what is the cause-and-effect relationship between absence of behavioural input caused by loss, and sudden appearance of this input in a new animal to make the loss good? If there is not some inner factor pushing animals to behave in a given way then there must be a pull from outside. The only pull could come from the animals that hitherto had been the recipients of the control animal's behaviour. These now have nothing to respond to. If, for example, the leader male is killed in a group of wild gorillas, the rest of the group might be said to 'pull' leadership behaviour out of one of their members by responding to minute tendencies on his (or her) part to perform leadership behaviour, or by responding simply to the physical appearance of one of their members in so far as it approximated to that of the lost leader. In any case their responses might lead the selected animal to begin to show some control behaviour and finally to become as fully fledged as his predecessor. As in the case of bees, physiological processes are undoubtedly involved in this transition, and current evidence indicates that hormonal changes may well be deeply implicated.

Michael Chance (1967) has described what he calls the 'attention structure' of a number of primate societies. This is the pattern of social relations resulting from the different amount of attention animals pay to each other in a social group. In the case where, as in gorillas, all eyes tend to look towards the biggest silverback male, you have a clear case of a 'centripetal' attention structure. If, in such a structure, this male dies, it is easy to imagine that it only requires a shift of predominant attention to a new animal (normally in actual fact the second-biggest silverback or largest blackback) *by the others* for a new control animal to appear. The animal selected initially does nothing, though later, unless he responds appropriately, he may be rejected in favour of an animal whose behaviour is more appropriate. In some captive groups that have been studied, such as the rhesus group I observed at Whipsnade, it looks more as if there is a hidden volcano of aggressive power in the second male that is suppressed by the control animal. But this may tell us more about the distortion of behaviour in captivity than about natural conditions. Or it may give us a clue about one of the conditions underlying role replacement in the wild. But 'bullies' can exert tyrannical control in captivity only when their subordinates cannot get away. In the wild there is probably a delicate behavioural balance between subordinate activities and leadership, with the ever-present underlying possibility that changes in one part of the system will be compensated by changes in another to bring the system back into a functional equilibrium with its environment.

Summing up so far, the general idea advanced is that in monkeys and other animals, society consists of a complex behavioural interaction system that has inbuilt physiological mechanisms for self-maintenance, and is functionally related to the environment. This system 'works' without any conceptualization on the part of any of the members of the society.

Let me give a final example of how such a system works. I take this example from my own study of a colony of rhesus monkeys living at Whipsnade Zoo (1962). In this colony there was a rank order of adult males and, associated with it, one for adult females. While I was observing the colony, the top-ranking female, Anne, died, leaving the top male, Henry, without a consort. He soon became interested in the bottom-ranking female, Blondie. At first she was afraid of him and withdrew, or gave fear responses to his approaches. But as time went by she became more confident, her behaviour and indeed her entire 'personality' underwent a complete change, and she eventually became top female, like her predecessor. What I observed in this case was the gradual emergence of aggressive, confident responses in this female, as a result partly of the attention being paid to her by Henry, and partly of the consequent caution with which other monkeys approached her.

This colony, as is often the case in captivity, was a quarrelsome and hierarchical one, with a lot of fighting and biting. Indeed this exacerbation of the agonistic mode is the common way that, for a group of animals, a resolution is found between naturally occurring behavioural tendencies and the captive environment. To an observer of the group rank was an important issue, as if the animals were preoccupied with status. But they were not, for they were unaware of status, rank and hierarchy. Each monkey was caught up in a pattern of reactions to other monkeys having its basis in the history of the relationships involved. Blondie's relationship with Henry had been one of submission: she was afraid of him. With Anne's death, his close presence slowly became, for Blondie, a normal feature of the environment; meanwhile the responses of other group members to Blondie changed from dominance to deference, as her 'dependent rank' (i.e. her rank as a close associate of Henry) rose. Blondie was whisked into power.

As an observer of externally manifested behaviour, I was struck by the changes in Blondie's behaviour. She had hitherto exhibited behavioural traits that I classified as fearful, submissive or subordinate—items such as 'look away', 'bare teeth', 'screech', 'flee' and 'scream'. As time went by, these items dropped out of her overt repertoire, and were replaced by threatening or aggressive or dominant items—'stare', 'bark', 'crouch', 'chase' and 'bite'. Corresponding to these changes in her behaviour, there were complementary changes in the other animals with whom she was interacting. I have investigated these changes as closely as possible and concluded that what was in fact happening was that Anne's social behaviour, her contribution to the total social fabric, was being replaced by the emergence of new behaviour in Blondie. The social system had suffered an upset by the loss of a key member, and the upset was being made good. Blondie was 'turning into' an Anne. Her latent aggressive responses were becoming overt, and her overt submissive ones were becoming latent. Once the change was made, the system was back where it had started, it had reverted to type, in the same way as the bee colony that loses its queen. With monkeys pheromones are probably not involved in this process, though they are important in sexual behaviour (Michael and Keverne 1968). Probably the stimuli involved in effecting role replacement are visually perceived behavioural signals, but how these affect physiological processes such as levels of hormone secretion from the adrenals and other glands, and their effects in the brain, are not known.

To sum up, the subject of this chapter has been that, whether we look at bee society or monkey society, we are faced with an essentially similar problem: how to explain changes in the behaviour of individuals that result from upsets in the social fabric and result in the re-establishment of a viable social system. We have sought to answer this problem without imputing any conceptualization of the social order, and the place of the self within it, to any of the animals involved in the process. And we have concluded that an explanation must be in terms of two processes: first, a tendency to respond to the behaviour signals of fellow group members with particular 'linking' or matched signals, and second, a tendency to respond in certain new ways when the input from other animals changes. This kind of approach is, I think, more valid than any kind of one-way deterministic theory that seeks to explain animal society as, say, the result of innate programming plus learning, or some basic 'force' of attraction. In the next chapter, we face the problem of how to bridge the gap between these animals systems and the very different case of human society.

CHAPTER 4

Hominid society before man

WE SAY THAT animal society 'runs' without conceptual awareness; we cannot say the same of human society. It is therefore easiest to do a point-by-point contrast between the two; we end up with a series of structural parallels between the groups and sub-groups of animal societies and the institutions of man. Indeed I would favour such an approach, and Callan (1970) has shown in her book *Ethology and Society* that it can give rise to meaningful problems, if undertaken in the appropriate way. Such studies should never be attempts to *reduce* human behaviour to animal processes but efforts to explore the parallels between the two.

But the problem which will concern us in this and the following chapters is a different one. It is how to explain the emergence of conceptual awareness in man. This is a question that has never been properly answered. Conceptual awareness is such a difficult concept that it has been neglected by most archaeologists and anthropologists, though there have been exceptions. But even then it has tended to be regarded as a by-product of increased brain expansion, this latter being associated with tool-use and new adaptations to a savannah way of life and a hunting economy, which necessitated cultural innovation and traditional learning.

I want to argue that conceptual thought needs to be considered as a primary datum causally underlying the development of the big brain in our genus, *Homo*. I want to spotlight its emergence as an event of equal or greater magnitude than the development of tool-using. And I want to discuss the manner of its emergence, the ecological context and the type of society which could have given it birth.

Human societal evolution

What can we say about man's prehistory and the prehistory of his society? We know precious few facts when it comes to the latter, but we can speculate in an informed way. We have two main sources of data to draw on in making these speculations: fossil evidence, and the comparative study of monkey and ape societies. Before *Homo* there was *Australopithecus*, who lived for several million years and on whose society most authors have rightly focused in explaining man's genetic programming. Before *Australopithecus* there were more ape-like forms. If we are to build up a coherent evolutionary picture we need to begin our analysis with these early ape-like forms and trace it forward from there. A useful procedure is as follows: we start by studying the fossils, then we compare the fossil bones with those of living primates and deduce similarities and relatedness, then we consider the behaviour and social life of living forms closely related to the fossil forms and make speculations about the fossil forms. But there is one major proviso: where it can be seen that the living and the fossil forms, however similar at the bone level, were living in different kinds of habitats, we can expect this to be reflected in different kinds of behaviour and society.

Man never was a chimpanzee, nor a gorilla, nor any other kind of living ape or monkey. These modern primates are our relatives in the sense that we and they share common ancestors who were different from any of us. Our early Miocene ancestors, the Dryopithecines, were apes in the technical sense (i.e. they are classified in the *Pongidae*) but were not identical with any modern apes, though some of them show remarkable similarities to the chimpanzee and gorilla. From the Dryopithecines, it is believed, arose the modern apes and the ancestors of *Australopithecus*, who in turn gave rise to *Homo*. The Dryopithecines were forest-living or woodland-living apes inhabiting first the warm sub-tropical forests of Africa, later Europe and Asia. Some of them probably looked not unlike modern chimpanzees, except that they were mostly somewhat smaller and their arms had not yet developed into the long, specialized structures of the modern apes. *Dryopithecus* was living in Africa some 18–23 million years ago, a widespread forest ape. In Eurasia, the species continued until 8 million years ago.

We have very little fact to go on in trying to determine what became of *Dryopithecus*. The fossil record is very incomplete, especially on the ape side, where we really know only the following: that at least two of the Dryopithecine species evolved into forms that became extinct (*Gigantopithecus*, the Pliocene–Pleistocene giant ape of Asia, and *Oreopithecus*, the 'abominable coal man' of Italy, from the late Miocene) and that many other lines of *Dryopithecus*, some that we know nothing of, also became extinct and others evolved into the modern chimpanzee (*Pan*), gorilla (*Gorilla*) and orang-utan (*Pongo*). Finally, and most importantly for us, one of the branches of *Dryopithecus* is thought to have led to *Ramapithecus*, who is possibly ancestral to *Australopithecus* and *Homo*. *Ramapithecus* is known from sites in India, East Africa, Europe and China, and although all the remains together amount to no more than a few pieces of jaws and teeth and some recently discovered post-cranial bones, it is clear from these than *Ramapithecus* had undergone certain 'progressive' changes towards smaller incisor and canine teeth—features characteristic of man. *Ramapithecus* is thus classified as a hominid, and is therefore the first creature on the branch, or coming off the branch, that led

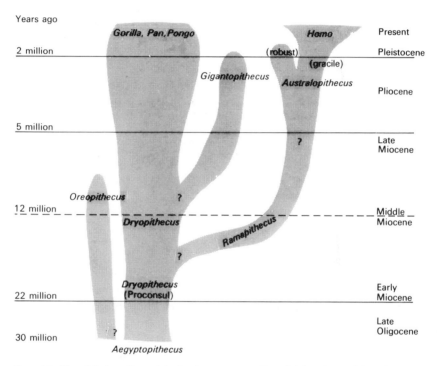

FIG. 4.1. Simplified outline of the basic structure of hominid and pongid evolution.

to *Australopithecus* and *Homo*. *Ramapithecus* lived in Africa some 14 million years ago but later in Eurasia, *Australopithecus* some 5 to 1 million years ago, and *Homo* arose between 3 and half a million years ago. All of us are hominids and we arose from or alongside the Dryopithecine pongids during the early Miocene or perhaps the late Oligocene, as shown in Fig. 4.1 (which is necessarily tentative and subject to revision in the light of further evidence).

So much for the barest bones of the story of human evolution. These give us the structure on which to pin our speculations. Our primary interest here is in the evolutionary aspects of human society and social behaviour. What can we read into, or build upon, the facts as presented above?

First, we need to remember our forest ancestry. We have not always been open-country creatures, and coming out into the open necessitated a transformation of behaviour that most authors have rightly made central to their understanding of human evolution. Secondly, we need to remember that we are derived from the same stock that gave rise to the modern apes, and that we are therefore more closely related to the apes than to any monkey species, such as baboons for example. This fact is borne out by our physical structure, which is much more like that of apes than of monkeys. Baboons, on which authors such as Morris (1967, 1969), DeVore and Washburn (1963), Tiger and Fox (1972), Campbell (1966), Jolly (1970), Ardrey (1961), Pfeiffer (1969) and others have focused their attention, show certain interesting parallels to human beings in their behaviour and social organization, but it may be that these and other authors have rather neglected the evidence from living apes in their efforts to trace the evolution of human society.

The baboon model

The appeal of a baboon-type social system in the search for a model of early hominid or pre-hominid society (see Fig. 4.2) seems to have been twofold. On the one hand, baboons live in open country in Africa and have therefore been subject to the same kinds of selection pressures as early man may have been. On the other, baboon society with its male dominance hierarchy, its tight-knit group cohesion and its reputation for high levels of aggression and sexuality, seems to accord to certain ideas of human society.

All this overlooks two crucial facts. However similar the African savanna environment in which modern baboons and early hominids may have lived, this in itself is no argument for similar adaptations to that environment, for different species adapt to a common environment in different ways, their particular adaptation depending mainly on the physical and behavioural characteristics they bring with them to the new environment in the first place. The giraffe and the zebra can share a savanna environment without coming into direct competition with each other because of their different adaptations, which are in turn based on their different ancestries. So, too, when early man, a hominid with pongid ancestry, came out on to the savannas of Africa and settled down there over a period of several million years, there is every reason to suppose that he adapted to his new environment on the basis of his pre-existing adaptations.

Monkeys (*Mesopithecus*) were already on the savanna when he arrived, exploiting it in their particular way, so there is an *a priori* reason to suppose that the successful early hominids evolved in ways that did not bring them into direct competition with them, but found their own particular niche.

It has always been supposed that the early hominid niche was in some way geared to hunting or scavenging, for we know that man eventually adapted to a way of life based on eating meat as well as vegetable foods. This view may, however, be wrong. The first adaptation made by the earliest hominids when they colonized the open country may have been quite different from their subsequent meat-eating adaptations: they may initially have been specialized *seed-eaters*. This at first sight unlikely hypothesis has been suggested by Jolly (1970) in explanation of a number of puzzling features of the earliest hominid fossils we possess, those named *Ramapithecus*.† Some 14 million years ago, *Ramapithecus* already had greatly reduced canine and incisor teeth. Canine reduction is characteristic of all hominids and is thus very ancient. Traditionally, it has been explained by the argument that tool-use rendered a dental armoury unnecessary and that such an armoury might be a disadvantage in intra-group conflicts. But there is a grave drawback to this theory— no tools have been found in association with *Ramapithecus*, and it seems most unlikely that *Ramapithecus* was more than a sporadic tool-user (like the chimpanzee, for example), since it antedates by some 10 million years the first evidence of systematic tool-use by hominids.

Jolly's argument is based on a point-by-point comparison between early hominids and *Theropithecus*, the gelada. He finds a large number of similarities between the two forms, especially in the skull, jaws and teeth. These similarities serve at the same time to distinguish the early hominids from chimpanzees and other pongids, and geladas from baboons. It thus looks as if there has been parallelism in the evolution of the early hominids and *Theropithecus*. We know that *Theropithecus* is a seed-eater, and Jolly suggests that the evidence shows that the earliest hominids were seed-eaters too. Dental reduction is an adaptation to seed-eating, as are a number of other features, e.g. manual dexterity, dexterity of tongue movements, emphasis on a sitting posture. On the social behaviour side, Jolly suggests that since geladas have evolved one-male units, this kind of organization may have been characteristic of the earliest hominids.

Early *Australopithecus* was thus, for Jolly, a product of the seed-eating adaptation 'phase 1'. During the time of *Australopithecus*, some

† Szàlay (1975) has recently argued against Jolly's hypothesis, but the issue remains undecided.

groups began to enter 'phase 2' of hominid differentiation, the exploitation of the meat resources of the savannas by hunting and scavenging, with more elaborate communication, more co-operation between groups and more extensive use of tools and weapons. *Austra-lopithecus africanus* was the form in which these adaptations were para-mount, as opposed to *A. robustus*, which persisted as a granivorous form in the old tradition, finally dying out while *A. africanus* evolved into *Homo*.

Jolly's hypothesis fits well with the view that hominids, in adapting to open country conditions, did not 'become baboon-like' in their social organization. His suggestion is that they 'became gelada-like', and, with regard to social organization, that they may have de-veloped all-male bands and one-male groups. This is an idea to which we shall return later. For the moment we need only note that gelada one-male groups are not spatially cohesive at all times; the male and his females form a loose and sometimes scattered unit in the troop, unlike the Hamadryas baboon where the one-male group is together all the time. This characteristic of males of leaving their females and not being with them all the time is, we shall see, an important factor in man's emergence and has never been sufficiently stressed. When, in due course, the hunting adaptation arose, it was dependent on male mobility. Had the early hominids evolved a baboon-like society, hunting by all-male teams could never have evolved, for savanna baboons take their females and infants with them wherever they go, thus limiting their mobility and largely ruling out a hunting way of life. One of early man's main achieve-ments seems to have been the transformation of males from vege-tarian food-finders to hunter-scavengers who left their females and young and went off in male groups, linking up with the other element of their society after the kill.

The chimpanzee model

The model I want to suggest in place of the baboon model for early hominid society is the chimpanzee model (see Fig. 4.2). I have already said that man never was a chimpanzee and I hope I have made it clear what man's relationship with the modern apes is. But the fact remains that if we want to find a living primate that physic-ally most nearly resembles the middle-range Dryopithecines of the early Miocene, the chimpanzee is the best candidate. Of the other living apes, the gorilla resembles a very large form of *Dryopithecus* (*D. major*); but such a large form would not be a likely candidate for ancestry to the pre-hominid pongids. And the orang-utan has adapted to arboreal life much more completely than the chimpanzee, so that its modern way of life is more specialized than that of our ancestors, with correlated physical modifications that make it less like *Dryopithecus* than the chimpanzee.

I want now to try to look at the societies of chimpanzees, baboons and early man, and to show that if we start with an understanding of the social life of chimpanzees as they live in the African forest today, and if we compare this with the social life of baboons, we get a better model for explaining the emergence of hominid society from chimpanzees than from baboons. Since modern chimpanzees are, physically, not so far removed from the ancestral Dryopithecines, then is it not logically necessary to work with a chimp-like model rather than a baboon-like model for the society and behaviour of early man? If the answer is 'yes', then a lot of the evolutionary underpinning of the view of man offered by Ardrey, Lorenz, Morris or Fox and Tiger has to be jettisoned and in its place we can build

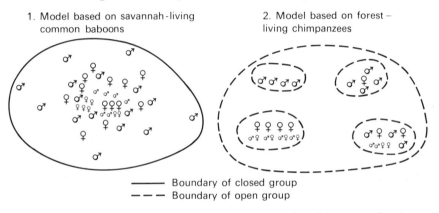

1. Model based on savannah-living common baboons

2. Model based on forest – living chimpanzees

———— Boundary of closed group
– – – – Boundary of open group

FIG. 4.2. Two non-human primate models for early man's social organization (see text).

up what I believe to be a new and exciting picture of the emergence of human culture.

Let us therefore begin with a sketch of what is known about forest chimpanzee society, based largely on the work of Henry Nissen (1931), Adriaan Kortlandt (1962), Jane van Lawick-Goodall (1968), myself and my wife in our field study in the Budongo Forest (Reynolds and Reynolds 1965), and a re-study there by the Japanese primatologist Sugiyama (1968, 1969). All these studies have concurred on the major issues, though some have naturally focused more particularly on one or other of them. In the description I shall endeavour to point out as we go along the main points of difference from savanna baboon-like society, and shall introduce some highly pertinent data concerning chimpanzee society in more open conditions.

Chimpanzees, in the first place, are *nomadic*. There is no territory ownership in them or any of the large apes. In savanna–woodland conditions distinct groups do form and keep apart, except that sexually receptive females move between the groups (Itani and Suzuki 1967). In the Budongo forest chimpanzees were free to travel widely, and did not do so only because social ties and familiarity with a certain part of the forest kept them to some extent in one place. We found no evidence that forest-living chimpanzees are attacked or chased away from certain areas by other members of their own species, but instead a potent *attraction* existed between the groups we observed.

The word 'group' raises immediately the most exciting feature of forest chimpanzee society, which I have called the 'open-group' system and which again is reported by most of those who have studied the species in its natural forest habitat. In a nutshell, no chimpanzee belongs to any one particular permanent social grouping which stays together all the time. The only exception is the infant or juvenile that stays with its mother. Apart from that, chimps are forever changing their associates, leaving some and joining others; they form a community within which spontaneous associations form and disband. Sometimes they change like this several times a day, or after a few days. Nothing could contrast more with the baboon's system whereby an individual belongs to a particular group or sometimes a set of sub-groups and is an outsider to all other groups. The savanna baboon is surrounded by familiar faces from birth to death; this in-group is a face-to-face context that provides all the stimuli and outlets for its social interactions. The chimpanzee, having left its mother at the age of 5 or 6, is free to join others of its own age and sex or to wander alone; an adolescent male can tag along with a bunch of mothers forming a nursery group, or study a mating pair and have a try for himself, or join some other adolescents for a romp. Or he can find his mother and spend the day with her. Chimpanzees meeting in the forest show all kinds of interactions, probably depending on their previous relationships with each other. Adult males sometimes get very excited and display to each other, but not always: sometimes they touch each other in affectionate greeting. Younger animals and females not in oestrus do not usually create much of a stir when they join groups, they appear to slot in without difficulty. Females in oestrus arouse males sexually and tend to attract a retinue of clients, or sometimes to form 'honeymoon' couples (Tutin 1974).

The question arises whether chimpanzee society is *wholly* open?

The most relevant and up-to-date work on this topic has been accomplished by a number of Japanese primatologists working in Western Tanzania (see Kawanaka and Nishida, 1974). In this area of riverine forests, woodlands, and open country, distinct social groups of chimpanzees have been found to exist. These groups consist of a core of adult males who, in the case of one well-studied group, have remained as the social core of the group for over eight years. During this same period, females have changed groups regularly. Are males antagonistic to 'outsider' males from other groups? On two occasions the Japanese workers have shown this to be the case, but each time an artificial feeding place was involved, and their behaviour was not wholly natural. Normally, rather than behaving aggressively, males from different groups avoid each other, and it may well be advantageous for such a mechanism to operate in these ecological circumstances. In the rainforest, by contrast, the richer food supply permits of a denser population, and instead of avoiding one another groups of males seem to interact much more. Nevertheless we still do not understand how far and wide chimpanzees actually do range in their normal forest lives. It seems to me that there would be no great gain and probably a loss in wandering *aimlessly* about the forest. The loss would be in terms of food-finding ability and reproductive success. Movements therefore are probably non-random and socially and geographically delineated.

This brings us to another characteristic of chimpanzee society. In the course of adapting to the food distribution in the forest, chimps have developed a division of labour in the food quest which has led to the existence of all-male groups, consisting of adult males only, and all-mother groups, consisting of females and their offspring only. These are permanent group *types* rather than permanent groups of particular individuals. Not all mothers are always in mother groups nor are all adult males in male groups. But such groups do form and are probably ever present in chimpanzee society, and they have a particular function in the food quest. Male groups in Budongo were, we found, highly exploratory and thus highly mobile, very excitable and very noisy. They made their way around the forest with hoots and shrieks, drumming on tree-buttresses and uprooting saplings as they went, rather like Hell's Angels. When they came to a fruiting tree they climbed and gorged themselves, but continued to hoot and keep up a merry din.

Nursery groups, by contrast, were quiet and extremely shy so that we had difficulty observing them. If one mother saw us she quickly took her infant to her breast and, her older offspring following, fled silently into the forest, other mothers following suit. If we managed to stay unobserved, we found that the mother groups were quiet and peaceful, the babies playing in small groups of two or three, the mothers feeding, dozing or grooming. Only when food was scarce did they move along. But if and when they heard the excited calling of other chimps nearby in the forest they visibly took notice, looking towards the calls, and very often a short while afterwards the whole group made a concerted move in the direction of the calls, joining the others to form a big mixed assemblage on a tree rich in figs or other fruit.

From this we deduced that chimpanzees have roles of the kind described in the previous chapter. The males, the mobile explorers, are the ones who find newly fruiting trees; females, rendered much less mobile by their infants (one, two or three per mother), home in on the food by following the calls of the males. Something on these lines could provide a basis for the emergence of a hominid division of labour on the savannas during the Pliocene, with males going out to scavenge or hunt, females staying behind to gather food and care for the young. Baboon-type societies seem to offer no such basis.

The last feature of chimpanzee society to which I want to draw attention briefly is what may be called the 'family'. By this I mean not a social institution but a cluster of offspring around a mother. Such a grouping is, as already stated, found in chimpanzees, and as the young stay with the mother longer than any other primate except man, the family can be quite large. Jane van Lawick-Goodall's work has shown that even after the young leave the mother, at the age of 5 or 6, they continue to return on visits to her, both sons and daughters. Right into adult life and presumably up to the mother's death, she is a central focus for family interaction and her young therefore have a high rate of interaction among themselves. In fact there is every reason to talk about brother–brother, brother–sister and sister–sister relations as being among the closest and warmest in chimpanzee society. With regard to mating, chimpanzee sons have rarely been known to mate with their mothers; brother–sister mating is also uncommon and there is obviously some kind of a block against it. Out-mating is preferred.

Australopithecine society

What may Australopithecine society have been like? *Australopithecus* was wholly savanna-adapted and it is this creature which has been characterized by a number of authors as having developed a baboon-like society in adaptation to open country conditions. Thus *Australopithecus* is variously said to have lived in closed troops, to have had dominance hierarchies, or to have been territorial. All this, I suggest, overlooks any preadaptations *Australopithecus* may have had.

What effects would the ecological pressures of a meat-oriented diet have had on a pongid type of social organisation? Moving further afield over the savannas in quest of game, the evolving hominid males could no longer communicate effectively with females and young. The mothers had to change too, not just eating but gathering food from their traditional food sources for their males as well as themselves, and gaining thereby the advantages of a diet including meat given to them by their mates, and at the same time increasing their dependence on males for protection and, in part, for food. Water now became scarcer and its locations in the dry season (water-holes) must have become foci of population at that time, especially since the hominid heat-loss adaptation, the bare-skin-and-sweat complex, necessitated a constant water intake. During the rainy season these aggregations doubtless split up and went their ways, coming together again at other or the same holes next year. When not at water-holes the women and children may have lived in smallish matrifocal family units in rock shelters or clumps of trees or caves for shade and security, foraging for vegetable produce, while the males were off hunting for days at a time, sometimes returning with meat, sometimes not. Relationships between the dispersed foraging and hunting groups were probably friendly, for the advantages of friendship would far outweigh those of hostility. Co-operation would benefit both females with young, who would perhaps need help with food or water at times of short supply, and males, who might well have to follow game in any direction for days on end as modern hunters like the Bushmen do, meeting other males as they went and joining forces in the hunt or to frighten away lions or hyenas from their kills. There seems no reason to suppose that *Australopithecus* was a hierarchical, troop-living species, defending his hunting grounds against other groups of his own kind.

It was probably with the transition of *Australopithecus* into *Homo* that the most exciting and most unexpected thing in the entire evolution of living matter happened. This was the emergence of conceptual awareness of social forms, the conceptualization of social relations and the prodigious effort to classify ongoing behaviour. This has led to the gradual emergence of norms and deviance, of a two-way interaction between social ideas and social behaviour. With all this went the development of a truly symbolic language, used first to express what was already happening but was only just becoming conceptualized, later to transmit norms to succeeding generations and thus create the social world for them, with all the possibilities for rapid change that this implies. The emergence of man was essentially a coming into self-awareness of what was already a highly complex social being, and I think that *this coming into conceptual awareness was the crucial and fundamental adaptation that enabled man to master first the savanna environment and later the rest of the world.* By it he was enabled to achieve a quite rigid and regular pattern of social relations without resorting to the face-to-face system of a baboon-like society. This was man's key social adaptation to the open country: the conscious ordering of social relations by conceptualization of the self and of the group, its structure and roles. This breakthrough, which may well have happened in Africa during the early Pleistocene as *Australopithecus*† evolved into *Homo*, enabled man to continue to operate and enjoy the advantages of an open-group system but to put much more structure and coherence into it, thus making his way of life as a hunter–gatherer more secure and less liable to succumb to the vagaries of climate and food shortages than it must have been hitherto.

What then happened as *Australopithecus* underwent a transition which changed him from a creature with a brain which, though of hominid form (see below), was scarcely larger than that of a chimpanzee (the cranial capacity of chimpanzees ranges from 300 to 480 cm³, of *Australopithecus* from 428 to 760 cm³) to a creature with a brain size ranging from 800 cm³ to 1250 cm³ (overlapping modern man's 1000–2000 cm³) and worthy of inclusion in the genus *Homo* as our immediate ancestor, *Homo erectus*? (Comparative brain sizes are shown in Fig. 4.3). Previous studies have linked brain expansion to the improvement in tool-making by *H. erectus*. *Australopithecus* undoubtedly did use tools and probably also *made* primitive stone choppers from pebbles crudely pointed at one end by chipping. *Homo erectus* went well beyond this, to make handsome hand-axes, carefully chipped on both sides. *H. erectus* also succeeded in controlling fire and using it to keep himself warm, to keep off predators and to cook his food, perhaps not in Africa in the early days, but certainly later when he had spread into Europe and Asia.

But can we accept as an explanation for the great expansion and development in the human brain, that it was related to the increasing use of tools? It is not an explanation to say that brain size (or complexity, or frontal lobe size, or a specific speech area) developed or increased in connection with increased tool-making. This is not a causal statement. It is not clear how tool-making could have caused

---

†For present purposes *Homo habilis* is bracketed with *Australopithecus*. A glance at Fig. 4.3 shows, however, that *H. habilis* is relatively big-brained. Further finds in E. Africa will doubtless shed more light on the complex relationships of these hominid forms.

conceptual development, the development of powers of abstraction and symbolic word-use. Tool-making could have evolved in a rather stereotyped 'animal' way not involving symbolic thought. The frontal lobes, where most brain development has occurred in the evolution of man, is in any case not much concerned with the sensorimotor co-ordination involved in the manufacture of material things; people with damage in this area and people congenitally incapable of conceptual and abstract thought can often, nevertheless, do manual tasks involving the same thought processes as were involved in the construction of tools, fires and dwellings of early man. Experiments by Richard Wright (1972) have shown that orang-utans are capable of making and using chipped stone implements. And speech,

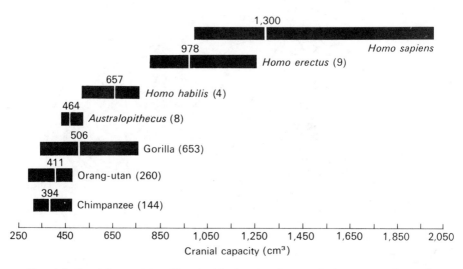

FIG. 4.3. Cranial capacities of hominoids, showing the sample size, mean value and range of values for each group. (Redrawn from Tobias, P. (1967), *Olduvai Gorge*, Vol. 2. Cambridge University Press. By permission of the publisher.)

surely, is in no clear way an *outcome* of tool-making. There is a danger of being misled in our efforts at understanding brain growth by the nature of the existing remains—worked stones and bones, man-made hand-axes—and of ending up by using the wrong evidence, leading to no explanation at all.

In this connection the work of Holloway (1972, 1974) is of considerable importance. He has compared endocasts of *Australopithecus* with those of living apes on the one hand, and man on the other. His conclusions are that the brain of *Australopithecus*, though of the same size as that of modern apes, was already distinctively hominid

in certain morphological respects. It has a larger and more con-
voluted third inferior frontal gyrus than that of apes, the frontal lobes
show 'a typically human morphology', brain height is proportion-
ately greater than in pongids and there are other similarities involving the temporal lobes and the position of the lunate sulcus.

The crucial areas of the brain for the study of language development would seem to be Broca's area and Wernicke's area (Geschwind 1972; see Fig. 4.4), neither of which is readily detectable from
endocasts. There is thus no direct proof or otherwise of the existence
of language in *Australopithecus*. Holloway's data indicate that the
Australopithecine brain 3 million years ago had certain hominid

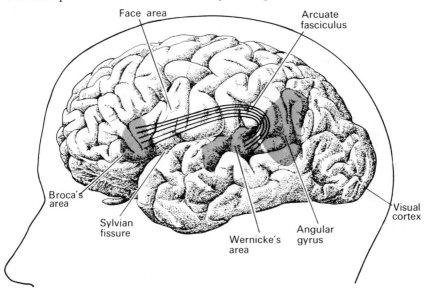

Fig. 4.4. Primary language areas of the human brain. (From Geschwind (1972).

characteristics, but what these amount to in functional terms we do
not know. In proportion to its body size, the brain size of *Australopithecus* was probably not, according to Holloway, greatly different from
the proportion found in modern man.

Thus part of the explanation of increased brain size in *Homo erectus*
and again in *Homo sapiens* is to be found in greater body size generally.
But it would be unwise to jump to the conclusion that *Australopithecus*
was already a competent symbol-user or linguistic creature. Perhaps
the wisest conclusion would be to see the brain of *Australopithecus* as
the essential preadaptation for the later symbolic/linguistic developments that characterized early *Homo*.

Thus the best brains in *Homo erectus* probably did not go in for either stone-working or pyrotechnics. More probably they worked on something that has left no trace—on sociology. In fact, if I had the chance to re-name *Homo erectus* (which ought on logical if not on taxonomic grounds to be done since the one thing that does not single out this form from its predecessors is its erect posture), then I would call him *Homo sociologicus*. For it was he who probably brought into existence the first systems of social rules that existed only in his own mind, who strove to give conscious structure and meaning to the complexity of proto-human life, and perhaps also to the phenomenon of death. As Lévi-Strauss (1968) has said, there have been men of the calibre of Einstein before the present time, and their achievements are with us still, unsung since they predate history itself.

CHAPTER 5

Man: constructor of his social world

SOMEHOW, at some time we can only guess at, early man achieved the distinction of bringing his social processes into his conscious mind and bringing his own inventive nature to bear on them. It cannot have been a quick process, it must have been a very slow one indeed, especially in the early stages. But we know it happened—that is the one certainty. All modern peoples everywhere have social systems consisting of social rules devised by their ancestors and perpetuated through their culture. What we do not know is the process by which this came to be.

Origins of the incest taboo

If, as Lévi-Strauss has said (1968, p. 351), there existed in bygone ages brilliant men with highly inventive minds, and these giant minds devised the rules of social life, marking by their efforts the transition between what was not yet man and what was man in the true sense, then what exactly did these giant minds do? Lévi-Strauss (1960) points at what he considers the first and crucial human social invention, the 'incest taboo'. Before man, he argues, mating occurred within families. Somewhere, sometime, the first men devised the taboo to regularize mating arrangements. Mating would henceforth, they decided, have to be with members of other families, and eventually other groups. These, he says, were the crucial first steps to human society. Women became the first goods to be used in social transactions, the first medium of exchange between social groups. Group A gave its women to group B and so hostility between them was avoided and they were allied by ties of kinship and affinity. The result of this was that they survived, having all the benefits of increased co-operation, larger scale, wider range of hunting territory, etc. (For a more detailed exposition of these ideas, see Leach (1970), Chapter 3.)

This may be an attractive theory of the emergence of human

society, but it is based on an assumption that is very probably wrong. This is that before man instituted the incest taboo, mating regularly occurred within the family. Today we know from well-documented studies of the society of a number of species, including Japanese macaques, rhesus macaques and chimpanzees, that even in species where mating is more or less wholly promiscuous, it is nevertheless rare, or at least uncommon, within families. Mother–son mating is extremely infrequent in wild primates, and brother–sister mating is less frequent than one would expect on a chance basis. Given the possibility of mating with a sibling or a less familiar associate the latter is preferred (Kortmulder 1968; Bischof 1972).

Chimpanzees are more or less promiscuous in their sexual relationships, apart from incest avoidance. Chimpanzee offspring continue to visit and associate, groom and play with their mothers right into adult life. Jane van Lawick-Goodall (1968) writes 'up to the time of writing (May 1968) no physically mature male has been observed to copulate with his mother ... Copulations have been recorded between known siblings but the female concerned (Fifi) tried to escape the first observed attempts of her two brothers to mount her in a sexual context.' This is a clear indication of incest avoidance: these chimpanzees had been under observation for many years, hundreds of copulations had been observed, and yet *none* of them occurred between a mother and her son, and only a few, apparently uneasy cases between siblings.

Not only do chimpanzees avoid incest; recent data (Kawanaka and Nishida, 1974) indicate that they practise consistent out-mating between groups in the open country conditions where such groups are found (see above). These authors have shown that whereas the males provide the social 'core' of groups, sexually active adult females very often move from one group to another and mate in the new group. In the case of two much-studied groups, these authors have found that an exchange system operates. 'The K- and the M-groups evidently exchange their females frequently ... even though the chimpanzees of the two unit-groups, especially adult males, are antagonistic to each other' (p. 181). Here then, or in some such system, we have a marvellous behavioural basis for the human institution of *exogamy*. But it is not only in chimpanzees that incest avoidance and kinship recognition are found.

In the case of rhesus monkeys living on Cayo Santiago in natural conditions, long-term studies have again led to the same conclusions. These monkeys live in more 'closed' groups than chimpanzees. Donald Sade (1965) has written: 'The most important relations a monkey develops are likely to be with its siblings and other relatives

... parent and offspring may maintain a distinct relation into the offspring's physical maturity.' He has documented this special relationship in terms of number of grooming contacts between monkeys. Duane Quiatt (1966) has again documented the closeness of family relations in rhesus monkeys by demonstrating the great amount of time related monkeys spend sitting near each other, and supporting each other in quarrels against members of other families. The same facts of family 'closeness' have again been documented by Virgo and Waterhouse (1969) in a rhesus colony at Bristol zoo. Family relations are intimate and supportive. Yet in all these cases, incest is avoided. In all the by now extensive literature on the rhesus groups living on Cayo Santiago there are relatively few cases on record of mother–son mating, and brother–sister mating is always infrequent; these groups, like the Gombe Stream chimpanzees, have been observed over many years. Japanese primatologists studying their own native macaques over more than a decade have reported the same (e.g. Imanishi 1965).

Donald Sade (1965) has already drawn the conclusion that I want to draw from the non-human primate data. He wrote:

> The fact that even rhesus monkeys can have correspondence as elaborate as they do between genealogical relation and behavioural relation suggests strongly that the immediate ancestors of the human species had at least as elaborate a system. The origins of the human family and of kinship should then be considered as being in the symbolic definition and generalization of statuses ... already present, as suggested by Count (1959, pp. 82–6). The variety of extant kinship systems would then be interpreted as results of millennia of cultural elaboration ... [of] ... the kinship system or systems that first appeared when our apish forefathers began to find their own behaviour suitable material for symbol-making.

I find this formulation of human social evolution very satisfactory in all its basic assumptions, much more so than that of Lévi-Strauss with its total ignorance of the primate data. I think it is precisely the conceptualizing of existing social relations and the formulating of them using symbolic 'tools', e.g. words, that mark the true transition from prehuman ancestor to man. It was when our ancestors began to gain awareness of the relationships they already recognized in terms of differential behaviour that man emerged.

The problem of concept formation is not just a problem of increased cortical power but also of communication. A selective advantage of such abilities would exist only if they enabled more efficient functioning for individuals, and for this to happen it was necessary from the start that concepts be communicable to others. Even such basic concepts as 'yes' and 'no', 'please' or, to borrow from Washoe, 'gimme' are essentially social communications, while object concepts, e.g. 'table', are of no use except in the context of social inter-action, and indeed we cannot acquire them except through social communication.

What was the mode of early man's concept communication? Some, e.g. Hewes (1973), and those who have been impressed with the abilities, demonstrated by Allen and Beatrice Gardner, of chim-panzees to use gestural language, would favour a gestural origin of language. Others, notably G. H. Mead, who as early as 1934 drew attention to the fact that words, because of their uniquely equal per-ceptibility to both speaker and hearer(s), would favour the view that human language was from the outset an oral–verbal phenomenon. No one would deny, of course, that such a development would be embedded in a whole set of non-verbal signals deriving from pre-linguistic millennia. Following Mead, I would favour a verbal origin for concept transmission, and would see in this further reason for brain growth, even to the point of developing a special brain area, now identified in the temporal lobe of the brain, for speech function-ing.

Certainly it has been with language that man has built up the structures and superstructures of his society. He has named his rela-tives and non-relatives, his seniors and juniors. He has named all sorts of different kinds of relationships from the most intimate through those of a formal kind to the most hostile. In so doing he initially gave conscious expression to what was there before, but in-creasingly with the passage of time produced new forms of social life by inventions and sub-divisions not hitherto existing at all. With sub-sequent transitions from a hunter–gatherer life-style, through an agricultural one to an industrial one, his social forms, though they may mirror those of his pre-human ancestors, are now his own pro-ducts. If there are similarities at the present time between human institutions and animal social organization we should not fall into the trap of concluding prematurely that homologous processes are at work.

Thus over the millennia man has shaped and constructed his society. He has himself created the immediate matrix of values and norms in which we live. And in so doing, he has effectively, in every society he has made, delimited the parameters of human personality, given content or meaning to social life, arbitrated between sanity and madness, conformity and deviance, good and bad. In this way he has created the social worlds in which each individual comes to have ideas about the nature of his own self, and about others. To this extent he has made himself the things he now is. He is still at the same time a product of evolution, a laughing, crying, loving and fighting member of the Hominidae. In seeing man as a self-made entity capable of social change in many directions, one must not overlook the constant interaction between the man-made social world and the non-man-made physical one. Human social interaction is the product of history, of economic forces, of a symbolic society-in-mind, but it also contains the remaining products of phylogeny.

If we accept Mead's insistence on language as an essential part of human social life and his explanation of how we develop into cultural beings and his designation of society as a complex of interacting minds, then this gives us a sufficiently distinct picture of human as opposed to animal society for us to go back to the crucial question: how did such a human system arise in the first place? What may have been the advantages of concept-based society?

Precisely because of the open-group system it was in the sphere of social relations that conceptualization was most important. Words such as 'mother', 'brother', 'sister', 'family', geared to the words for 'own' and 'other', must be basic to any conceptualization of social relations, and with the distinction 'here'/'over there' quite accurate designations of the whereabouts of a large number of the kin of local people could be formulated. At that moment a remarkable thing could be achieved: *the open-group system could be given a structure not based on face-to-face relations but on conceptualized relationships.* For the first time ever group A could be distinguished from group B not on the basis of its whereabouts but purely on the basis of its genealogical connections. We know that monkeys can distinguish between their own and other kin at a behavioural level; now it would become possible for early man to distinguish between them conceptually as well, formulating his ongoing behaviour in symbols. Having distinguished grandmother A from grandmother B you can then distinguish the offspring of grandmother A from those of grandmother B as two distinct social groups, and then you can create a word for a system of out-mating between the two. You can harden up an existing tendency for out-mating into a normative system, and you can proceed to punish 'deviants' who mate with their sisters.

Again, regulating relationships in this way only makes sense in an open-group system. If, as in the case of troop-living monkeys, all your family is around you full-time there is little to be gained by being able to refer to them all by name. By contrast, if your family is scattered around the place it will help you to co-operate with them if you can designate them and discover from other visitors who arrive in your group where they are. And if you are a young man in search of mates you can find out where these may be available before setting off. The process of conceptualization of social relations was man's key adaption to the savannas, his alternative to other methods of 'structuring up' society—the closed, face-to-face troop, the closed one-male group system or any other such system. The breakthrough into conceptual awareness enabled man to continue to operate an open-group system with all the advantages of co-operation and dispersion that we see in modern hunter–gatherers while avoiding the risks of loss of contact that might have been sufficient to eliminate an open-group system otherwise.

The categorizing animal

If Lévi-Strauss can be criticized for having ignored the evidence pertaining to the biological bases of human society, he must be praised for his devoted attention to the specifically human practice of categorizing things and creating rules about them. His analyses of this topic have a great bearing on the matter in hand. What is valuable in Lévi-Strauss is that he has shown something that is basic to man, so basic that it comes to be taken for granted, namely that man is a *categorizing* and a *rule-making* creature (Lévi-Strauss 1962). No other creature is like this. Put man in an environment and he will begin putting symbolic labels on the bits and pieces that he can distinguish in it and then making rules about them, i.e. regulating his conduct with respect to them.

Now, as Lévi-Strauss has shown, one of the primary areas of categorization and rule-making is man himself, in particular his social life. Lévi-Strauss has always argued that in structuring his social world man uses the same kinds of relationships he discovers in his interaction with the natural world. While it ignores the biological derivation of social relationships this idea nevertheless offers us a guideline as to the source from which early man drew some of his ideas about social structure. Totemism, for example, involves the use of animals to distinguish between human groups. And Lévi-Strauss has written about the symbolic significance of the ideas of 'raw' and 'cooked' (1964). Edmund Leach (1970), in his book *Lévi-Strauss*, writes:

Primitive man, before he had any writing, perhaps even before he had developed his spoken language to a point where it could be used as a refined instrument of logic, was already using things 'out there' as instruments with which to think. This is the essence of Lévi-Strauss' arguments about totemic species categories, and food preparation categories—they are categories which refer to things 'out there' in the human environment and they are things good for thinking not just things good to eat [p. 114].

This chapter makes one point only, which is nevertheless crucial to the thesis of the book as a whole, namely that during the course of human evolution an essential and characteristic development, found in no other species, was the conceptual formulation and subsequent constant reformulations of social relationships. We cannot ever know for sure what the pattern of initial formulations may have been nor how it has changed over the millennia. Morgan in 1871 posited a primitive form of matriliny, with subsequent development of patrilineal forms of society, and his thinking influenced Engels and Marx, for it buttressed the central Marxist notion that social forms emerge as a superstructure to an economic base, in this case the emergence of property ownership by males, transmission from father to son, and the development of male-dominated society with the rise of feudal and capitalist systems. A social anthropologist has difficulty in accepting this as a *general* theory because he knows of so many societies in which matrilineal organization is quite compatible with property transmission between males; Malinowski, for instance, in 1922 described just such a society in the Trobriand Islands in his famous book *Argonauts of the Western Pacific*. Other early speculators such as MacLennan, Tylor and Westermarck wrote in a similar vein, though differing in political persuasion and the inferences they drew. Behind such theories lay Darwinian evolutionary theory and concepts of social process as a form of competitive struggle, perhaps most thoroughly integrated into social theory by Spencer and Galton. The study of late nineteenth–early twentieth-century thought about biology and society is worthy of extensive study and has been written about by authors such as Burrow (1966), Banton (1967), Freeman (1974) and Young (1971). Now is not the moment to enter into that debate or to consider how it looks in retrospect. Suffice it to say that the point this chapter makes is of a more general kind; it concerns the erection of sociological edifices by human minds as a new departure from the pre-existing animal arrangements, and it does not concern the actual nature of those edifices, their subsequent transformations and the reasons for those transformations.

Having said that, let us now move on to the next section of this book, which returns to our primary concern: the organic, evolved nature of man. Having by now repeated *ad nauseam* the development by him of a man-made social world in which he subsequently lived, we must now rebound forcibly to the undeniable and fascinating fact that in his physical make-up he is incredibly close to other mammalian life-forms in general and to his fellow primates in particular. Man continues and will always continue to be an organic being. Though living in an ideas-world of his own making, he remains very much an organism, an evolved part of the natural world as Freeman

(1965) has forcibly reminded us. Rebounding to that side of the dialectic confronts one again with the question that this book sets out to explore and if possible to answer: how far does this organic side of man determine his behaviour, even his social arrangements? Simply to say he has constructed them might not rule out the possibility that he has constructed them within a set of evolved limits. To what extent, and in what respects, are Fox, Tiger, Ardrey, Lorenz and Morris right after all?

The only way to proceed would appear to be to examine with more than passing interest the known facts of human biology, in particular of genetics, processes of physical growth and development, and of the development of social behaviour from birth onwards, in so far as this can be seen as a biological process. Ultimately, from a knowledge of what exactly those who have studied human developmental biology have discovered about it, we can come both to appreciate something of the complexity of human biology, and to see more clearly its place in the explanation of human action. We need to study with great care the *mechanisms* by which, from their beginnings in the newly conceived fertilized ovum, the necessary transitions occur to result in the formation of adult human beings engaged in the perpetuation of social structures. In all this we must exercise the utmost caution in jumping further than is legitimate from the known available causal mechanisms. There can be, as we shall see, no conceivable justification for jumping from genes to human actions. An enormous number of intervening variables has to be considered along the way. Yet from a finite number of tiny unicellular beginnings all of history, all of poetry, and all of technology have arisen. What are the processes of human life that have enabled this to happen?

PART III

The physical mechanisms of human action

Introduction to Part III

In Part I a set of ideas and supporting evidence about the biology of human action was presented and critically reviewed. In Part II a speculative evolutionary argument was formulated. In Part III an effort is made to seek out and present the hard side of the evidence bearing on human development. The emphasis is on *physical* development, not only because the evidence is 'harder', but because the physical side of development has implications for action which, though often neglected and still unclear, must nevertheless be carefully sought out. This is the main rationale for the part as a whole, and its place in the book.

There is another reason, which relates back to the book's central arguments. Students of human action working outside the biological sciences often feel mystified about the extent of biological 'control' of behaviour and consequently tend to dismiss that side altogether, or alternatively to overstate it. In part this is because of a lack of acquaintance with the level of inferences about causation that can be legitimately drawn from the data we now have. The second objective in setting out the data in this part is to clarify this matter of level of inferences. We cannot jump from genes to actions. Genes have their functions and to deny or ignore this (as often happens) is folly. But it is equally wrong to overstate the 'power' of genetic control. Likewise with the other processes of development included here. The third objective of this part is thus to give the student outside the biological sciences but interested in human biology in relation to action a reasonable idea of the level and extent of our knowledge in this field.

CHAPTER 6

Genes and individuality

CULTURES HAVE to have something to mould. What they in fact have is an exceedingly complex arrangement of biochemical machinery, each piece containing certain instructions of a highly specific kind about its own development. Culture, too, provides a set of instructions about development. Man is thus subject to two sets of instructions, a cultural set and an organic set, both of which are with him from conception to death. The organic set is in the ascendancy before birth; after birth the cultural set becomes steadily more potent, until eventually, towards death, the organic set regains the ascendancy. Cells are 'born' in two ways: by fusion (this occurs once only for each of us, at the moment of conception) and by division (this occurs many millions of times throughout life during growth and replacement processes).

Growth leads eventually to loss of function, or senescence. Both growth and senescence are accompanied by disease. Disease in the sense in which authors such as May (1958) use the term is a tipping of the scales in favour of those substances that are destructive of our tissues or those organisms that feed on our tissues. Between them, senescence and disease constitute the anti-life or life-depleting aspects of our organic existence, just as cell division, differentiation and function constitute the dynamic aspect of the life process. Both aspects act alongside each other during infancy, childhood and adolescence, but after maturity mitosis and differentiation are much reduced, function continues though for the most part with reduced efficiency, and the process of senescence is accompanied by the build-up of constitutional disease processes. Occasional onslaughts from infectious disease are a further source of breakdown of body functions at all ages, and may have weakening constitutional effects in later life, as in the case of cardiac scar tissue left after infectious rheumatoid arthritis.

The nature of genes

Let us look first at the most elementary of the life-sustaining processes: the organization of those substances that are responsible for

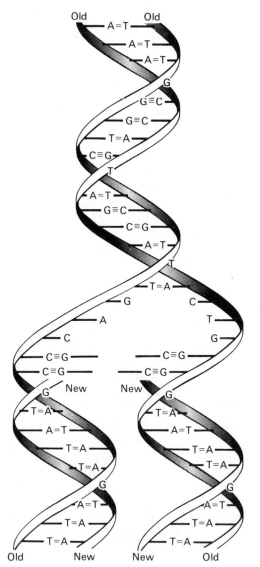

FIG. 6.1. The replication of DNA. A, adenine; C, cytosine; G, guanine; T, thymine.
(Redrawn from J. Z. Young (1971).)

the inherited aspects of our organic nature. Such is the universality of these basic processes that they are the same, or nearly so, for all forms of life from bacterium to man. A typical cell consists of a nucleus and a surrounding cytoplasm. Within the nucleus are bundles of the substance DNA (deoxyribonucleic acid) wrapped in proteins. This DNA is in the form of double strands made up of pairs of nucleotides. There are only four nucleotides: adenine, thymine, guanine and cytosine, and only two types of pairs: adenine–thymine and guanine–cytosine. The nucleotides along one strand work in triplets (i.e. three neighbouring nucleotides) to synthesize amino acids. There are 64 theoretical triplets, but in fact only 20 kinds of amino acid are produced because several different triplets frequently work to produce the same amino acid; in addition three of the triplets determine not amino acids but termination of amino-acid production. The combinations of DNA nucleotide triplets and the 20 amino acids they synthesize are known as the genetic code (see Table 6.1). The amino acids produced by a given set of nucleotide triplets form together into a chain known as a polypeptide, and this chain ends when a 'termination' triplet occurs on the DNA strand. Thus when DNA is active in amino-acid production (e.g. during cell division (Fig. 6.1)) a large number of polypeptide chains is being produced according to the instructions coded in triplets along the DNA strand, or chromosome (see Table 6.1). Messenger RNA carries the information encoded in DNA on the chromosomes from the nucleus of the cell to the sites of protein synthesis in the cytoplasm. Each human body cell contains 46 chromosomes, consisting of 23 pairs, one of each pair from the mother and one from the father. The maternal and paternal chromosomes in any given pair are homologous, i.e. of the same type, though not identical. In only one case is the pair not homologous, and that is in the case of the sex chromosomes of males, who have one X and one Y chromosome (see Fig. 6.2).

During embryonic and postnatal development, cell division is occurring and nucleotides are producing polypeptide chains of amino acids. These polypetide chains are already fairly complex, consisting as they do of up to 20 amino acids in various combinations with one another. The polypeptides themselves are then linked together to form proteins. Some of these proteins are in the nucleus with the DNA, others (most of them) are in the surrounding cytoplasm and in other parts of the body. There are myriads of types of proteins, some very common in the body, e.g. the several million protein molecules of haemoglobin, others rare. Most of the proteins have a specific function to serve as catalysts, i.e. to speed up biochemical reactions; these proteins are called enzymes. Other pro-

TABLE 6.1

The genetic code

First letter

Third letter

		Second letter				
		a	b	A	B	
a		Phe	Ser	Tyr	Cys	a
		Phe	Ser	Tyr	Cys	b
		Leu	Ser	chain end	chain end	A
		Leu	Ser	chain end	Try	B
b		Leu	Pro	His	Arg	a
		Leu	Pro	His	Arg	b
		Leu	Pro	Gln	Arg	A
		Leu	Pro	Gln	Arg	B
A		Ile	Thr	Asn	Ser	a
		Ile	Thr	Asn	Ser	b
		Ile	Thr	Lys	Arg	A
		Met	Thr	Lys	Arg	B
B		Val	Ala	Asp	Gly	a
		Val	Ala	Asp	Gly	b
		Val	Ala	Glu	Gly	A
		Val	Ala	Glu	Gly	B

Note. Each amino acid is coded by a triplet of three bases, as shown in the table, which is a compact way of setting out the 64 possible triplets.

The four bases are denoted by the letters a, b, A and B. In DNA the four bases are:

a = adenine   A = thymine
b = guanine   B = cytosine

In messenger-RNA they are:

a = uracil   A = adenine
b = cytosine   B = guanine

The 20 amino acids are identified as follows:

Ala = Alanine
Arg = Arginine   Lys = Lysine
Asn = Asparagine   Met = Methionine
Asp = Aspartic acid   Phe = Phenylalanine
Cys = Cysteine   Pro = Proline
Glu = Glutamic acid   Ser = Serine
Gln = Glutamine   Thr = Threonine
Gly = Glycine   Try = Tryptophan
His = Histidine   Tyr = Tyrosine
Ile = Isoleucine   Val = Valine
Leu = Leucine   Chain end

For example the triplet bAB stands for Gln = glutamine. This implies that guanine–thymine–cytosine codes for glutamine in DNA and cytosine–adenine–guanine codes for glutamine in RNA.

(From *The Genetics of Human Populations* by Cavalli-Sforza and Bodmer. W. H. Freeman and Company. Copyright © 1971.)

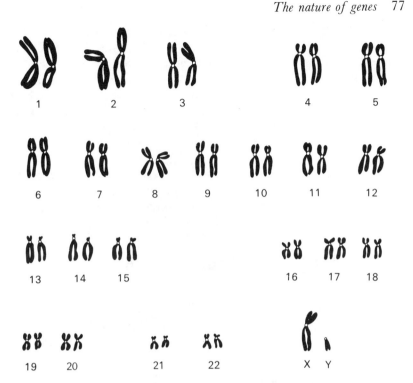

FIG. 6.2. The chromosomes of a normal male body cell, arranged in a karyotype. (Victor A. McKusick, *Human Genetics*, © 1969; reprinted by permission of Prentice-Hall Inc., Englewood Cliffs, New Jersey, U.S.A.)

teins function for transport (e.g. of oxygen or iron), for mechanical purposes (e.g. elasticity) and for defence (e.g. capture of antigens).

We are now in something of a position to see what genes are. Genes are those neighbouring nucleotide triplets that operate to produce, eventually, proteins. But we have noted that there is a *pair* of homologous chromosomes in each body cell, so that in each cell two sets of instructions are being issued about amino-acid production. If the maternal and paternal loci are identical then only one type of amino-acid chain will result and the genes at this locus are called homozygous. If the maternal and paternal chromosomes differ with regard to the arrangement of nucleotides at a given locus, then the instructions will differ, and one of two things may happen. First, the instructions from one chromosome may inhibit or suppress those of the other. Thus in the case of haemophilia, a gene producing a blood-clotting deficiency occurs in both males and females but its effects are seen only in males because it occurs on the X chromosome and its effects are masked by the corresponding normal gene on the other

X chromosome in females. This is a case of a sex-linked recessive deleterious gene in which the normal gene is dominant. (We know the gene is not carried by the Y chromosome because it can be transmitted through the mother.) Secondly, two different genes at a given locus may act in such a way that each contributes something to the result. An example of this is the pigment of petals of certain sweet peas: when a red strain is crossed with a white strain the offspring in the first generation are all pink. In this case the genes are co-dominant.

The above discussion of genetic processes has two purposes. On the one hand it seeks to clarify what genes are and how they act. An understanding of their protein-making properties is essential before we can assess their significance in wider organic processes,

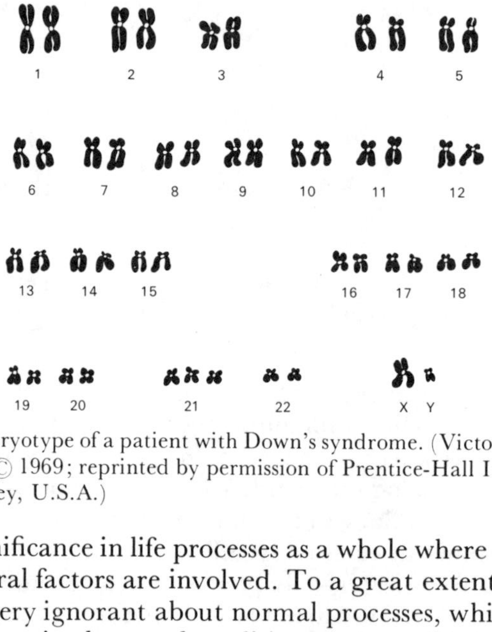

FIG. 6.3. The karyotype of a patient with Down's syndrome. (Victor A. McKusick, *Human Genetics*, © 1969; reprinted by permission of Prentice-Hall Inc., Englewood Cliffs, New Jersey, U.S.A.)

and their significance in life processes as a whole where environmental and cultural factors are involved. To a great extent we discover that we are very ignorant about normal processes, while our knowledge about certain abnormal conditions such as albinism, phenylketonuria and others is often rather complete, as a result of a knowledge of the underlying genetic fault and the resultant protein or enzyme deficiency, and a clinical understanding of the expression of such 'inborn errors of metabolism' in the phenotype. In other cases we know that the fault is not just genetic but chromosomal: Down's syndrome, or mongolism (Fig. 6.3), is known to be caused by trisomy 21 (an extra no. 21 chromosome), while Turner's syndrome (see Fig. 8.1) is known to be caused by monosomy of the sex chromosomes, i.e. one of the sex chromosomes is missing, leaving one X chromosome only. The excess, or absence, of large quantities of genetic instructions involved in these cases has ramifying effects on the individual's physical and mental development. The effect of these known errors is a good indication to us of the degree of genetic control involved in normal development.

The second purpose of our discussion of genetic processes is dealt with in the following section.

Human diversity

A knowledge of genetics raises an issue of profound importance: the question of individual uniqueness and the nature and extent of inter-individual differences. As far as genetics is concerned the only differences of interest are heritable differences. Despite the complexities of genetic and developmental processes it is possible for all individuals of a group to have the same genes or the same nucleotide sequences on their DNA molecules. Such tends indeed to be the case in so-called genetic 'pure lines': highly inbred strains of mice, flies or plants, members of which are in fact largely genetically identical with one another. In these cases the results have been achieved by generations of highly selective inbreeding of offspring. In the case of man, eugenicists have envisaged selective inbreeding programmes and a start was made towards the production of all-Aryan children in Germany in the 1930s. No such programme has been successful, for a number of excellent reasons, and in consequence we are faced with the unquestionable fact that with one kind of exception *each living human being is genetically unique*, and furthermore, so slim are the chances of duplication, that each living human being is genetically different from all previous (now dead) humans and all individuals as yet unborn. The exception, mentioned above, is the case of identical twins, who are genetically identical.

Of the number of genes in man, Cavalli-Sforza and Bodmer (1971) write as follows: 'Taking the average size of a polypeptide to be about 100 amino acids, the number of nucleotides coding for the average polypeptide will be 300, and therefore 600 in double-stranded DNA. The number of nucleotides in a haploid human cell is about 3×10^9; thus the number of cistrons should be $3 \times 10^9/600$ or approximately five million. This may be an overestimate ...' (pp. 35–6). In this sentence the word 'cistron' means the minimal functional unit of DNA nucleotides concerned in production of a polypeptide chain and is thus effectively the same as the 'gene' concept. In any case, whether we refer to genes or cistrons, the number involved in man is such that, given the immense possibilities of assortment that can be ascertained by means of Mendelian and post-Mendelian genetic theory, genetic uniqueness not in one but in very many respects is assured for each of us.

Likewise it warns us that any theory of human development must reckon with this basic diversity of our make-up. What is perhaps remarkable and calls most for explanation is the extent of similarities between members of human populations. This implies that individuals, though uniquely different from one another at the genetic level, nevertheless have much in common. Some genetic characters are common to all mankind, others to specific populations. The fact that all mankind is reproductively inter-fertile implies a fundamental compatibility between the organization of the DNA molecules of each individual and each other individual everywhere. Genes for the ABO blood group O have been found in every human population studied, whereas those for groups A and B are rare among the aboriginal inhabitants of the Americas. The Rhesus blood group allele R_O (cDe) is common among African Negroes but rare elsewhere, while the allele r (cde) is widely prevalent only in Europeans (this is the gene responsible for haemolytic disease of the newborn, caused by inter-parental rhesus incompatibility).

Within any given population, e.g. in Britain or the U.S.A., extent of sharing of the overall gene pool will depend on the extent to which actual matings approximate to a theoretical model of random mating. Under random mating gene-flow is continuous throughout the population; genetic differences between individuals are at their greatest since all the available genetic material is constantly being shifted around. In reality mating is never at random in any human population because of a variety of cultural rules, norms and expectations about who may mate with whom and who may marry whom. Homogamy, or preferential marriage with a person of one's own socio-economic class, caste or religion, is well established in many societies including our own and is clearly restrictive of gene-flow, tending to promote a closure of gene pools and, for a variety of reasons, to cause differences between the groups to increase over time. However, we should note that sub-groups within human populations frequently do mix and produce offspring whatever the cultural rules. And secondly, we should be cautious about jumping from theoretical propositions about the genetic differences likely to exist between sub-groups to statements about phenotypic differences between those groups, since in very few cases do we know the causal links between the genetic bases and their eventual outcomes.

For example it is known that age at first menstruation (menarche) is highly correlated between twins, especially identical twins, thus indicating the possibility of a strong genetic component. The correlation coefficient for heritability has been estimated at 0·9 and 0·93 in two studies (Petri 1935; Tisserand-Perrier 1953). Differences in age at menarche have also been shown to exist between socio-economic classes (see Chapter 7). Are these genetic? It might be predicted from the high estimates of heritability based on twin studies that they show genetic differences between classes. However, we also know that nutrition is an important determinant of age at menarche. This is shown, for instance, by the secular trend for this factor: average age at menarche has been declining at the rate of 4 months per decade during most of this century, a period during which a number of other changes in body size and maturation rates have been changing and for which the commonly accepted explanation is improved diet, hygiene and medical treatment. If nutrition and other environmental factors are heavily involved in the determination of age at menarche then the data on identical twins and other relatives are capable of an alternative interpretation in terms of relative similarity of dietary intake (it seems likely that twins would share most of their meals during the pre-menarcheal period). Heritability might in fact have quite a small effect on age at menarche. Since the secular trend appears to have operated across the board for the population as a whole, it seems not unreasonable to suppose that most or all genotypes are predisposing of a wide range of age at menarche but that actual age within this range is determined for each individual by her prior nutritional and other relevant environmental experiences. This would reduce the estimate of the effect of heritability on age at menarche considerably.

Thus, in making genetic comparisons between populations or subgroups of populations within which there is preferential mating, we are on safe ground only when the genotype–phenotype relationship is clear-cut. This excludes most multifactorial characters, where gene–environment interaction complicates the issue. If we go back to age at menarche, what exactly is the relationship between this and the genetic basis? It is certainly very complex. We need to consider the sex chromosomes (**XX**), the early differentiation of the foetus into a female, with ovaries and follicles, the actions of the pre-menstrual pituitary gland in secreting the sex hormones appropriate to bringing the menstrual cycle into existence, the higher brain centres that act on the pituitary, and the rest of the body which, according to how well it is nourished, can expedite or delay the onset of puberty. Co-ordination of all these parts is needed, some 13 or more years after the basic instructions in the form of nucleotide arrangements were laid down, in order to bring about a state of sexual preparedness essential for the continuation of the species. The exact way in which it all happens is still largely unknown in terms of the genetic loci and systems of interacting proteins that bring about the transitions of puberty. Clearly, hormones are of central importance but something has to trigger off increased levels of hormone production. And something has to trigger that something off, etc.

What is the contribution of genetic material to modern civilization? It is similar to the contribution of the sun to life on earth. Without the one, the other would cease to exist. In that sense genes are basic. But the sun has at various times nourished quite other *forms* of life than those that now exist, and perhaps in the future equally great transitions will again occur. Is it equally true that genes exert no specific control over the *forms* of human action and society? If there are genetic or other organic controls, what are they and how do they work? In particular, are they to be thought of as predispositions or limitations? These are questions to which we shall return again and again in this book.

Let us for the moment return to our theme of individuality. What are its implications for physical development?

First, we must be careful, while giving the fact of individual uniqueness due weight in any argument about 'average' or 'normal' behaviour, not to exaggerate its significance. Each cow, horse, frog and toad is genetically unique in the same way as each human is, yet a cow remains very much a cow and a toad a toad. The genotype for what we call a 'cow' thus has very distinct characteristics that to a great extent mask the characteristics of individuals. Despite their different coat colours and patterns, a herd of cows looks rather uniform. Close acquaintance, such as the farmer has, leads to the recognition of many differences, of temperament and physical appearance. But never is a cow so different that it more closely resembles a horse than its fellow kine.

So it is with man. There is a great difference between a pygmy and a Nilote, in some respects the greatest difference to be found between humans (Fig. 6.4), but the difference falls a long way short of the difference between either of them and man's closest relative, the chimpanzee. In the proportions of limbs, relative size of hand and foot to body, relative size of fingers and toes, size of incisors, canine and molar teeth, distribution of body hair, size of brain, structure of skull, position of foramen magnum and other cranial points, curvature of spine, shape of pelvis as well as in behaviour, all men are more akin to each other than to any other species. In addition all humans are inter-fertile, the surest indication of chromo-

FIG. 6.4. The shortest and the tallest people in the world—Congo pygmies and Nilotic Negroes such as the Dinka. Both live in tropical Africa. (Redrawn from Cole (1963).)

somal and genetic compatibility. The differences that do exist between populations are primarily the result of social and geographical isolation and failure to combine gene pools; the differences that exist between individuals within a breeding population are the result of differential distribution of some of the genetic material in its gene pool. Individual differences are greatest between people who belong to gene pools that have been isolated from each other for long periods and have in that time become modifed by a number of processes (mutation, natural selection and perhaps genetic drift) and have thus differentiated. These differences are least in members of one gene pool and in particular in small gene pools that are highly inbred (e.g. in small communities where there is a high level of inter-marriage between members).

In separating gene pools, social barriers can be just as effective as geographical ones, as has for example been shown by Hiernaux (1966) for the Tutsi, Hutu and Twa groups of people living cheek by jowl in the small country of Rwanda, in Central Africa. The three social groups are clearly distinct in terms of their ABO blood-group frequencies as well as in other, grosser morphological respects. The three groups have in fact come to live in Rwanda at different times and have not mixed but have remained as separate strata in a very rigid caste system, and as a result their gene pools have remained distinct. Further study beyond Rwanda indicates an affinity between the Tutsi and certain West African tribes; this is borne out by genetic and morphological similarities, and by linguistic connections. The Hutu are genetically similar to their Bantu-speaking neighbours in the nearby Congo; while the Twa are probably related to the Congolese pygmies.

The question of differences between individuals within a breeding population thus concerns the distribution of a limited sample of human genetic material. In most cases it seems probable that those genes that are available within a population have survived either because of a selective advantage or because there has been no disadvantage. Thus genes controlling reduced skin pigmentation probably arose and spread with the migration of humans to more northerly latitudes from more southerly ones, in response to the need to synthesize adequate amounts of vitamin D from the available sunlight. If, however, we look at the distribution of eye colour we find that although all people of tropical regions with high levels of ultraviolet radiation have dark eyes, a significant number of people in more northerly latitudes have dark eyes although their skin colour is light. We must therefore assume that selection pressure for light eyes has not been as intense as for light skin. The result is that there is greater inter-individual variation in eye colour than there is in skin colour in the indigenous population of a country like Britain. The same is true for hair colour: like eye colour it varies from light to dark in the British and other populations of north-west Europe, while skin colour does not. This example serves to show that the extent of genetic individuality within a breeding community is not uniform across the genetic board; on the contrary there are very many universal genes that all members share in common, others that are polymorphic and occur with greater or lesser frequency, such as the ABO blood-group genes, and some that occur in a few individuals only, such as the recessive gene that in the homozygote causes albinism, which itself has a frequency of 1 in 20,000, the gene frequency being 1 in 141.

This basic genetic individuality is the starting point of development. During development this genotype interacts constantly with what must in many respects be an equally unique environment. There are clear limits to the allowable variation on both sides, transgression of which leads to non-viability of the organism. The rules of individual development are a set of rules about the limits of tolerance within which a genotype can give rise to a viable individual. These limits are in some respects wide, in other respects narrow. The narrowest are often of the chemical kind, where the next step in development at a given point calls for a certain biochemical substance, and absence of this substance causes development to stop. Many spontaneous abortions are undoubtedly the rejection of a foetus whose progress has stopped in this way. On the other hand the overall nutritional needs of a developing embryo or child are such that there is great flexibility and a large measure of recovery is possible after severe food shortage.

Developmental processes

The narrow kinds of developmental steps that are best understood are the metabolic transformations in which substrates are transformed by enzymes into a form suitable for a specific body function. These 'metabolic pathways' have frequently been discovered as a result of study of metabolic errors, some of them genetic. Not all development can be seen in terms of proteins and their transformations, however. Nor is growth and development fully comprehensible if we add to an understanding of the protein transformations the replication process of cell division accomplished by DNA and RNA. There is still another, third part, and that is the process by which body tissues in course of development appear to 'instruct' neighbouring tissues how to develop. It was first shown with skin from a developing frog that removal of 'eye' tissue before the eye developed and its transplantation to the back of the body led to the development of that tissue into typical 'back' tissue. This is a fair indication of the flexibility of certain developmental processes of body tissue. In other cases there is inflexibility: a person with the genotype for cleft-palate/hare-lip develops this characteristic and the surrounding normal tissue does not compensate in any way; in fact, given this genotype, the surrounding tissue sees the deformity as 'normal'.

The detailed processes of development await elucidation. One puzzle is the nature of the feed-back mechanisms by which the genes controlling development of a given body part 'know' when to start and when to stop acting. Unless one assumes that all the information is present in the zygote it is necessary to conclude that the post-zygotic organism develops characteristics which themselves serve to trigger off further developments, etc.

We can take as an example neural development. This is already well advanced by the first time we are able to study it in the 4-mm-long, 4-week-old human foetus. The neural fibres present at this stage and those that subsequently appear are described by Windle (1971). Sensory development is described by Gottlieb (1971). Around day 49 after fertilization an overt response to tactile stimulation is present in the human foetus, consisting of bending the head away from the site of stimulation when the oral region is touched lightly (Hooker 1952). At about 6 months the human foetus is capable of responding to auditory stimulation, by which time the relevant receptor organ of Corti is fully developed. Visual function is slower to develop, so that true visual responsiveness is not present at birth but develops shortly after birth and accommodation of the eye reaches adult performance at around 4 months.

The actual process of growth of nerve fibres has been extensively studied by Sperry and others. What is perhaps most remarkable is that nerve fibres develop exceedingly complex connections with one another without the influence of any actual functioning at all. Sperry (1971) writes as follows:

In brief, as we now see it, the complicated nerve fiber circuits of the brain grow, assemble, and organize themselves through the use of intricate chemical codes under genetic control. Early in development the nerve cells, numbering in the billions, acquire individual identification tags, molecular in nature, by which they can be recognized and distinguished one from another.

As the differentiating neurons and their elongating fibers begin to form functional interconnections to weave the complex communication networks of behavior, the outgrowing fibers become extremely selective about the molecular identity of other cells and fibers with which they will associate. Lasting functional hookups are established only with cells to which the growing fibers find themselves selectively matched by inherent chemical affinities. In many cases the proper molecular match may be restricted further to particular membrane regions of the dendritic tree or soma of the target neuron.

The outgrowing fibers in the developing brain are guided by a kind of probing chemical touch system that leads them along exact pathways in an enormously intricate guidance program that involves millions, in the higher mammals presumably billions, of different, chemically distinct brain cells. By selective molecular preferences expressed through differential adhesivity the respective nerve fibers are guided correctly into their separate channels at each of the numerous forks or decision points which they encounter as they travel through what is essentially a three-dimensional multiple Y-maze of possible channel choices.

Each fiber in the brain pathways has its own preferential affinity for particular prescribed trails in the differentiating surround. Both pushed and pulled along these trails, the probing fiber tip eventually locates and connects with certain other neurons, often far distant, that have the appropriate molecular labels. The potential pathways and terminal connection zones have their own individual biochemical constitution by which each is recognized and distinguished from all others in the same half of the brain and cord. Indications are that right and left halves are chemical mirror maps.

This entire process is achieved without actual functioning, i.e. without conducting nervous impulses as part of a motor or sensory system. This view directly contradicts the earlier view that functioning was the process that brought into existence neural connections. Sperry's view is that the behavioural functioning of a species is very much determined by the genetically programmed network of nerve circuits and connections. Thus a given species brings its particular sensory–neural–motor arrangements into the world at birth, and with this equipment reacts to postnatal external environments. As Sperry points out, this view of things corresponds well with the data known from ethological studies of the natural behaviour of animals, which are always found to have species-specific or species-characteristic responses to certain features of the external environment. Von Uexküll (1934) early on described the selective responsiveness of the tick to the presence of a warm mammalian host; and reports of other such specific behavioural responses to selectively perceived parts of the environment abound in the ethological literature.

Since man's neural development consists of essentially the same processes as that of other mammalian species (differing in the much greater extent to which those processes go on, to produce a relatively gigantic brain with a greatly exaggerated frontal portion and a number of other characteristic features) we can expect that our brains too develop along genetically programmed lines. In the case of animals this was postulated because behavioural responses tended to be species specific. Is the same true for man? This is the central question already asked and to which we shall return. Without wanting to prejudge the issue, it seems to be the case that some universal responses are clearly present in early life, but that they become less and less clearly evident as childhood proceeds; the conclusion that would appear to follow is that the relatively exaggerated growth of certain brain areas is concerned not so much with behaviour determination and restriction as with the opposite: the keeping open of options for behaviour to be modified and adjusted by conditioning of basic programmes.

Has Sperry over-emphasized the contribution of genetic material to the development of the brain? Eisenberg (1971), in the same volume (Tobach, Aronson and Shaw 1971), writes as follows:

> I would argue that there is no behavior, certainly nothing like intelligence, or mating behavior, or display patterns, or even stature, in the zygote. Such notions are utterly absurd carryovers from preformationism. What the DNA specifies are chemical constituents. These constituent enzymes and substrates interact with one another and with the internal and external environment of the developing organism to produce successive stages of ever greater complexity with the sequential emergence of new properties at each succeeding stage of development. It is the nature of the interactions that must concern us, not so that we can disregard the genetic code, but so that we can understand it and its environmental dependency.
>
> The code, for example, may specify galactosemia in a newborn, but the galactosemic infant is distinguishable from his genetically unmarred brother only in an outer world in which his diet contains milk. Remove the offending disaccharide, the development of the infant is phenotypically normal. Or, it may dictate, as it did in all of us, the capacity for language *acquisition*, something that I would argue is specifically human, but the language acquisition occurs *only* in a verbal environment. Remove the speakers, no language appears.

This at first sight is in every respect the opposite of what Sperry has been arguing. And yet a moment's reflection is enough to convince one that both are right, and that the contradiction is a matter of emphasis and of semantics, with Sperry emphasizing the extent of genetic control and Eisenberg emphasizing the inevitability in development of environmental inputs.

Accepting that morphogenesis and cell differentiation are under genetic control in a given environment, it is clear from the fact that both the genetic make-up and the environment of individuals differ (except in identical twins where only the latter differs) that we have to contend with a series of individuals each of whom has certain attributes in common with the rest and certain attributes of his or her own. How great are these differences? It depends on the 'attribute' one looks at. In the case of those attributes, or phenotypes, that are related to single genes or single loci, variation is limited to a few clear-cut forms. But many of the phenotypes studied by biologists are controlled by many genes. If we take whole brains, then according to Sperry 'experts who work intimately with brains in large numbers come to recognize in the surface fissuration of the cerebral cortex ... almost the same order of individual variation that the average person perceives in faces'.

Biochemical and morphological variation

R. J. Williams, in his book *Biochemical Individuality* (1956) is at pains to stress the extent of individual variability and the fact that this aspect is often neglected in studies of performance or behaviour which often treat animals as if they were constitutionally identical, chiefly, he feels, because of the desire of research workers to make generalizations. He includes a table (Table 6.2) from a 1926 study to show the great differences that were found simply by measuring the relative weights of individual organs in the bodies of 645 normal rabbits. All the rabbits in this study were males and all were adults. They were not genetically homogenous and thus may have been of any breed or variety of rabbit. In so far as rabbit variability reflects that found in man the results are an indication of the variability of human organs. We should note that the figures in the Table are already adjusted to take account of overall body weight.

TABLE 6.2

Range of relative organ weights of rabbits

Organ	Grams per kilogram of net body weight		Ratio: maximum/minimum
	Minimum	Maximum	
Gastrointestinal mass	70·4	452·0	6
Heart	1·95	4·42	2
Liver	23·2	117·0	5
Kidneys	3·45	17·28	5
Spleen	0·035	2·93	80
Thymus	0·248	3·315	13
Testicles	0·47	4·93	10
Brain	3·33	8·16	2·5
Thyroid	0·048	1·23	25
Parathyroid	0·001	0·022	22
Hypophysis	0·007	0·035	5
Suprarenals	0·080	0·572	7
Pineal	0·002	0·025	12
Popliteal lymph nodes	0·05	0·382	8
Axillary lymph nodes	0·019	0·24	13
Deep cervical lymph nodes	0·02	0·295	15
Mesenteric lymph nodes	0·67	6·91	10

Williams gives further data on a number of biochemical items in man. Both inorganic and organic constituents of human blood show wide ranges of variation, and where studies have been made of particular individuals over long periods of time they have tended to indicate constancy of levels for those individuals. This is true for protein-bound iodine, copper, histamine, lipids, cholesterol, amino acids and vitamins. Besides blood, a similar situation is found in the composition of saliva, gastric juice, duodenal juice, bone and in the DNA content of spermatozoa. Williams concludes that if enough measures of any individual are taken, that individual will be found to be 'abnormal' in some respect or other.

Besides the above, Williams examines individual enzymic patterns and finds, in summary, that 'the cumulative evidence that each individual human being has a distinctive pattern of enzyme efficiencies is hard to refute'. Inter-individual variation in enzyme efficiencies tends to be three- or four-fold, and can be ten- to fifty-fold (in normal individuals).

Of special interest in view of their relevance to the study of action are individual endocrine activities. The location of the thyroid glands is variable in man, as is their output. The number of parathyroid glands in humans is most often four (perhaps in some 50 per cent of a population), but there may be anything from two to twelve and their positions are variable. Insulin production by the pancreas varies from insufficiency in diabetics to over-production in hyperinsulinism, and these abnormal conditions may show up early in life, in middle age or in old age depending on the extent of genetic determination and the threshold for manifestation of the condition, which probably depends on the rest of the genome.

Oestrogen production in women doubtless varies with the weight of the ovaries, which is from 2 g to 10 g in normal women. It also varies according to age, time of month and particular circumstances, so there is a wide range of intra-individual variation, but a wider one between individuals. In men, testes weight may vary from 10 g to 45 g; and daily androgen excretion in the urine in one study of normal men was 20–225 International Units, an eleven-fold variation. Again, as with oestrogens there is much intra-individual variation, and the same is true for women's androgen and men's oestrogen production.

Adrenal-gland weight varies from 7 g to 20 g and the thickness of the adrenal cortex varies from 0·5 mm to 5·0 mm in normal individuals. Adrenocortical-hormone production varies more between individuals than in single subjects (Fox, Murawski, Bartholomay and Gifford 1961), a fact to which we shall return later. The levels of catecholamines (the products of sympathetic nerve endings and of the adrenal medulla) likewise vary between individuals and show consistency within individuals (Patkai and Frankenhaeuser 1964). In a current study of 5–6-year-old children my colleagues and I have found that inter-individual differences exceeded intra-individual differences for excretion rates of adrenalin,[†] metadrenalin and VMA (vanillyl mandelic acid).

[†] Adrenalin = epinephrine; metadrenalin = metanephrine; noradrenalin = norepinephrine; normetadrenalin = normetanephrine.

The pituitary gland is of the utmost importance in that it is heavily involved in the control of the thyroid, adrenal and sex glands. Its total weight varies from 350 mg to 1100 mg, but this overall difference still masks differences between different functional areas: the anterior lobe constitutes between 56 per cent and 92 per cent of the total gland weight, the posterior lobe 7–41 per cent, the epithelium 0·13–3·6 per cent and the colloid 0·02–10·4 per cent.

One could continue on these lines *ad infinitum*, for the number of features that show variability are as legion as the number of features themselves. It is not the object of this chapter to list all the characteristics that vary and how much they do so. I wish merely to demonstrate that human biology is a complex matter that does not lead quickly to generalizations about human body processes, let alone behaviour or social organization. Viewed against the wealth of data now in existence in the fields of genetics, embryology, biochemistry, biopsychology and anthropology, statements such as 'man is by nature an aggressive animal' look as problematic as statements that 'at birth man is a *tabula rasa* on which culture writes its instructions'. We shall come back to these arguments from time to time, as they are still to be found in both the scientific and the lay communities. But besides these extreme positions, there seem to be some studies in developmental psychology that take little or no account of biological differences in their examination of developmental processes, laying great weight on environmental causes; while other studies, especially medical studies, often ignore the environment almost completely. We shall look at some of these in subsequent chapters.

CHAPTER 7

Postnatal growth

IN THE LAST CHAPTER much emphasis was placed on individual variability at the organic level. Such variability was seen as a proved fact at both the genetic and the morphological levels. Nevertheless, we did not over-emphasize that argument, as it was shown that in every case there were limits to variability beyond which survival was probably not possible. In this chapter we come to a consideration of morphological developments after birth. The emphasis here will tend to revert to norms and averages, but the lessons of the last chapter will, hopefully, not be forgotten.

Maturation of the body

J. M. Tanner (1962), whose books and papers on human growth summarize much of our knowledge on the subject, is fond of illustrating what must be the earliest scientific record of the growth of a human child—a series of measurements every 6 months from birth to 18 years of age made by Count Philibert de Montbeillard upon his son, over the years 1759–77 (Fig. 7.1). When plotted in terms of height gains rather than actual heights we can see that the rate of gain fell sharply from birth to the age of 4, that it then steadied but continued to fall slowly until the age of 12, when it rose sharply for a couple of years, afterwards falling again. This pattern is typical for boys, the sudden increase in height being part of what is called the 'adolescent growth spurt'. This occurs in girls too, though at an earlier age.

De Montbeillard began his measurements at birth, and the falling height gain (or length gain) shown by his data is in fact a continuation of a trend which starts in the fourth month of pregnancy— growth velocity increases until this time, after which it declines fairly steadily (when average figures for large samples are considered) until the adolescent spurt.

If we take a different measure of growth, namely weight, then the peak velocity comes later, usually shortly after birth. There appears to be a slowing down of the growth rate during the last month before

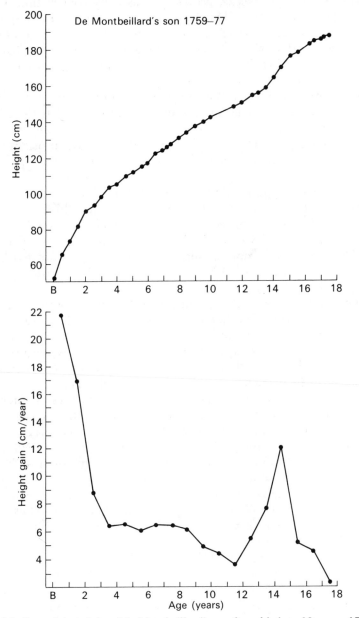

F IG. 7.1. Growth in height of de Montbeillard's son from birth to 18 years, 1759–1777. *Above:* distance curve, height attained at each age. *Below:* velocity curve, increments in height from year to year. (Redrawn from Tanner (1962).)

birth from 36 to 40 weeks, probably caused by constriction of the foetus inside the uterus. This slowing down is most clearly seen in the case of twins, in which it occurs earlier, when their combined weight equals that of a 36-week-old singleton. In both cases (singleton and twins) birth is followed by a 'catch-up' phase of increased growth rate until the child is on its prenatal curve again.

Besides growth, there is the separate matter of maturity. The chief sex difference here—a faster rate of maturation in girls than boys amounting to one week in every ten from conception on, building up to about 2 years at puberty—is probably genetic in origin. It is found in other primates such as chimpanzees and rhesus monkeys, and also in rats, and may be a general characteristic of mammals. Tanner (1960) suggests that the slower maturation of males may be due to a retardation factor on the Y chromosome; this is indicated by results of measurements of skeletal age on individuals with Klinefelter's syndrome (XXY) and Turner's syndrome (XO) (see Chapter 8). The former were not significantly different from normal boys, i.e. XXY matures like XY; the latter resembled girls' growth patterns, i.e. XO matures like XX.

Detailed findings resulting from various measures of maturity are presented by Tanner. From these, one or two points of general significance arise. The first is that there appears to be some general process of body maturation such that children who are slow maturers on one scale are slow on all others too. Thus children tend to be either advanced or retarded in terms of size factor, skeletal ossification, permanent dental eruption, and physiological processes such as menstruation. This is not true, however, of some pathological conditions where discrepancies of growth occur. Secondly, correlation of certain measures of the onset of puberty, notably age of menarche, with other developmental ages, e.g. skeletal age, show a higher correlation coefficient than they do with chronological age. Thus girls who reach menarche earlier have already reached a greater skeletal age than those who reach it later, and projecting backwards it can be shown that they already had done so by age 7 if not before (Fig. 7.2). This generalization does not, however, hold for all sex characteristics (Marshall 1974).

Thus the human body follows certain well-defined patterns in its progress from birth to maturity. The next step will be to examine the variability of these growth processes, and discuss some of the evidence for genetic and environmental influences that cause this variability.

Studies of different racial groups point to the existence of genetic factors underlying growth processes. The greatest contrast in height

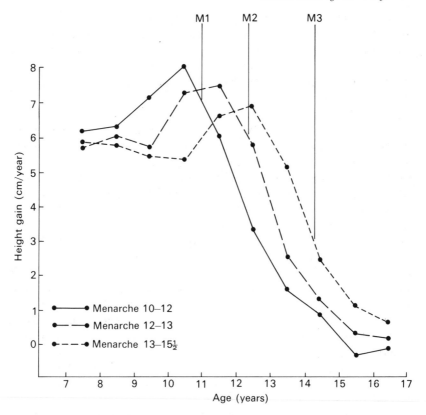

F IG. 7.2. Relation of peak velocities in height for early, average and late maturing girls; and of time elapsing between peak velocity and menarche for the three groups. M1, M2, M3, average time of menarche for each group. (Redrawn from Tanner (1962).)

exists between the Dinka tribe of the Sudan, a Nilotic people, and the nearby pygmy tribes of the Congo (see Chapter 6, p. 83). Undoubtedly these differences are the outcome of a considerable period of natural (and perhaps also sexual) selection. It has been suggested that the shape and size of Nilotes is a dry-heat adaptation promoting heat loss by sweat evaporation by maximizing the surface area of skin relative to the body volume. In the case of pygmies, the selective advantage of small size has been related to hunting success in the tropical rainforest.

There may be a genetic factor in the faster rate of maturation of Negro than of white children in infancy. Studies made in West Africa, East Africa and the U.S.A. have shown that Negro babies grow faster and are ahead at sitting up and crawling during the first year or so of life; the difference declines and disappears by the fourth year. Such precocity as exists may of course be environmental. Nevertheless the permanent dentition of Negroes erupts about a year earlier on average than that of whites, again indicating genetic factors rather than nutritional ones, which would in many African cases be expected to cause a retardation.

Climate has been shown to affect development in a number of ways. In mice, experiments have shown that cold conditions retard sexual development. One reason may be that more oxygen is needed for metabolism and is not therefore so freely available for growth purposes. In man, climate has little or no effect on overall growth rate. The great difficulty in comparing human populations is to equate nutritional inputs and other socio-economic aspects. When these are held equal, climate has been said to have little or no influence on age at menarche. For example, Alaskan Eskimo girls and upper-class Nigerian schoolgirls, each of whom have above average nutrition, share an almost identical age of menarche: 14·4 for Eskimos; 14·43 for Nigerians. But it can equally be argued that, given a very different genetic endowment of the Nigerians and Eskimos, the climatic difference is the crucial factor that equates them for age of menarche! There are too many unknowns in the equation for firm conclusions.

In one study (Ito 1942) Japanese-American children born in California were divided into two groups—those born and reared in California and those born in California and reared in Japan. The former group reached age of menarche $1\frac{1}{2}$ years earlier than the latter. Skeletally, another study (Greulich 1957) has shown that Californian Japanese are 1–2 years advanced over Japanese in Japan, and are taller and heavier. However, though body size and rate of maturity increased to European standards in the Californian environment, the body shape, both as regards leg length relative to trunk and stockiness or weight in relation to height, remained typically Japanese. Better nutrition in particular is thought to speed up development and hasten maturity.

Developmental 'catch-up'

In order to establish the effects of malnutrition on growth, nutritional studies need to be made on children who share a common gene pool. Studies of humans who have been subject to famine in wartime, and experimental work on animals, show that malnutrition during childhood delays growth, and delays the appearance of the adolescent spurt. Fig. 7.3. shows height and weight data for boys and girls in Stuttgart from 1911 to 1953. The decline in World War

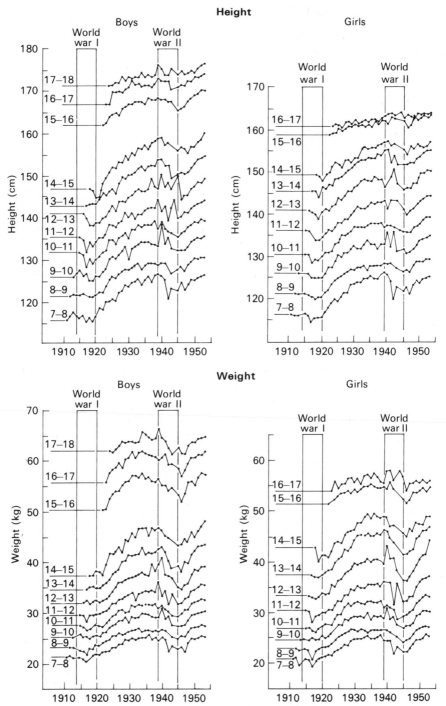

FIG. 7.3. Effect of malnutrition on growth in height and weight. Heights and weights of Stuttgart schoolchildren (7–8 to 14–15 : Volkschule; 15–16 upwards : Oberschule) from 1911 to 1953. Lines connect points for children of same age, and express secular trend and effect of war conditions. (Redrawn from Tanner (1962).)

II is clear-cut, as is the recovery after 1946, to heights and weights that by 1953 were in advance to pre-war figures.

These data indicate directly that whole populations or 'cohorts' can recover from a severe nutritional setback. Indirectly we can tie this recovery to other data indicating that there are mechanisms in the body that put into action a 'catch-up' process after a period of retardation caused by poor conditions.

It has been shown that girls are more resistant to adverse circumstances— are less easily thrown off their growth curves—than boys. In a post-war study (Greulich 1951) of children on Guam, it was found that all children were retarded, because of wartime hardships, in height, weight and skeletal maturity, but that girls were less retarded than boys. The same was shown in a study of child survivors of the atomic bombings of Nagasaki and Hiroshima (Greulich, Crismon and Turner 1953). A study in Oxford has shown that boys are more responsive than girls to poor home conditions (Acheson and Hewitt 1954) and to illness (Hewitt, Westropp and Acheson 1955). Waddington has termed this difference one of 'canalization'—girls' growth processes are better canalized, i.e. less variable, than those of boys. A similar sex difference has been observed in malnutrition experiments on rats.

Illness is usually thought to have an adverse effect on growth, but in the case of minor childhood illnesses no such effect has been demonstrated, at least not in weight gain during the first 3 years. This could be a result of the 'catch-up' phase referred to above. Where studies focus on poor families and exclude others, however, weight differences have been found, and again one could speculate that adequate nutrition is needed for the adverse effects of illness to be made good, though data on the details of the process are not available. For example, it has not been possible to ascertain whether children who are anyway growing more slowly are also subject to more illness, thus turning a cause–effect relation into a simple association. Genetic and environmental effects are very hard if not impossible to disentangle. Again, within any sample there is much individual variation and we need to know more about the causes of this—some children's growth is affected by a severe measles or pneumonia attack, others' is not.

In the case of major illnesses growth can be severely retarded— but there is a strong tendency to make up all that is lost. In one study (Bauer 1954) a group of 34 children suffering from nephrosis fell from being 100 per cent of the average height for their age to 71 per cent after 2 years. Extreme cases died, but of those who recovered, height for age was back to 94 per cent of average only 18 months after the start of recovery. It is not known whether it rose further, perhaps back to the 100 per cent mark, because no further measurements were taken. Another example of failure of illness to reduce growth permanently comes from the tropics. In a study in Gambia, children with repeated malarial infections grew less in their first 2 years than those protected by anti-malarial drugs. By $3\frac{1}{2}$ years, however, they had developed immunity and had caught up in terms of growth (MacGregor, Gilles, Walters, Davies and Pearson, 1956).

Social class, nutrition and development

Two factors known to affect growth are socio-economic class and the so-called 'secular trend'. Most class-based studies use the Registrar General's categories or some other such system that makes the basic distinctions between salaried people, people earning wages for non-manual work, manual, skilled and unskilled workers. Such studies generally show children with fathers from the higher-income

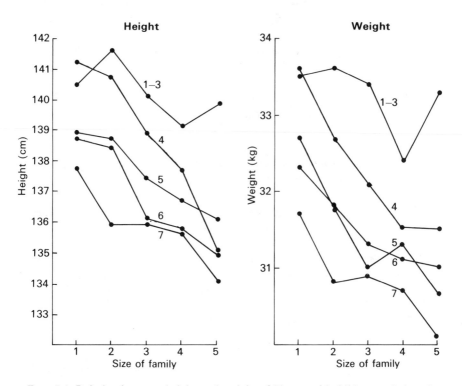

FIG. 7.4. Relation between height and weight of 11-year-old children and size of family, in different socio-economic classes in Scotland, in 1947. Classes marked 1–3, 4, 5, 6 and 7. (Redrawn from Tanner (1962).)

groups to be bigger than children with fathers from the lower-income groups. A fairly extreme case is that shown in Fig. 7.4. Here, height is plotted against size of family for a number of Scottish 11-year-olds, and the curves show the breakdown of results according to socio-economic class. Height is seen to differ as much as 6 cm and weight as much as 3 kg in extreme cases, but this is double the range found in most studies in Canada, England and the U.S.A. Cross-sectional and longitudinal studies show that the class differences increase with age, e.g. from 2·5 cm at 2 years to 3·5 cm at 4 years.

The greater part of the social-class differences is due to earlier maturation, the smaller part to an overall adult differential. Menarche occurred 3 months earlier in girls at high schools than in secondary modern schools in a 1958 study in Bristol (Wofinden and Smallwood, 1958). A 2-month difference is reported from Denmark (Bojlén, Rasch and Weis-Bentzon 1954), an 8-month difference between rich New York Negroes and Negroes in the South (Michelson 1944); a 6-month difference between rich and poor Indians in Durban (Kark 1956). Height, weight and genital development differences follow the same pattern. So does permanent-tooth eruption. The main reason for this is probably mainly better nutrition. A secondary factor, also related to nutrition, is family size. This has at various times and places been larger in lower status groups than in higher, and large family size is known to be related to a slower rate of development (as the Fig. 7.4 showed).

The secular trend

Next we can consider the 'secular trend'. This is the very clear evidence that the whole process of growth and maturation has become speeded up continuously, with a few exceptions, throughout the present century in rich countries, but that now there are signs that it is levelling off.

Fig. 7.5 shows this trend by contrasting data for 1883 with data for 1938–9 and 1965–71, for all ages from 7 years to 18 years, in Swedish school-children. For example, looking at the top left graph, 11-year-old girls in 1965–71 were already the same height as 13-year-old girls in 1883; in general the height and weight differences amount to 1½ or 2 years between the two earlier dates, and there is also an overall increase in final height and weight except in the case of girls' weight, which was less in 1965–71 than in 1938–9.

Data from a variety of countries—including North America, Britain, Sweden, Poland and Germany—all show similar secular trends. Outside Europe and the U.S.A. data show the same trend in Australia, New Zealand and Japan. The oldest set of records is from

Height

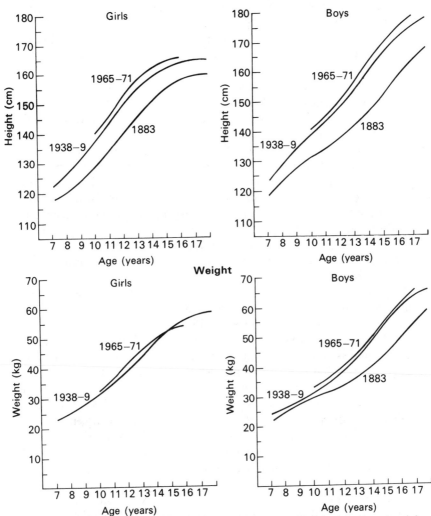

FIG. 7.5. Secular trend in growth of height and weight. Height (*above*) and weight (*below*) of Swedish girls and boys measured in 1883, 1938–9 and 1965–71. (Redrawn from Ljung, Bergsten-Brucefors and Lindgren (1974), *Annals of Human Biology* **1**, 248–9.)

Norway, where a continuous set of measurements of soldiers' heights has been kept since 1741. This series shows that from 1760 until 1830 there was a small gain of 1·5 cm, or 0·2 cm per decade. From 1875 to 1935 there was a gain of 4 cm, or 0·6 cm per decade. The data for Europe and the U.S.A. generally show an adult increase of 1·0 cm per decade since 1880, with an even greater increase for selected age groups: $1\frac{1}{2}$ cm for age 5–7; $2\frac{1}{2}$ cm for adolescents. For these two groups weight gains during the same period were $\frac{1}{2}$ kg per decade and 2 kg per decade respectively.

Why the secular trend? Better nutrition and improved child care are probably the main factors at work. The data indicate that the rate of increase has been greater among the lower socio-economic classes than the higher. Nevertheless it has occurred in all groups. There is no reason to think that the change in the wealthy sector has been one of getting *more* to eat but it may be that today's diets are richer in vitamins than those of the last century. Another contributory factor is the overall decline in family size, but even assuming a halving of family size the expected result would not explain the enormous change that has occurred. Another factor that has been suggested is heterosis ('hybrid vigour'), assuming that outbreeding has occurred to an ever greater extent during the period concerned. There is good evidence of this, but less evidence that the genetic basis of height or weight is such that heterosis could be included as a viable explanation. In any case, heterosis could not account for more than a fraction of the secular trend.

Besides the increase in height and weight and the earlier adolescent spurt there has, as expected, been an increasingly early age at menarche. This is seen in Fig. 7.6. The data used for the various countries were the best and most reliable available. The overall trend shown is remarkable for its linearity and it is only in recent years that there has been any tendency for it to level off. The general picture is a fall in average age of menarche from 16 or more a hundred years ago to 13 or less at the present time. In a recently published study of a sample of 8261 girls in Naples, Italy, the mean age of menarche was 12·49 years. The study was made in 1969–70 and the mean age of menarche found was the lowest so far recorded in Europe (Carfagna, Figurelli, Matarese and Matarese 1972).

Just how early normal menarche can be we do not yet really know. In the meantime we have to face and plan for the fact that sexual maturity in our children is occurring long before full social maturity; in fact long before the earliest permissible school-leaving age. It is perhaps a demonstration of the flexibility of the human organism that reproduction can be, as it normally is in our culture, withheld for many years after sexual maturity. Indeed, heterosexual behaviour is often delayed by a variety of cultural means—single-sex schools, secrecy and taboos, etc. But the intense emotional difficulties of so many adolescents must, one suspects, be related to the conflict between physical readiness and cultural taboos.

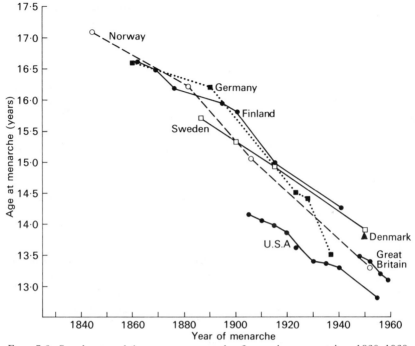

F IG. 7.6. Secular trend in age at menarche for various countries, 1830–1960. (Redrawn from Tanner (1962).)

Sex developments at adolescence

Let us make a closer consideration of the physical aspects of adolescence. In Tanner's words, 'every muscular and skeletal dimension of the body seems to take part in the adolescent spurt. Even the head diameters, practically dormant since a few years after birth, accelerate somewhat in most individuals. The cartilages of the wrist grow and ossify more rapidly. The heart grows faster; so also do the abdominal viscera. The reproductive organs in particular enlarge, strength increases and the face quite noticeably changes. . . .' However lymphatic tissue and, in boys, subcutaneous limb fat decrease during the spurt.

We can look at these changes in more detail. First, in what order do various body changes occur? In fact there is a fairly regular order: leg length reaches its peak first (i.e. peak growth velocity) followed 4 months later by hip width and chest breadth. Shoulder breadth follows a few months later, with trunk length and chest depth last. Within the limbs there is a gradient of timing: the foot grows earlier than the calf and the calf earlier than the thigh, while the forearm grows earlier than the upper arm—thus peripheral parts are more advanced than proximal parts.

Head and face changes at adolescence show the typical adolescent spurt, even though absolute rates of growth are small. Much of the growth is caused by thickening of the skull and of scalp tissues, but it seems likely that in addition there is some growth of the brain itself. Forward growth of the skull is mainly caused by development of the brow ridges and the frontal sinuses, but there is also a lowering of the base of the brain case and some occipital growth that appears to accompany brain development; Tanner, however, stresses problems of measurement and inadequacy of data on this point. Growth of the eye follows the same pattern as that for the brain, most growth being completed before adolescence; however, at adolescence there is a slight acceleration, especially of sagittal or axial length, and this growth may in part help to explain the high frequency of myopia that occurs in this age group.

Most parts of the face show a growth spurt a few months after the stature peak. The mandible grows fastest. This lags behind the face during childhood and 'catches up', as it were, during adolescence. Growth of the mandible is in thickness, length and height, and is greater, as expected, in boys than girls. It is associated with growth of the maxilla so that in all the prognathism of both upper and lower jaws increases. The nose also grows, both in bone and soft tissue, bringing the point of the nose further forward and downward. The pharynx grows rapidly in length and its inmate, the hyoid bone, descends rapidly.

I shall mention only briefly the other features of adolescent growth besides reproductive changes: these are the decline of thymus size at puberty associated with the decline of lymphatic tissue, and the loss of subcutaneous fat at adolescence in boys. Growth in general is complete by about $17\frac{3}{4}$ years for boys, $16\frac{1}{4}$ years for girls; after this age no more than 2 per cent is added to stature. Among the last skeletal growth points are the bony epiphyses which close between the ages of 18 and 26 years.

At puberty and during adolescence the most significant changes the body undergoes are those concerned with bringing it into a state of reproductive capacity. The times of development of male sexual characteristics are shown in Fig. 7.7. This diagram is based on average figures derived from longitudinal data; the figures show the range of variation of individuals for the start and finish of the various growth spurts. As can be seen, there is a great range of variation between early and late starters, and acceleration in penis growth, for example, is already over for some children at the age of $13\frac{1}{2}$, while

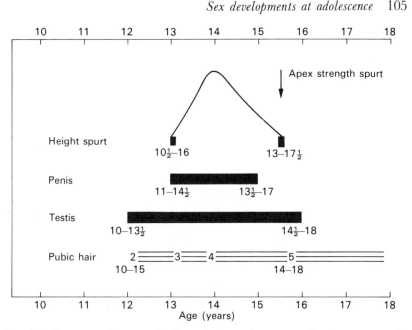

F IG. 7.7. Sequence of events of puberty in boys. An average boy is represented: the range of ages within which each event charted may begin and end is given by the figures placed directly below its start and finish. (Redrawn from Tanner (1962).)

in others it does not begin until $14\frac{1}{2}$. Fig. 7.8 shows three boys all aged 14, indicating the normal range of variation for this age group.

The normal pattern of development of sexual characteristics is as follows. In the case of boys, there is an initial enlargement of the scrotum and testes, followed by penis growth which accompanies further growth of scrotum and testes until full adult size is reached. This whole process takes on average around 4 years. Facial hair begins to grow towards the middle of this period, starting at the corners of the upper lip and spreading to form the moustache, and growing from the upper cheeks and lower lip to form the beard, which covers the lower border of the chin last. The larynx is enlarged and the voice deepens gradually. There is some breast development in males, the areola growing from a width of 12·5 mm before puberty to 21·5 mm in mature males. In about a third of boys there is breast development not unlike that of girls on a minor scale—the areola projects as a result of the development of mammary gland tissue. This lasts from a year to 18 months, then subsides. The cause is thought to be an increase of oestrogen excretion from the adrenal cortex.

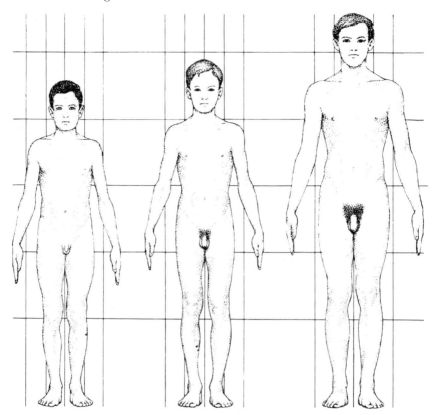

F IG. 7.8. Three boys, all of the chronological age of 14·75 years, to show variation in the range of their development. (From Tanner (1973a). Copyright © 1973 by Scientific American, Inc. All rights reserved.)

In the case of girls the most marked changes in morphology concern breast development. At first there is the appearance of a 'breast bud' with elevation of the breast and papilla as a small mound and enlargement of the areolar diameter. This growth continues, with projection of the areola and papilla to form a secondary mound above the level of the breast. Finally, at the mature stage with the development of the full-grown breast the areola recedes so that only the papilla projects. Areolar width is on average 35·5 mm in girls.

Pubic hair growth follows much the same pattern in both sexes. At first there is a sparse growth of long, slightly pigmented downy hair; this in due course becomes darker, coarser and more curled but remains sparse, until the adult hair form is reached. The area is now covered somewhat more thickly as more hair appears, and the distribution ends as a straight horizontal line at the top of the pubic area. In 80 per cent of men and 10 per cent of women there is a final development as the hair spreads further upwards and outwards in other directions.

Axillary (armpit) hair is a further development for both sexes at puberty. It develops at the same time as the apocrine sweat glands, which are absent or non-functional before puberty. These glands, located under the armpits and in various other parts of the body, produce a form of highly scented secretion and resemble the true eccrine sweat glands in their mode of operation, but probably do not serve a cooling function. Instead, their responsiveness to emotional arousal suggests that they may have a function in sexual interaction, and the otherwise puzzling occurrence of armpit hair may have the function of concentrating and holding the apocrine aroma.

Besides the reproductive and other differences described above there are certain overall differences of size and shape that develop during adolescence, resulting in the sexual dimorphism characteristic of many primate species including man. In the context of other primates man is not particularly dimorphic for overall body size— he is about as dimorphic as chimpanzees, less so than baboons or gorillas. And as in the case of other dimorphic species, the female matures faster than the male. In the case of species such as baboons it is argued that smaller size and earlier maturity in females is advantageous in terms of reproductive capacity and biomass. Sex differences in physique can arise in four ways:

1. By differential growth rates operating only at adolescence, as a result of differential hormone secretion then (e.g. hip and shoulder breadths).
2. By the male delay in the growth spurt, so that males grow over a longer period, achieve a larger size and retain less pedomorphism in adult life.
3. By differential growth rates all through growth, from birth or earlier (e.g. forearm grows relatively faster in male than female).
4. By differential growth rates at some particular time other than adolescence (e.g. development of sex organs in foetus).

The sexual *size* difference is largely due to mechanism 2 above. Up to age 10 average size differences are small and inconclusive. From age $10\frac{1}{2}$ to 13 girls come to be larger in almost all dimensions than boys. At this age the girls' growth spurt is exhausted and the boys' just starting. By now boys are often already somewhat larger than girls were at the start of their spurt, and the boys' spurt is longer and greater than the girls', so that boys finish some 10 per cent greater in weight and most body measurements.

The chief skeletal *shape* sex differences are that men have broader shoulders, narrower hips, longer legs and longer arms (particularly forearms). The shoulder–hip distinction is a result of a large spurt in hip width for girls, which is as great as that for boys, coupled with a much greater shoulder spurt for boys (see Fig. 7.9).

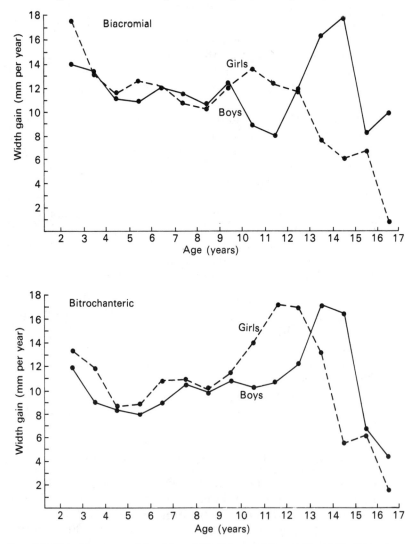

F I G. 7.9. Velocity curves of shoulder width (biacromial) and hip width (bitrochanteric) in girls and boys. (Redrawn from Tanner (1962).)

Differential leg length is not a result of spurts of different intensity but simply of delayed acceleration. The pre-growth-spurt period is one of intensive leg growth anyway and in boys this means that the legs have 2 extra years of normal, fairly rapid growth before the spurt.

In the case of the arm the same process is at work, but there is in addition a life-long sex difference in forearm length, males exceeding females from age 2 or even earlier, the difference being continuously greater throughout development.

Further sex differences include the density of the skeleton, male bone being heavier than female. This is due to male bones having thicker cortices than female bones, a difference that probably arises

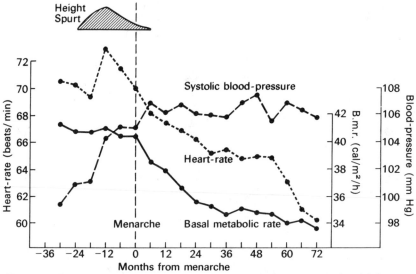

FIG. 7.10. Physiological changes at adolescence in relation to menarche. Adolescent height spurt indicated at top figure. (Redrawn from Tanner (1962).)

at adolescence, also there are certain cranial sex differences, e.g. in the size of the mandible.

One of the main sex differences in *soft tissue* is fat. At birth the difference is negligible. During the first year girls have slightly more fat than boys, from 1–6 girls lose fat less rapidly than boys, and from 6 onwards they gain it more rapidly, especially during the adolescent spurt.

So far we have concentrated on morphological changes. Besides these, a very large number of physiological changes occur at adolescence, and some of these have been subjected to measurement. For instance (Fig. 7.10) systolic blood-pressure (high peaks) rises slowly during the pre-adolescent period, rises steeply during the period of the growth spurt, and in girls steadies at the time of menarche, by which time adult values have been reached. The same figure shows that basal metabolic rate (measured in terms of heat produced per square metre of body surface) and heart-rate both decline at this time.

There is a sex difference in systolic blood-pressure, boys showing higher values than girls. This difference is probably caused by greater growth of the heart at adolescence in males, with a consequently greater stroke volume. Diastolic (low peak) pressure shows no change and no sex difference at adolescence.

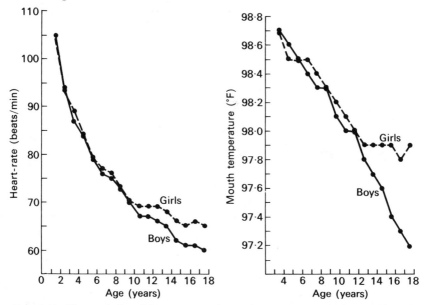

F IG. 7.11. Change in basal heart-rate and mouth temperature during childhood, showing the development of sex differences at adolescence. (Redrawn from Tanner (1962).)

Heart-rate (basal) falls gradually during growth. At adolescence a sex difference is established, so that after this time women have a 10 per cent faster heart-rate than men (see Fig. 7.11). This difference in heart-rate may be related to the previously mentioned difference in heart size, or to a further difference in body temperature. The same figure shows that girls level off at this final adult temperature considerably earlier than boys, whose basal temperature (i.e. temperature in the mouth after resting for 40 mins) remains about $\frac{1}{2}$°F lower than girls' during early adult life. The relation between

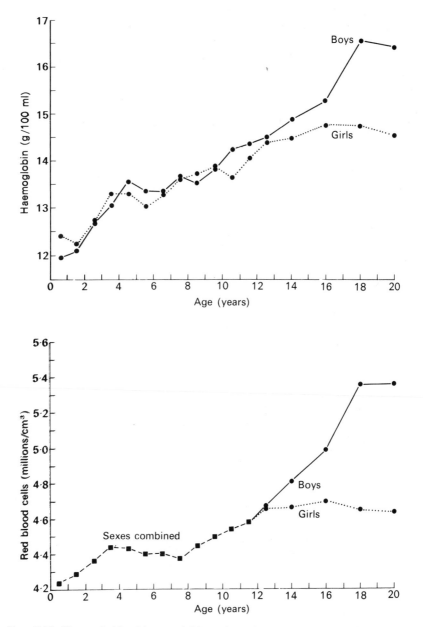

FIG. 7.12. Change in blood haemoglobin and number of circulating red blood cor-puscles during childhood, showing the development of the sex difference at adole-scence. (Redrawn from Tanner (1962).)

heart-rate and body temperature is such that for every degree Fahrenheit increase of temperature there is on average an 11-beat increase (per min) of heart-rate. In the sex difference at adolescence the temperature difference of half a degree or so would seem to be closely related to the slower heart-rate (5 beats per min slower in boys). Tanner regards the temperature difference as cause and the heart-rate difference as effect. The cause of the temperature difference is, he says, unknown—it may be endocrinological or it may reflect hypothalamic function.

A further sex difference concerns the constitution of the blood. At adolescence, the haemoglobin content of the blood, which has been increasing slowly during childhood, increases more rapidly in boys and tends to level off in girls (Fig. 7.12). This difference persists during adult life and is not changed by exercise or athletic activity on the part of girls. It seems to be a result of testosterone secretion, since this hormone causes red-cell production in eunuchs and certain forms of anaemia. There is also an increase not only in haemoglobin *concentration* and red-cell count but also in the actual *volume* of blood in the body at puberty, and this increase is more marked in boys than girls. One explanation for this may be that a greater percentage of the body volume in boys consists of muscle, and blood volume is related to muscularity.

A further change at adolescence concerns the amount of total body water, which becomes greater in males than females. The amount of potassium in the body, mostly occurring in muscle tissue, shows a sex difference after puberty, with males having 15 per cent more than females. The concentration of plasma proteins undergoes no change at puberty, whereas that of plasma lipoproteins shows an increase in boys over girls, a difference that is continued into adult life.

There are changes in respiration at puberty. The basal respiration rate continues its childhood fall and there are no changes of rate or sex difference here. But the respiratory volume increases considerably in boys, not in girls, as does the *'vital capacity'* (maximum expiration following a maximum inspiration) and the 'maximum breathing capacity'. Fig. 7.13 shows the difference in vital capacity according to age (left) and surface area of the body (right). The surface-area chart shows that the vital capacity increase exceeds the amount due to overall body growth and the explanation would seem to be a greater growth of the increased male shoulder and chest width at this time. A further sex difference in respiratory function that arises at adolescence is the ratio of carbon dioxide to oxygen in the expired air—this increases more in boys than girls.

Vital Capacity

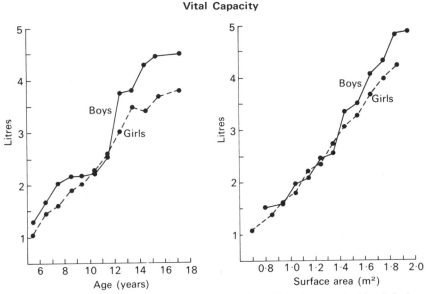

FIG. 7.13. Change in vital capacity from age 5 to 17 in boys and girls. *Left:* in relation to age. *Right:* in relation to surface area. (Redrawn from Tanner (1962).)

It has already been stated that *basal metabolic rate* (heat produced per square metre of body surface) falls at adolescence. This is part of a general decline in basal metabolic rate from birth to old age (see Fig. 7.14). The upper graph shows the actual basal metabolic rate at each age; the lower graph shows the rate of change. This shows that the rate of decrease of basal metabolic rate slows down and almost stops in boys between 11 and 13 years of age. In girls, this check occurs some 2 years earlier. This maintenance of high basal metabolic rate at puberty thus coincides with the adolescent growth spurt and probably reflects extra heat production involved in the building of new tissue, or it may be in part hormonally produced. The overall sex difference throughout childhood is such that boys' basal metabolic rate is always higher than girls', but according to Passmore (1968) this sex difference is not apparent if *lean* body weight is used to make the comparison.

With regard to brain activity, a certain amount is reported by Tanner with regard to changes during growth, but he stresses the need for more work in this area. In early childhood the predominant rhythms are the low-frequency delta and theta rhythms, which are gradually replaced by alpha rhythms, arising first in the parieto-occipital area at rhythms of 8–13 Hz (cycles per second). The frequency of the alpha rhythm increases from a mode of about 8 Hz

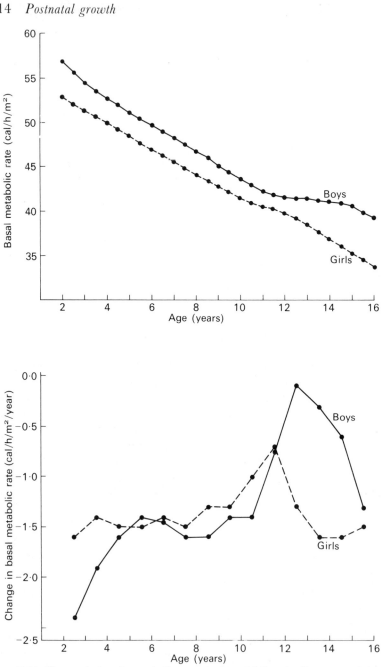

Fɪɢ. 7.14. Change in basal metabolic rate during childhood. *Above:* actual metabolic rate at each year of age. *Below:* rate of change of basal metabolic rate. (Redrawn from Tanner (1962).)

at 6 years to 9½ Hz at 18 years. High-frequency rhythms of 15–27 Hz are more common in women than men, but it is not certain when this difference arises. There is also slight evidence for a higher frequency of the alpha rhythm in girls than boys.

Recent developments in the field of human growth endocrinology are described in Tanner (1973), from which we can judge both the extent of our knowledge and of our ignorance of even such basic processes as puberty. Among the reasons for this are both the technical difficulty of measuring the often minute quantities of hormones involved, the fact that their rate of production varies from individual to individual and according to time of day, and the sheer complexity of the interactions of the various hormones with one another.

Endocrines and growth

One interesting sex difference at puberty concerns the anterior pituitary, which contains acidophil cells that secrete growth hormone and prolactin: this organ grows considerably at puberty in girls but barely, if at all, in boys.

The pituitary is greatly involved in the events of puberty. Two of its products, follicle-stimulating hormone (FSH) and luteinising hormone (LH), have been present at low levels during childhood but now increase until a point is reached where FSH stimulates either the tubules of the testes or the ovarian follicles to develop, and LH causes testosterone secretion from the Leydig cells in the testis. Oestrogen, again present in children, also rises slowly until adolescence, when there is a marked increase in girls, a lesser one in boys.

The adrenal cortex produces three groups of hormones—cortisol, aldosterone and androgens. Of these, the former two show no spurt at adolescence, but the last shows a great increase in both sexes. The cause of this increase is not known, but its effects include the growth of pubic and axillary (armpit) hair. It seems that pubic hair, which develops earliest, has the lowest threshold to adrenal androgenic stimulation, axillary hair has a higher threshold and is also more responsive to testosterone, the beard has an even higher threshold and a more pronounced preference for testosterone. As these thresholds are reached by the hormones, so the particular type of hair growth is 'switched on'. However, there is probably an additional factor—a sequence of changes in the receptivity of the target organs themselves.

The cause of the adolescent body growth spurt is not yet known. The excess of male over female growth is probably due to testosterone, which is probably also responsible for the greater muscle and bone development of boys. The general spurt of both sexes is probably the result of growth hormone level, adrenal androgen level, or both.

Motor development

It is known that boys are stronger than girls, but few people have much idea when these differences develop or how far they go. A number of studies have attempted to measure strength changes around the time of adolescence and these have been conveniently summarized by Tanner.

Fig. 7.15 shows strength of hand grip, arm pull and arm thrust. The instrument used is known as a dynamometer, and results show the best score obtained in competition with a classmate of similar ability in a Californian study. Data are plotted at 6-monthly intervals over a period of 6 years and are longitudinal. The four boys' curves all show an upwards swing characteristic of the adolescent spurt, from age 13 to 16 years. No clear swing of this sort is clearly visible in the results for girls. In hand grip boys already exceed girls at age 11, despite the fact that they have at this age not yet reached their growth spurt while the girls have. Tanner relates this to the difference in length and breadth of the forearm, which is greater in boys than girls throughout childhood, from age 2 on. The increase in the difference after age $13\frac{1}{2}$ is presumably due to the specific adolescent growth spurt. In the case of arm thrust there is no pre-adolescent sex difference, but the extra growth of boys' shoulder, back and pectoral muscles at adolescence takes effect at the time of their growth spurt.

Strength curves such as these have been shown to resemble the curves for morphological and physiological characters, in that early developers are also physically stronger than later developers at any given age. Also, there is a seasonal effect which is the same as that for height—strength increases more in the spring than in the autumn, and of course there are cultural effects, e.g. occupation.

Examination of curves for muscle growth in comparison with the increase of strength indicates that there is a delay between the peak growth in size and the peak for strength. This indicates that the strength increase is in these cases due to factors besides mere muscle size due to growth hormone, and the action of sex hormones and adrenocortical hormones is indicated. It is known that injections of testosterone can increase strength in eunuchs and in 70-year-old men, given suitable training procedures. This '*trainability*' of muscle becomes greater in boys than girls after puberty but is not present before; it reaches its maximum in men in the 25–35 age group, after which it declines. In the case of girls there is no change in the amount

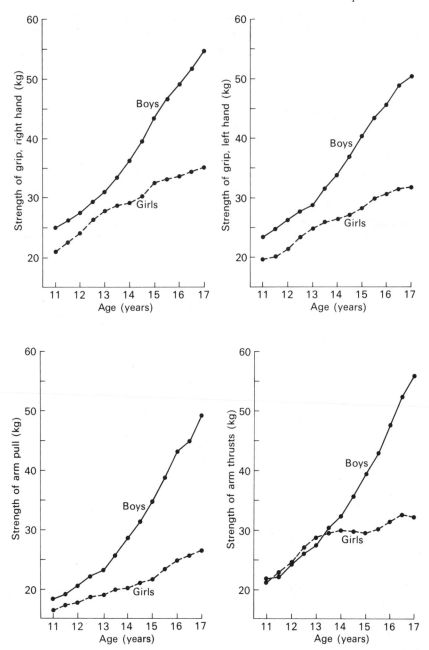

FIG. 7.15. Strength of hand grip, arm pull and arm thrust from age 11 to 17. (Redrawn from Tanner (1962).)

of trainability as between immature and mature persons, i.e. women do not become more capable of increased strength due to muscular activity as adults than they were as children. The 'trainability' curve for men declines and there is no sex difference after age 60.

This chapter has been concerned with the morphological, physiological, endocrine and motor changes accompanying development. A question not raised so far, however, concerns the nature of the external factors influencing masculinity and femininity, raising an important distinction between 'sex' and 'gender'. Here we begin to re-emerge into the main theme of the book: the part played by ideas of appropriateness, expectations arising from cultural ideas, and their interaction with ongoing organic body processes, in determining courses of action. In the next chapter we continue to emphasize the organic, physical side of development, but continually run into inevitable entanglements with cultural prescriptions.

CHAPTER 8

Sex and gender

LET US CONSIDER the distinction between 'sex' and 'gender'. 'Sex' is used to refer to those aspects of maleness and femaleness of an organic kind. Thus the physical construction of a naked man or woman is 'sexual'. Gender is used to refer to the societal or cultural side of things—thus a sexual female may be assigned to a masculine gender, either in a transvestite show or in 'real life'. Such a person wears man's clothes and may be generally accepted as a man.

Let us look at sex first, and later at the question of gender. We are nearly all born with the external physical characteristics of one

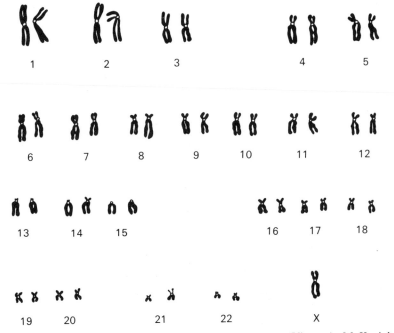

FIG. 8.1. Karyotype of a patient with Turner's syndrome. (Victor A. McKusick, *Human Genetics*, © 1969; reprinted by permission of Prentice-Hall Inc., Englewood Cliffs, New Jersey, U.S.A.)

sex or the other, so our *sex* is announced at birth and often the first thing a mother hears (and wants to know) is the sex of her baby. This knowledge influences her responsivity to the baby and she will normally encourage by what she says and does those subsequent activities of the infant's that seem to her to be appropriate for a boy or a girl. Thus in effect she is assigning her child a *gender* and conditioning it into an appropriate role. However, it does not necessarily follow that everything the child does is the result of her assignment. On the contrary, the infant, as we have seen, arrives with its own set of instructions for further organic development.

Chromosome anomalies

In some cases these instructions contain 'mistakes'. The field of sex differences provides some examples of biochemical–behavioural upsets of which the genetic, or at least the chromosomal, basis is known. I refer in particular to the conditions usually known as Turner's syndrome (Fig. 8.1) and Klinefelter's syndrome (Fig. 8.2). Both of these anomalies, known for many years at the clinical level, were shown in 1959 to result from an abnormal number of sex chro-

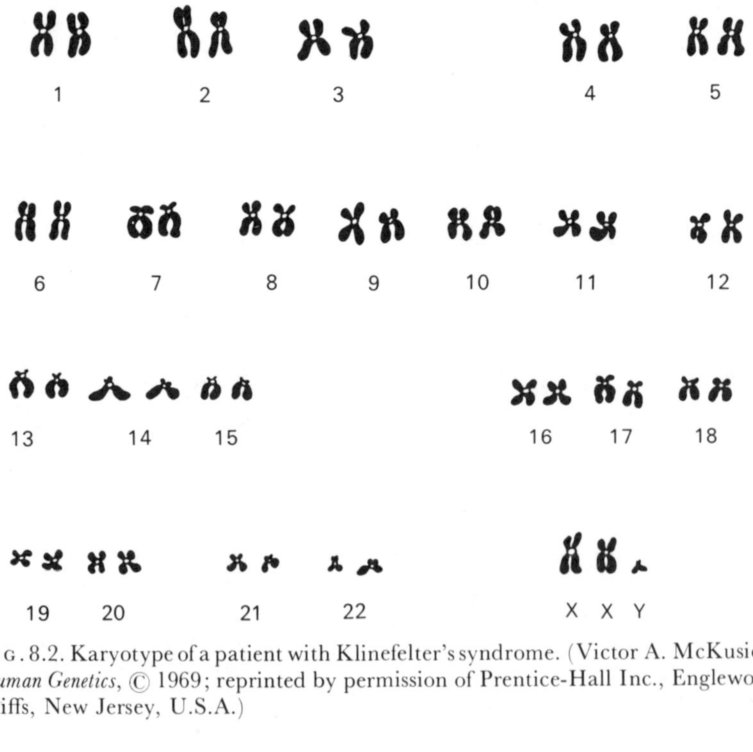

FIG. 8.2. Karyotype of a patient with Klinefelter's syndrome. (Victor A. McKusick, *Human Genetics*, © 1969; reprinted by permission of Prentice-Hall Inc., Englewood Cliffs, New Jersey, U.S.A.)

mosomes, one too few in the case of Turner's syndrome (X0) and one too many in Klinefelter's syndrome (XXY).† These abnormalities in turn result from errors that occur during meiosis, such that the sex cell that one parent brings to the zygote either has no sex chromosome in it (0) or has two X chromosomes in it (XX). X0 is caused by a normal female sex cell from father or mother fusing with an abnormal 0 cell; XXY results from a normal male sex cell from the father fusing with a double X sex cell from the mother, or a normal X cell from the mother fusing with an abnormal XY cell from the father. There are two further well-known anomalies of this type, resulting in individuals who are XXX and XYY, and in addition there is a wide variation of anomalies, some based on perfectly normal sex chromosome arrangements (XX and XY) but with abnormal embryonic development of the foetal gonads. Where there are errors not of primary sex chromosome complement but of subsequent differentiation, the resulting individual has characteristics of both sexes.

Turner's syndrome (X0) has an estimated frequency of about 0·75 per cent among conceptions but is associated with a high prenatal mortality as early spontaneous abortion which may be as high as 97 per cent, resulting in a live birth rate of 1:5000. At birth the infant, in appearance a girl, has loose and redundant skin at the nape of the neck, and this develops during childhood into neck 'webbing'; a second characteristic in childhood is short stature; but the condition manifests itself most clearly at puberty when there is a lack of secondary sex characters with continued short stature. By the time of puberty the ovaries are reduced to vestigial organs, having diminished in size from the age of 3 months post-conception.

Klinefelter's syndrome (XXY) occurs in 1:700 newborn males. It is not detected during development of the child, but in the adult the testis is very small, with (usually) absence of spermatogenesis, atrophy of testicular tubules and disturbance of sex hormone activity.

The triple X anomaly (XXX)‡ has a frequency of 1:1250 among newborn girls and is not marked by any clear-cut syndrome of externally observable physical characteristics. The individuals concerned have been called 'super-females', but in fact their pubertal development appears to be normal (Ganong 1973, p. 317).

† X0 and XXY are the commonest chromosome abnormalities in Turner's and Klinefelter's syndrome respectively. Others now known are as follows. Turner's syndrome: X0/XX mosaicism and X0/XX/XXX mosaicism (a mosaicism is a condition in which the chromosomal complement of different autosomal cells is different). Klinefelter's syndrome: XXYY, XXXY, XXXYY, XXXXY and XY/XXY mosaicism (see Ganong 1973, p. 317).

‡XXXX and XXXXX are also known.

The XYY anomaly, which has an incidence of about 1:700 in newborn males, is, like XXX, not clearly evidenced by external morphological characteristics. A correlation with tall stature has been suggested, but recent data tend not to support this (Murken 1973). Gonadal development is sometimes imperfect, ranging from hypospadias and hypogonadism to undescended testes; but it may be normal. XYY males are reported to be normally fertile, but detailed studies of meiosis in XYY sperm have shown certain anomalies.

Owing to the fact that the XYY condition was first revealed in a study of a criminal population, it was originally suggested that there might be some causal connection between the presence of an extra Y chromosome and criminal tendencies. The idea achieved wide circulation mainly because of the ongoing debate about human aggressiveness and the theory, based largely on ethological data from other species, that aggression was a male characteristic. Here, then, appeared to be strong evidence that an extra male chromosome produced an excessively aggressive male who in consequence landed up in prison. Eugenicists likewise rejoiced at the prospect of spotting the future criminal at birth (or before).

Further studies have served to diminish to zero the likelihood that the XYY chromosome type increases aggressiveness. In particular it has been shown that the incidence of XYY is no higher in criminals than it is in the rest of the population. Secondly, it has never been shown that those criminals who are XYY are in fact more aggressive than those who are XY. The strength of the association between criminal behaviour and XYY sex chromosomes was never proved; Murken's definitive study (1973) disposes of the idea completely.

Social factors and gender identity

'Gender' differences differ from sex differences in that gender is a social or sociological or psychological condition in which a person finds himself, whereas sex is socially neutral, being a fact to be established by examination of the individual's chromosomes and/or sexual anatomy. Gender is related to sex in the following way: an individual's sex, determined at birth by inspection of his/her genitalia, determines in turn the attitudes and actions of the parents, relatives, friends, playmates, and other aspects of the environment—the toys he or she will be given, the activities that will be rewarded and those that will not.

This set of social factors by no means rules out the possibility or probability that the infant will bring sex-related behaviours into the social world with him on the basis of his or her physical endowments.

Such differences are properly called sex differences and for the most part they are still to be adequately documented. It is well known in our culture that boys fight more than girls, and differences in level of aggressiveness have emerged from a number of studies made on ethological lines by the method of direct observation of ongoing behaviour in children (Blurton-Jones 1967; Grant 1969; McGrew 1972, etc.). Such studies, mostly on pre-school children in the 3–5-year-old age group, do not and cannot by their nature distinguish between sex differences and gender differences. To do that we need cross-cultural studies where gender differences are great. In one such study (the only adequate one to date) of the Bushmen, boys were found to be significantly more aggressive than girls, using the same techniques as those used in studies in Britain (see Blurton-Jones and Konner 1973, pp. 703–77, for further details). We need more studies, made in cultures where aggressiveness is discouraged and frowned upon, to indicate whether differences in overt aggressiveness between boys and girls are inevitably found. This would still not mean that they were true sex differences in aggressiveness, for it is hard to see how such differences in regard to any human characteristic that involved a heavy component of intervention by adults could be clearly shown not to have gender elements. Human differences in action between boys and girls or between men and women are probably best regarded as gender differences in the present state of understanding.

In regard to abnormal sexual development, it is scientifically of great interest (though in human terms often saddening) to note the pattern of gender identification by others, and of gender identity by themselves, of affected individuals. Money, Hampson and Hampson (1955) drew attention to the influence of environmental factors, in the case of people whose sex organs were ambiguous, in determining the gender to which they were assigned and with which they identified themselves. At that time, they stated that 'psychologically, sexuality is undifferentiated at birth'. Hutt (1972) points out that this position was modified subsequently to the view that 'there may well be a fetal hormonal effect on ... psycho-sexual differentiation' (Money and Erhardt 1968). This latter position was doubtless necessitated by two sorts of data for which evidence has accrued in recent years, first the pervasive and long-continued effects of sex hormones in the organization of personality and sexual identity, and secondly the fact that in a good number of cases, people whose assigned gender was at variance with their genetic sex or their physical appearance were often extremely unhappy with their assigned gender and strove desperately to change it to the gender they felt was correct for themselves. Let us look at evidence on this point, which is of interest in its own right but also has great significance in understanding the nature of human development as a product of biological and cultural forces.

Mensh (1972) discusses some of the findings in regard to gender differences and gender identity on the basis of studies made at the University of California at Los Angeles Gender Identity Research Clinic, and I shall refer to those data briefly here. Other data are to be found in the psychiatric and psychosomatic literature, often written up at great length in the form of individual case histories.

Following work by Stoller, Mensh (1972) contrasts two types of cross-gender behaviour, transexualism and transvestism. The transexual has the physical characteristics of one sex but the psychological identity, the actions and dress of the other. Most transexuals are males physically. They act like women and want to be women, and in some cases can undergo surgery to bring this hoped-for condition nearer to reality. Transvestites share the characteristics of transexuals except that they do not want to be physically transformed into the opposite sex, in other words they are content to be one sex masquerading as the other. It is the former category, the transexuals, who are thus of greater interest in the present context since the question arises: why should a person who is biologically male desire to be a woman to such an extent that he will undergo surgery to bring this about?

This is to some extent a false way of presenting the question. In most of these cases sexual development is not wholly normal. Excessive adrenal output of androgens in females both *in utero* and after birth can give rise to the adrenogenital syndrome in which male characteristics as well as female ones are present in the genitalia. Testicular feminization may occur in males as a result of excessive oestrogen. Individuals who are genetically XX may, because of 'male' autosomes that play a role in gonad development, develop male gonads and ultimately more-or-less complete male sexual anatomy while remaining XX in every cell of their body; or the reverse may occur where a genetic male appears to all intents and purposes to be a female.

Stoller earlier described the case of an apparently normal girl, reared as such, who did not develop normally at puberty but underwent a voice change of male type. Genitally 'she' was predominantly female but chromosomally she was male, and physical examination showed certain male characteristics including a normal prostate. Told 'she' was a male, 'she went home, took off her girl's clothing and became a boy, immediately beginning to behave like other boys in the community'. Further development in this case was satisfactory, and the boy changed 'from being a mediocre to an excellent student'.

A second case described by Stoller is, however, extremely puzzling. A child reared as a boy with normal male genitals developed along female lines at puberty, but disguised her feminine appearance (breasts) by becoming withdrawn until the age of 17 when she changed her gender role to being a woman, subsequently at the age of 20 undergoing surgery to transform her male genitalia into female. In this case the individual was genetically male but was apparently somehow producing massive amounts of oestrogen leading to the female developments at puberty. How was the massive oestrogen output achieved? The answer came unexpectedly, during a follow-up interview some years after the 'sex-change' operation: the patient had been *taking* oestrogens since puberty. He had, it appears, deceived everybody on this point, having been driven all along by an obsession to be a woman. Whence came this obsession in a genetically and anatomically normal male? The answer is not known. This child was reared as a boy, so the case does not conform to Money and Hampson's expectations, whatever the somatic base. Genetically and ontogenetically there was no evidence of female developments. However, this person did play, during childhood, at being a female. Why he did this is not known. Ultimately it seems he took his unsatisfactory condition in his own hands and by a conscious decision set about changing it. If any theory is able to account for this it must be a theory that places much weight on conscious personal autonomy; perhaps the philosophy of Sartre would provide a starting point. Clearly we have here an exception to the vast majority of cases where organic predisposing factors underlie gender confusion.

We have mentioned just one such case; there are undoubtedly others. Their significance to the present work is the strength with which they argue the case of the cognitive self-construct in the mind of the individual over his or her organic programme in the determination of action. There is, however, something else, a 'driving force' behind such action and indeed underlying all action. This force or impetus is most often referred to as 'emotion'. We conclude this part of the book with a closer look at emotion from a physiological standpoint.

CHAPTER 9

The 'emotions' and the physiology of stress

The nature of emotions

The word 'emotions' is in inverted commas because there is at present some debate about the nature and number of separable arousal states constituting 'the emotions' and the degree to which both they and their associated facial expressions vary across cultures (cf. Ekman and Friesen 1971; Eibl-Eibesfeldt 1970). Considerable problems of semantics are involved here, and these lie outside the confines of this book.

What, in evolutionary terms, are emotions? According to Lorenz aggression has been the phylogenetically first and most important emotion, from which, during evolution, the other emotions, in particular love, have developed. Eibl-Eibesfeldt by contrast holds that love and hate are equally ancient and basic, competition and co-operation being equally essential ingredients for social coexistence and survival. Fear is clearly ancient, being well developed in fish, which for instance will dart around rapidly in a tank if a stream of water is let into it containing the smell of a predator species. Maternal emotion is doubtless a more recent phenomenon dating back no further than the mammals. Sex seems well developed in fish and birds, judging from the intensity and oblivion with which they pursue their mating rituals; insects too, and indeed all sexually reproducing species that need to move and copulate, may qualify for the possession of this basic emotion.

What, in physiological terms, are emotions? William James (1890) described emotional states as the perception by the mind of visceral physiological states, but this view was disputed by Cannon (1929) (see further discussion below). There is, however, no doubt that visceral physiological changes do accompany subjectively experienced emotional states. This can be shown, for instance, by the use of an instrument measuring skin resistance. A small electric current is passed between two points on the surface of the skin, for instance between the second and third fingers, and the baseline resistance to the current is measured. On experiencing 'emotion' of some kind, e.g. mild fear or shock at hearing a loud bang, or shame, jealousy or anger arising from experimental procedures or mere thought, skin resistance declines and the amount of current passed between the two poles increases. The reason for the change is a slight increase in sweat output accompanying emotional arousal.

Quite how useful this measure is seems questionable. Problems arise of a practical kind. What one is measuring is, after all, sweating, not emotion. Individuals are known to differ markedly in their base-line sweating rate, but it is hard to determine differences in respon-siveness of individuals' sweat glands to a common stimulus because between the stimulus and the response are a number of unknowns, including the perceived meaning as well as the perceptual ability of the subject. Also it is known that skin resistance is affected by rate and depth of breathing, which are hard to equate between subjects. While precision is impossible, it is nevertheless clear that skin resist-ance changes with emotional arousal.

A list of physiological variables that co-vary with 'anxiety' is given by Cattell (1966) as follows:†

> increase in systolic pulse pressure
> increase in heart-rate
> increase in respiration rate
> increase in basal and current metabolic rate
> increase in phenylhydracrylic acid in urine
> decrease in electrical skin resistance
> increase in hippuric acid in the urine
> increase in 17-OH-ketosteroid excretion
> decrease in alkalinity of saliva
> decrease in cholinesterase in serum
> decrease in neutrophils and, less clearly, eosinophils
> increase in phenylalanine, leucine, glycine and serine
> increase in histidine in urine
> decrease in urea concentration
> decrease in glucuronidase in urine and in serum

In a review of the ontogeny of emotional behaviour Candland (1971) draws attention to an early paper by Ray 'who studied a number of physiological variables, including pulse rate, respiration and blood pressure, in children reacting to a sudden loss of physical support. His findings indicated that in such an apparently emotion-provoking situation some children showed an increase in the re-sponses measured and others a decrease' (p. 114). Candland con-

† Physiological associations are listed in approximate order of degree of association and degree of confidence in confirmation.

cludes that while individuals may have characteristic patterns of physiological reactivity to a given situation, different patterns of reactivity will be found between individuals.

The work of Miller and his colleagues on learned patterns of control of autonomic functioning is relevant here—it could help to explain individual differences where these are not constitutional. By ingenious experiments with rats these workers have been able to show that the animals can learn to slow down or speed up their heart-rate, intestinal contractions, rate of kidney blood-flow, rate of blood-flow through the stomach wall, stomach contractions, and blood-pressure. One particularly unexpected result was that rats could be trained to increase vasodilation of *a single ear*, leaving the other unaffected! (Miller 1969).

In certain rodent species, notably voles, physiological changes of the reproductive system (e.g. foetus resorption) accompany conditions of overcrowding. Such conditions appear in many rodent species, as well as in other mammals, to accompany conditions of high emotional arousal, with aggression a common concomitant in rats and mice, and infant killing and eating in rats. In these cases, the emotional-cum-physiological events probably have a selective advantage in controlling population growth. Possibly the same is true of all such changes—the very existence of emotions and their physiological correlates must, one assumes, be the outcome of natural selection.

A selective advantage was in fact posited by W. B. Cannon, whose book *Bodily Changes in Pain, Hunger, Fear and Rage* (1929) remains a monument in the field of physiology and emotion. Cannon's researches were directed at the interplay of emotional feeling and actions of the autonomic nervous system, especially the sympathetic nerves from the cerebrospinal system to the viscera and certain other organs. Pavlov had early shown that psychic stimuli, such as the anticipation of food by dogs, could produce copious salivary and gastric secretions. It had also been shown that fear could inhibit such secretions. Cannon investigated the two-way excitatory–inhibitory action of the autonomic system, concluding that there were certain rather specific responses of the system to states of high emotional arousal, especially on the heart, the liver and the adrenals, together with associated effects on muscle tissue, red blood cell count, and speed of coagulation of the blood. The heart was speeded up, the liver released more glycogen (stored starch) for conversion into blood sugar, and the adrenals produced an increased flow of adrenalin from their medullary or central portion.

Cannon was especially interested in the flow of adrenalin. He showed that its function was to augment and prolong the effects of the sympathetic nervous system. Adrenalin acts, he showed, in the same way as increased sympathetic arousal, producing essentially similar effects on organs and smooth muscle but over a longer period of time. In particular it could cause continuous liver action to liberate sugar, it could improve the performance of fatigued muscle and could hasten blood coagulation.

Why should emotional excitement produce these effects? Cannon's answer was as follows:

Every one of the visceral changes that have been noted—the cessation of processes in the alimentary canal (thus freeing the energy supply for other parts); the shifting of blood from the abdominal organs to the organs immediately essential to muscular exertion; the increased vigor of contraction of the heart; the discharge of extra blood corpuscles from the spleen; the deeper respiration; the dilation of the bronchioles; the quick abolition of the effects of muscular fatigue; the mobilizing of sugar in the circulation—these changes are *directly serviceable in making the organism more effective in the violent display of energy which fear or rage or pain may involve*.

The experience of emotion, then, according to Cannon, leads to physiological changes that give the individual a better chance of responding to a challenge and hence of surviving.

To Cannon, 'emotion' is not the subjective experience of visceral physiological changes, nor are different emotions the perceptions of different physiological changes. This view, called by Cannon the 'James–Lange' theory, is rejected for a number of reasons. First, almost all the outward signs of emotional experience can be observed in animals after surgical removal of all connections between the brain and the sympathetic nervous system. Secondly, the whole process of emotional reactivity is too quick to depend on impulses coming back from the rather poorly innervated viscera. Thirdly, the artificial induction of body changes, for example by the injection of adrenalin, fails to induce specific emotions, producing instead vague feelings of tension or feelings 'as if something is about to happen'. Thus physiological correlates of emotion must be seen to some extent as effects rather than causes of heightened emotional arousal.

One might suppose that if emotion did not come from 'below' it would come from 'above', i.e. from higher cortical brain areas, but this again is not so. Two lines of evidence are adduced by Cannon. First, the outward signs of an emotion such as rage can be induced in decorticated experimental animals. Secondly, certain types of facial paralysis (hemiplegia) cause loss of cortical control of facial musculature, yet in emotion the affected muscles may behave in the normal way. In another condition which he calls 'pseudo-bulbar palsy', 'voluntary pursing of the lips as in whistling, or wrinkling of the forehead, or making a grimace may be impossible. The intractable facial muscles, however, function normally in laughing and crying, scowling or frowning' (p. 364). Thus a subcortical region is held by Cannon to be the 'seat of the emotions' and he points to the thalamus as the region in question. This is not to deny that cortical processes may, in everyday life, be crucial for the initiation or control of emotional expression. Indeed, as Cannon says, 'cortical processes may start thalamic processes' (p. 371).

These views, derived from experimental evidence, are very much in line with modern research. Subjective perceptions arising in the interpretation of the environment can stimulate the hypothalamus, which in turn acts on the adrenals; autonomic effects occur as Cannon described; and there are in addition effects on facial and other musculature that have communicative significance. The body responds appropriately for survival, but the perception of factors that lead to an emotional response occurs via the cognitive, ideational cortex in normal circumstances. It may be generated there—e.g. a sudden thought sets in motion the processes Cannon described. Or it may arrive there from perceptions of the external environment arriving via the sense organs.

Cognitive aspects of emotion

Some of the most pertinent research in this field in recent years has been that of Schachter and his colleagues. A summary of the findings of this work can be found in Schachter (1966). Schachter and Singer (1962) devised a series of ingenious experiments that involved administering injections of adrenalin or placebo to subjects who were completely misinformed about the nature of the experiment, being told it was a study of vision. Before being given the adrenalin injection, some subjects were correctly informed about the side effects they were likely to experience, some were told there were no side effects and some were misinformed. The placebo group, who were given saline, were told (correctly) there would be no side effects.

After the injections subjects were left sitting in a room where they were joined by a specially trained stooge who acted in such a way as to produce an atmosphere of euphoria for certain subjects, anger for others. The ideas behind the experiment were (a) to see whether the groups who had been injected with adrenalin would be more emotionally aroused by the stooge than those who had not; (b) to see what the effects of the information about side effects would be on the subjects' reactions; (c) to see whether the subjects' reactions would reflect those of the stooge.

The experimenters found a much higher level of responsiveness to the stooge in the 'ignorant' and 'misinformed' groups that had received the adrenalin injection than in the groups that had been told what effects to expect. The latter group reacted less markedly than the placebo group, in fact.

The authors' conclusions were that, given a state of physiological arousal from the injection, subjects who were either not expecting this or had been misinformed (they were in fact told to expect itching sensations, numbness and a slight headache) did show a marked emotional response to a social situation, and that this response was of the same kind as that of the stooge. Where they knew what to expect, however, this knowledge seems to have completely inhibited their emotional responsiveness.

In more general terms, Schachter takes these results to show that the actual type and degree of emotion shown by a person is an out-come of both physiological and cognitive inputs:

A general pattern of sympathetic discharge is characteristic of emotional states. Given such a state of arousal, it is suggested that one labels, interprets, and identifies this stirred-up state in terms of the characteristics of the precipitating situation and one's apperceptive mass. This suggests, then, that an emotional state may be con-sidered a function of a state of physiological arousal and of a cognition appropriate to this state of arousal. The cognition, in a sense, exerts a steering function. Cogni-tions arising from the immediate situation as interpreted by past experience provide the framework within which one understands and labels his feelings. It is the cogni-tion which determines whether the state of physiological arousal will be labeled 'anger', 'joy', or whatever. [Schachter 1966, pp. 194–5.]

Again: 'Should he at the time [e.g. of physiological arousal] be with a beautiful woman, he might decide that he was wildly in love or sexually excited. Should he be at a gay party, he might, by com-paring himself to others, decide that he was extremely happy and euphoric. Should he be arguing with his wife, he might explode in fury and hatred' (Schachter 1966, pp. 196–7). '. . . it could be antici-pated that precisely the same state of physiological arousal could be labelled 'joy' or 'fury' or any of a great diversity of emotional labels, depending on the cognitive aspects of the situation' (p. 197).

For Schachter, then, a general level of physiological arousal is an essential ingredient of what we call an emotional state, but the actual state, or label we attach to it, is cognitively determined by our inter-pretation of the (social) circumstances and our ideas of appropriate-ness, acquired through cultural learning. Indeed, later in the chapter we have been looking at, Schachter, following Becker (1953), de-scribes the process of learning to smoke marihauna, learning to label the ensuing physiological symptoms as being 'high', and learning to enjoy these symptoms or sensations.

The work described above is clearly of central interest in the study of the biology of human action. When the social context is taken fully into account, as in the study I have referred to by the sociologist Becker, one can see the individual body and its functions, the individual mind and its interpretative processes and the prevailing cultural context of ideas of appropriateness combining to form a unified scheme of action. Probably one needs to add qualifiers to Schachter's view that a single general kind of physiological arousal underlies differently labelled emotional states; that could be only partly true, and there could be extra physiological components in particular circumstances. Thus in sexual arousal a male experiencing concomitant penile erection would be subject to local parasympathetic activity, whereas a male having a row with his wife would probably not. Miller and Banuazizi (1968) have shown that, in rats, visceral learning can be specific to particular organ systems; they trained one group of rats to adjust (either speed up or slow down) heart-rate but not intestinal contractions, and another to respond the other way. There is thus no *a priori* reason to think of autonomic functioning (whether sympathetic or parasympathetic or a mixture of both) as all of a piece; indeed the available evidence indicates that this is not the case (Miller 1969). But the tripartite view that emerges from the studies we have looked at—two parts, the physiological and the cognitive, at the individual level, and the third part, the normative, at the cultural level—seems the most useful for the understanding not only of what the so-called emotions are and how they work, but of human action in general.

Endocrinology of the emotions

A field of great interest with regard to emotional physiology is the study of neuro-endocrine substances. These, it is widely believed, are very closely bound up with emotional states. Indeed it is possible that an individual's baseline emotionality and his patterns of emotional reactiveness are coincident with the particular and unique functioning of the many complex hormones he produces and their numerous metabolites. This hormonal system works together with the cognitive structuring by which he perceives the world, which is equally unique, to make up what we can call his 'personality'.

We are a long way from understanding much of this, but there are a number of promising empirical studies in both the non-human and the human field, the hormones mostly studied being the products of the adrenal glands—the catecholamines adrenalin and noradrenalin produced by the medullary or central part of the adrenals,

and the corticosteroids, especially 17-OHCS (17-hydroxycortico-
steroid) and cortisol itself, produced by the outer area of the adrenals
or adrenal cortex.

In mice, for instance, Christian (1964) described a linear correlation between rank order and adrenocortical function: the latter is
least in most dominant and greatest in most subordinate mice and
'increases more or less linearly with descending rank between these
two extremes' (p. 169). The same relation between rank order and
adrenocortical level of functioning has been shown in rats, rabbits
and dogs. If a number of animals whose baseline levels are known
are grouped together, the animals with lower baseline levels are
dominant and their levels do not change much in response to grouping, whereas those with higher baseline levels are subordinate and
their levels rise as a result of grouping before subsequent stabiliza-
tion. The more animals that are grouped in a given space, i.e. the
greater the population density, the greater the overall level of adrenalin and noradrenalin secretion by all animals, especially subordinates. Behaviourally one sees the increasing density correlated with
increasing aggressiveness on the part of dominants, while subordinates flee or crouch in fear. Reproduction may at this stage cease,
young may be eaten and in general the entire set of changes may
be seen as a selective spacing mechanism (Christian 1964).

In primates Southwick (1967) has shown an increase in aggressiveness resulting from increased density in rhesus monkeys. Endocrine
correlations with rank order seem to be non-linear, at least in the
case of the squirrel monkeys studied by Candland and Leshner
(1974). These authors found that monkeys with high dominance
status had *high* 17-OHCS (i.e. adrenocorticosteroid) levels, the
reverse being true of subordinates. This was true both before introduction to a group situation (i.e. it was true of their baseline levels)
and it was still true 9 weeks later and 4 years later in the group
studied. The only time it was not true was shortly after being put
together, when the levels of the two top-ranking monkeys fell below
those of the other three monkeys in the group (see Fig. 9.1).

Regarding total catecholamine levels in this group, a remarkable
transformation occurred during socialization. This concerned the
animals of intermediate rank. Before being put together certain animals had low relative catecholamine levels. During socialization,
levels for these animals went up to such an extent that they were
the highest in the group. Subsequently the picture was unclear, but
after 4 years high rankers had lower levels, low rankers high levels,
and mid-rankers were in between (Fig. 9.2).

Studies of wild squirrel monkeys have indicated that intermediate

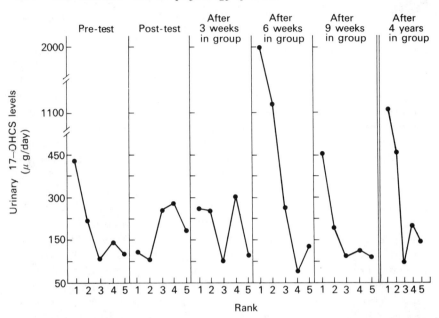

F IG. 9.1. The relationship of dominance rank to urinary 17-OHCS-levels as a function of duration of group-living. (Redrawn from Candland and Leshner (1974).)

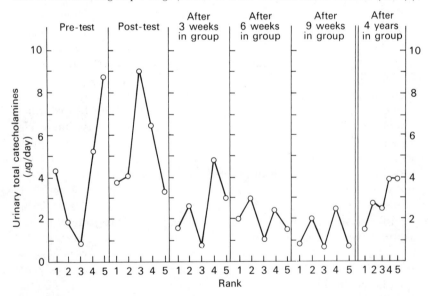

F IG. 9.2. The relationship of dominance rank to urinary total catecholamines as a function of duration of group-living. (Redrawn from Candland and Leshner (1974).)

ranking animals have more reproductive success than either high rankers (who are too busy with agonistic interactions) or low rankers (who are pushed out). Some corroboration of this idea for another species can perhaps be found in Kaufmann's (1965) study of free-ranging rhesus-monkeys, where dominant males often focused their sexual activity on one or a very few females while those of slightly lower rank had more mates. It is possible to suggest that in natural conditions those individuals who show adrenomedullary *responsiveness* rather than high or low *chronic* levels are at a selective advantage, i.e. they produce more offspring, even if they do not appear to have all the immediate advantages conferred by dominant status.

Studies on normal human subjects in their everyday lives have shown that individuals do have fairly constant catecholamine excretion rates over periods of days or weeks or longer, and the same is reported for adrenocorticosteroids (see p. 90). Such studies additionally report the existence of considerable inter-individual differences. Such differences are doubtless in part of constitutional/genetic origin.

Tentative correlations have been suggested between endocrine secretion rates and personality. Fox *et al.* (1961) suggested a correlation between high 17-OHCS levels and relatively uncontrolled emotional expressiveness, and between low 17-OHCS levels and highly controlled emotional expression. In a study of 18 healthy male college students whose urine was collected for analysis continuously for 5 weeks, these investigators found that of the two subjects with the highest excreted 17-OHCS one was characterized by an 'urgent, indiscriminate quality' in his social relations, and a 'need for unusual closeness', while the other was 'persistently suspicious' and 'aware of his vulnerability'. The four lowest excretors were on the contrary characterized by 'emotional detachment, inhibition of feelings and impulses, or emphasis on orderliness and self-regulation'. Personality was assessed on the basis of psychiatric interviews and Rorschach tests. The authors concluded that 'the more a person reacts emotionally, the higher the level of the 17-OHCS. The more guarded the individual ... the lower the 17-OHCS.'

It is known that adrenocortical activity is stimulated by ACTH—(adrenocorticotrophic hormone)—a hormone secreted into the blood stream by the pituitary gland. The pituitary in turn is stimulated by hormones from the hypothalamus in the brain stem, and this receives neuronal–chemical information from higher brain centres, including the cortex. Besides, there appears to be a feed-back loop controlling ACTH secretion once a certain level of adrenocortical products or their metabolites is present in the blood-stream, but, as chronic inter-individual differences in excretion rates show, the level of cut-off varies from one person to another.

What, in point of fact, do excretion rates really mean? It is generally assumed that an increase in excretion reflects an increase in secretion and to some extent this must be so. Studies of the effects of viewing exciting films that cause anxiety (horror films) or hilarity (comedies) indicate increases in catecholamine excretion rates that appear to be a direct reflection of increased secretion rates (Levi 1968).

In these studies groups of people, under properly controlled conditions, give a urine sample, have a drink, then watch a film after which they give a second urine sample, then have another drink and finally give a third sample. The drinks are all identical quantities of water. The whole experiment lasts about 6 hours. What the results show is that, in most people, in the case of bland, natural-scenery films catecholamine levels remain more or less constant or even go down, whereas in the case of arousing films, whether they be hilariously funny, very frightening, or frankly erotic, catecholamine levels go up (Fig. 9.3). Interestingly, a sex difference was found in relation to the sex films—men were more responsive to these than women (see Fig. 9.3 (e) and (f)). Such a difference was not found in the other kinds of film studied.

One thing to note in connection with these film studies is that the subjects involved are all volunteers, i.e. we are dealing with a voluntary involvement and not an enforced one. This means that people are letting themselves get excited, not just passively being aroused. The latter can, of course, happen too, as in the case of, say, traffic accidents in which one is personally involved as a bystander, but in the film studies people are actively seeking arousal. Lazarus (1971) distinguishes between 'eustress' and 'dystress'—the former is pleasant and sought, the latter unpleasant and avoided—following Bernard (1968), and the distinction seems analytically useful. These two psychological terms can be used in distinction from physiological stress. Lazarus too writes interestingly about individuals' coping ability, and notes how they make efforts to overcome 'dystress' by re-ordering 'reality' and thus restoring 'self-esteem'.

But do long-term or chronic excretion differences between individuals tell us about their relative secretion rates or their *utilization* rates? Circadian rhythms are known to occur for most physiological processes, including endocrine secretion (Conroy and Mills 1970). For instance there is a lower level of catecholamines in the plasma and in the urine during the night than during the day and a higher

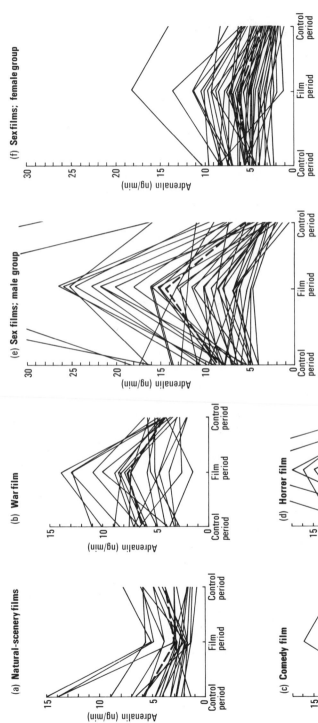

(f) **Sex films: female group**

(e) **Sex films: male group**

(b) **War film**

(d) **Horror film**

(a) **Natural-scenery films**

(c) **Comedy film**

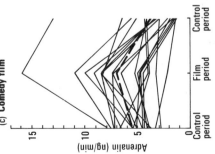

FIG. 9.3. Urinary adrenalin excretion rates before, during and after viewing various types of films. Solid lines are individual values, dashed lines indicate mean values. (Redrawn from Levi (1972).)

level of plasma and urinary 17-OHCS in the morning than later in the day or at night. Since it is improbable that catecholamine or cortisol is utilized faster or more fully at night, and in any case the plasma levels are low, not just the urinary levels, we can assume lower production rates by night. But the difficulty with measuring just adrenalin or just adrenalin and noradrenalin, as is often done in studies of adrenomedullary activity, or of measuring just 17-OHCS or just 17-ketosteroids or just cortisol (or even all three) in studying adrenocortical activity, is that this leaves some of the metabolites unaccounted for. In fact over 90 per cent of secreted catecholamine is metabolized before it reaches the urine (Barchas, Caranello, Stolk, Brodie and Hamburg 1972). To get at actual secretion rates direct it is necessary to insert a catheter into the adrenal vein, a procedure that interferes with normal functioning in laboratory animal experiments and is unethical in man. And then the rate and pattern of breakdown into metabolites is left unexplored. In our own recent work at Oxford, my colleagues and I are measuring excretion rates of the primary catecholamines and as many of their metabolites as possible, in order to obtain indirect evidence of secretion rates and direct evidence of patterns of breakdown.

Despite the difficulties there are a number of further studies that merit attention because of the suggestive nature of the results. On the adrenalin–noradrenalin side much current work derives from Levi and his co-workers at Stockholm. The tradition of this work is to relate findings to what Levi refers to as 'stress (Selye)', i.e. to the hypothesis first put forward by Selye and now widely accepted that adrenal cortex function is a stress response, using stress in a strictly physiological sense to refer to a 'non-specific response of the body to any demand made upon it' (Selye 1971). Cannon showed that much the same process occurred in the adrenal medulla. In the case of a sudden burst of muscular activity with increased heart-rate and a sudden need for oxygen in muscle tissue, adrenalin causes (among other things) dilation of arterial walls and increased blood-flow and blood-pressure. The original (adaptive) context of this was, he considered, the stressful 'fight-or-flight' situation frequently met by our early hunting ancestors; and one present-day research tradition following this is to search for stressful situations in modern life and ascertain the extent to which it is non-adaptive or even positively harmful in the modern context.

The viewing of exciting films already referred to is a good example of a situation in which adrenal activity increases but there is no physical activity and so the action of adrenalin is non-adaptive. Adrenalin causes release of free fatty acids; it also raises the blood-sugar level

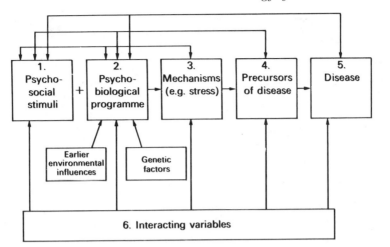

F I G. 9.4. A theoretical model for psycho-socially mediated disease. The combined effect of psycho-social stimuli (1) and the psycho-biological program (2) determines the psychological and physiological reactions (mechanisms (3), e.g. stress) of each individual. These may, under certain circumstances, lead to precursors of disease (4) and to disease itself (5). This sequence of events can be promoted or counteracted by interacting variables (6). The sequence is not a one-way process but constitutes part of a cybernetic system with continuous feed-back. (Redrawn from Kagan and Levi (1971).)

by mobilizing glycogen from the liver; these actions may be mal-adaptive because unused sugars are converted for storage into fats in the blood and may promote atheroma formation and thus hasten the processes leading to coronary artery disease (see Fig. 9.4).

In what other situations does catecholamine excretion rate change in a regular fashion? Frankenhäuser (1971) reports that adrenalin excretion increases as a result of electric shock and riding a centrifuge. Other situations include car driving, taking exams, dental treatment, admission to hospital, and sensory deprivation (see Kagan and Levi 1971). Frankenhäuser tested adrenalin excretion in 98 students who had to do mental work against a background of workshop noise. There was a significant overall rise in adrenalin activity above baseline levels for the group as a whole; and individuals differed from each other in the extent to which they responded. She concluded that those subjects who had the greatest adrenalin increase (a) performed better than the others and (b) subjectively experienced less stress than the others. She refers to another study by Johannson, Frankenhäuser and Magnusson (1973) which showed the same result for a group of children: those who showed an adrenalin increase relative to their base levels during a mathematics test performed better than those who showed no such increase. Thus it may be that in modern working conditions those do best who are adrenally responsive while subjectively unstressed.

Other situations studied by workers in the U.S.A., Britain and elsewhere will be mentioned only briefly, for reasons of space. Many of them are reviewed by Mason (1968). Taking adrenal cortex studies first, he includes studies of oarsmen and the coxswain in Harvard boat races, aircraft pilots in flight (an English study this, by Carruthers (1973)), pre-operative patients, including dental patients awaiting treatment, and students before their final examinations at university. An often-drawn conclusion is that it is the amount of *unpredictability* of the anticipated situation that determines the extent of adrenal response, i.e. if you believe you can cope you do not respond as much as if you are not so sure you can cope; but what if you are *sure* you *can not* cope? Then, surely we have what Bruner (1966) refers to as 'defending', i.e. the building of walls of indifference or sheer retreat into oneself or into fantasy, etc. What does this look like endocrinologically?

We come on inevitably to the examination of what are rightly or wrongly classed as 'psychiatric cases'—a contentious phrase in view of the strictures of Szasz (1972) or Laing (1967). But a mention of the evidence is not an endorsement of psychiatric labelling, rather it is an opportunity to find out what we really *are* talking about and as such a *replacement* of the jargon of which complaint is often made (e.g. by Szasz).

Such studies have shown that in intense cases 'anxiety' and 'personality disintegration' go with unusually high levels of excreted 17-OHCS. In the case of 'depressives' there has been reported an initially high level of excreted 17-OHCS levels during the mental 'turmoil' phase followed by a marked and permanent lowering of levels which characterize the 'depressed' phase. A study of a single manic-depressive patient showed fluctuations in these directions of excreted 17-OHCS to be correlated with phases of the manic-depressive cycle. But we should note (a) certain contradictions in the data (e.g. in some studies a 'manic' state has gone with *low* 17-OHCS levels), (b) differences in usage of such terms as 'manic' by different observers, (c) differences between patients, and (d) that 17-OHCS, though accurately measurable, is an end-product of an exceedingly long chain of metabolic processes and urinary *excretion* rates do not tell us *directly* about *secretion* rates or utilisation of metabolites in the body and/or brain, which is what we really need to know.

If we now come to the adrenal medulla, again, taking studies of 'normal' people first, aircraft flight has been shown to affect medullary end-products, being correlated with increases over baseline expectations of excreted adrenalin and noradrenalin in pilots, whereas the same study showed an increase in adrenalin but not noradrenalin in passengers. In a study of athletes it was shown that increased levels of both products were present in the urine both before and after their physical exertions. Other situations giving a similar picture that have been studied include 'gravity-stress' in a centrifuge, sleep loss, and combat situations. Most such studies have been on urinary catecholamines, not plasma catecholamines, for a number of reasons, one of the main ones being that the mere collection of blood-samples and preparatory procedures in 'normal' situations is a contradiction in terms, whereas people do urinate anyway and so one can collect samples relatively easily for analysis. It is, however, necessary to guard against 'over-interpretation' of results.

With regard to psychiatric patients, findings seem to concur that adrenalin is excreted in larger amounts in 'manic' than in 'depressed' phases, and that in particular emotional outbursts are associated with increased adrenalin excretion. Certainly catecholamines, including adrenalin as well as noradrenalin, are usually excreted in greater quantities as a result of motoric body activity, although there are studies that have dissented on this point. It remains to be fully ascertained how far excreted catecholamines, especially adrenalin, which is the exclusively adrenal product, and its metabolite metadrenalin, are true reflections of psychological activity.

Returning to the adrenal cortex, we have already referred to one finding that greater emotionality went with a higher level of excreted 17-OHCS. In this study (Fox *et al.* 1961) there was no examination of the actual cognitions of the subjects relative to a standard situation—they were studied during the course of their ordinary lives. Other studies have tried to look at individual differences in responsiveness to a standard situation, and especially a stressful one. Such studies have come up with interesting confirmation that it is the perception of situations as 'manageable' or 'unmanageable', and especially the subjectively experienced ability to cope with situations that correlate most closely with adrenocortical response. Two examples show this.

As a first example there is a study by Bourne (1971) of 7 helicopter ambulance medical-aid men in the Vietnam war, and of 12 men in an isolated camp in Vietcong-held territory. Bourne found from measures of urinary 17-OHCS that in the first group levels did *not* rise on flying days, when the men had to go to battle areas to bring out wounded, as opposed to non-flying days. He also found that overall levels were *below* those for average individuals in training camps in the U.S.A. In the second group were 2 officers and 10 men. On the day when an attack was expected the 17-OHCS levels of the 2 officers rose while those of the rest of the group, on average, went *down*.

In explanation of these levels Bourne relies heavily on the concept of subjectively experienced stress. He points out that these soldiers universally had cognitive coping processes by means of which they were able to go into action and overcome any fear of danger. One man had a strong belief in divine protection, another in self-reliance, a third in his own invincibility. The two officers, by contrast, lacked such firm beliefs, on top of which they had to make decisions involving consideration of alternative plans, and felt responsible for others.

The second study to which I shall refer is that by Wolff, Hofer and Mason (1964) of 31 parents (19 mothers, 12 fathers) of children suffering from fatal illnesses (mostly leukaemia). These parents were initially interviewed with a view to establishing the effectiveness of their psychological defences against the prolonged crisis with which they were faced. Following these interviews they were grouped according to the extent to which the interviewer felt they had come to terms with their predicament. It was predicted that urinary 17-OHCS levels would be lower in those parents with more effective psychological defences than in those without. This prediction was borne out; significant differences in the expected direction were found. The typical high 17-OHCS excretor had little 'defensive reserve', was a poor sleeper and lived in dread of the inevitable day, or refused to accept its inevitability and instead searched for a miracle cure. Low 17-OHCS excretors on the contrary exhibited a controlled factuality with which they were able to face the situation; in several cases this included a belief in God's will or a fatalistic acceptance of events.

Follow-up studies reported more recently (Hofer, Wolff, Friedman and Mason 1972) show that long after the child's death differences remain between the parents, but the picture is by no means a simple one. The authors find that each of the four logical possibilities occurs in actual fact. There are those parents whose pre-death levels were low and are still low; those whose pre-death levels were low and are now higher; those whose pre-death levels were high and are now low; and those whose pre-death levels were high and are still high. In terms of psychological mechanisms that now have had to deal with grief at loss, and mourning, the picture remains unclear; hypotheses abound but it will be a long time before we can be sure what actually has been going on. In this case there were two follow-up urine collections, several months after the child's death. Such procedures, necessitated by circumstantial constraints of all sorts, are clearly too crude to take account of the precise events of such complex processes as grief and mourning.

With regard to the physical effects of emotional *deprivation*, a subject which is further discussed in Chapter 10, the work of Patton and Gardner (1969) and of Gardner (1972) is of importance. They have documented cases where infants have, for a variety of reasons, been without maternal or other adequate care during early life, especially from the seventh to the twelfth month, and who have, apparently as a result of emotional and not nutritive starvation, failed to grow adequately and become appreciably stunted. They call this syndrome 'deprivation dwarfism'. Such children appear to go into a protracted state of immobility and unresponsiveness akin to depression, and physiologically produce little hydrochloric acid in the stomach. Patton and Gardner suggest that impulses from the higher brain centres associated with the deprivation reach the hypothalamus which then reduces the functioning of the pituitary. One such effect is on ACTH production, another is on production of somatotrophin, or growth hormone. In most cases, when children whose growth has been stunted in this way are restored to a normal emotional environment they catch up again rapidly, but they may never completely recover. Six children who were studied intensively over a number of years by these authors did not recover fully: they tended to remain below average in height, weight and skeletal maturation.

Another psychosomatic disorder which calls for attention is the condition of *anorexia nervosa*. This condition especially affects adolescent girls. It is probably ultimately of psychogenic origin, either due to difficult family conditions or fear of examinations or other emotional upsets. There is loss of appetite, and the resulting loss of weight can eventually lead to cessation of menstruation. Again, as with 'deprivation dwarfism' it may well be that the underlying physiology of this condition involves a reduction of pituitary hormones since certain of these are known to control the female sex cycle. Although *anorexia nervosa* may be a very severe disease and difficult to cure, the process concerned, once reversed, usually leads to complete recovery of the functions lost.

A head for the body

In focusing attention on the physiology of the adrenals and other body organs as indicative of emotional states, we have been following the path mapped out in the first place by Cannon and Selye. Certainly the adrenals seem to be closely involved in emotional reactivity. But we have to be careful to avoid the implication that other body systems are not involved or even that they are less closely involved. The body's systems are but sub-systems that work together; even the whole body is but a sub-system that works together with its external environment to form a whole system.

Thus it is clear that emotional state affects not only adrenal functioning but also, for instance, the functioning of the entire reproductive system, implicating the hypothalamus, the releasing factors for LH and FSH, the pituitary, its hormones, the functioning of the ovaries (perhaps less so the testes), and the autonomic nervous system and its links with the sex organs. We see this clearly from such facts as that *fear* of pregnancy can, alone and unaided, bring about a cessation of the menstrual cycle and several of the physiological manifestations of pregnancy itself; or that fear of sex can bring about sexual inadequacies and failures of various sorts such as failure to achieve or maintain erection or failure to achieve ejaculation, behaviours that have a clear-cut and well-known physiological and largely reflexive basis.

Such data, however, continue to focus on the regions below the

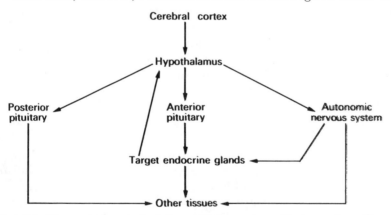

FIG. 9.5. The central control of the endocrine system. (Redrawn from Greene (1970).)

neck for evidence of emotional effects, and as a result we find ourselves with something of a headless body, or perhaps a shadowy head consisting of a hypothalamus connected to 'higher' centres on the one hand (but how connected exactly?) and, more clearly, to 'lower' ones, in particular the pituitary and thyroid glands and thence to the rest of the body (Fig. 9.5).

To leave the brain as a shadowy hypothalamus with higher connections is a wholly inadequate procedure and the next step is therefore to try to clarify the picture. This is easier said than done because of the complexity of the brain and its interconnections. The brains of octopuses, snails and moths have turned out, on close study, to be exceedingly complex organs. How much more so, then, the brain of the rat, and that of man. Yet an effort has to be made. The folllowing is an attempt to sketch the outlines of the functioning brain, without getting lost in the details of neurophysiology. It follows to some extent the pattern laid out by Gray (1971).

Our present understanding of neural connections and functioning has been largely achieved by experimental procedures involving animals. Such experiments can be divided into two main kinds. First, there are experiments in which animals are conditioned to respond in particular ways to particular environmental stimuli. Conditioning involves associating particular objects in the animal's environment with a reward (positive reinforcement) or a punishment (negative reinforcement). Secondly, there are experiments of a surgical kind in which lesions are made between brain areas or alternatively in which micro-electrodes are introduced into the brain at known sites and these sites are stimulated with minute electrical pulses at or near physiological levels. The effects of lesions and electrode stimulation on behaviour are either studied in their own right, or in relation to previously acquired information about the animal's pre-operative performance in conditioning experiments.

One major contribution to the understanding of brain action is the discovery of two areas in the limbic system that have been called the 'reward' and 'punishment' areas (Gray 1971) or the 'pleasure'

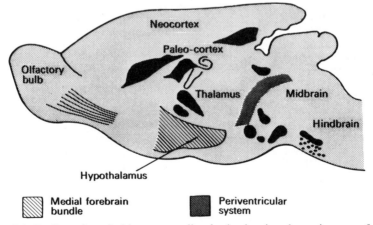

FIG. 9.6. Outline of a primitive mammalian brain showing the major areas from which Olds obtains electrical self-stimulation of the brain (the medial forebrain bundle) or where the animal will work to terminate electrical stimulation applied by the experimenter (the periventricular system). (Redrawn from Gray (1971).)

and 'displeasure' areas (Campbell 1973), originally discovered by James Olds. These areas are shown in Fig. 9.6.

The significance of the discovery and localization of these areas (in both rats and humans) in relation to behaviour is that it seems more than a little likely that reward-conditioning and punishment-conditioning are the behavioural concomitants of brain activities establishing links between performed activities and the pleasure areas and displeasure areas respectively. This neurophysiological hypothesis (backed by substantial amounts of evidence but still best thought of as a hypothesis rather than a fact) gives us an essential link between higher cortical functioning and lower brain activity close to or involving the hypothalamic functioning that we know to be linked to pituitary and hormonal activity. In what Gray calls the 'Gray and Smith' model, it is the joint operation of the reward and punishment areas on a positive and negative feed-back basis to the brain areas that is concerned in the conditioning or learning process that, together with a 'decision process', determines whether the subject will approach or avoid any given stimulus (Fig. 9.7).

Continuing in terms of the Gray and Smith model, the 'reward'

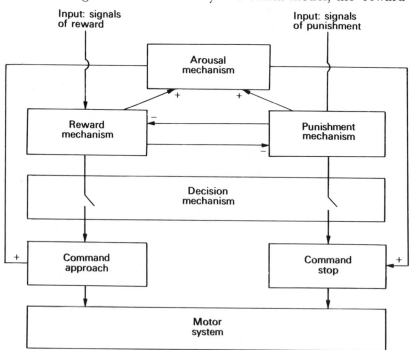

F IG. 9.7. Part of the Gray and Smith model for conflict and discrimination learning. (Redrawn from Gray (1971).)

areas are in the forebrain (including the hypothalamus) and the 'punishment' areas are in the midbrain (periventricular system). Thus it is only necessary to connect these to the hypothalamus–pituitary system to achieve an explanatory model for adrenocortical effects, and to the sympathetic nervous system to explain adrenal medulla effects. Our head and our body are beginning to fit together. We are in fact beginning to connect up the world of culturally learned categories and concepts of appropriateness, conformity and deviance, all of which are the outcome of many minute steps in a life-long conditioning process, with the world of whole-body physiology.

We can see culture, in its historical aspect 'outside' of particular individuals, as a universe of rewards and punishments for appropriate and inappropriate actions. Parts of this universe, in course of socialization, become incorporated into the brains of individuals as their 'minds'. As this happens, the brain becomes the agency instructing the body how to respond to life situations; the body functions smoothly and efficiently if it receives clear, unequivocal instructions, but if the instructions are contradictory because the 'mind' cannot cope then whole-body effects can make people impotent, chronically apathetic as in prolonged depression, or cause other severe disabilities. Most people undoubtedly live between these two extremes, in worlds where they can cope reasonably adequately with life situations; sometimes we cope well and 'feel good', at other times we fail to cope and 'feel bad'. It is clear, looking around, that some people are highly motivated to pursue culturally approved ends, others are highly motivated to pursue ends that main-stream culture labels 'deviant', others still are not highly motivated and some (who in our culture are normally hospitalized) lack all motivation and will not, for example, dress themselves, feed themselves or excrete in culturally approved ways. We take so much for granted, and yet to explain even the most ordinary of our actions we need a conceptual framework of causes, effects and feed-backs that is quite fantastic in its complexity.

But we must end with a caveat. Just because cultural or sub-cultural orthodoxy makes for physiological efficiency and what can be summarized by the word 'health', that *alone* can never validate it. There are powerful arguments going well beyond the confines of this book that the easiest way in life is not always the best one. The fact that well-organized belief systems make for efficient biological functioning tells us nothing at all about the ethical or moral aspects of those beliefs, an aspect we need to consider more than a little before accepting them. Where choice of beliefs exists, it cannot be made on biological grounds. Biology alone is neutral to moral content.

PART IV

The psycho-social development of human action

Introduction to Part IV

The data presented in this part, like those in Part III, have two purposes: to expose the foundations that have so far been laid concerning the manner of functioning of the growing human organism, and to stress the level, often quite a humble one, at which hypotheses can be usefully formulated.

As the focus here is on psychological and social development we are clearly closer to the processes of action than we were in Part III. We are, in fact, talking about action itself, looking at it from the perspectives of certain 'disciplines' that have over the years developed techniques and accompanying jargons to bring precision to bear on the difficult subject of their study. In particular I shall discuss the work of child ethologists and child psychologists.

CHAPTER 10

Mother–infant interaction

THE INFANT ENTERS the world at birth not, as was once thought, as 'a blank sheet on which culture writes its instructions' but as a creature programmed by evolutionary selective forces for survival. It is programmed for survival in a group of nomadic hunter–gatherers living on the African savannas, for survival without medical aid or cow's milk. It comes not helpless but armed with a number of powerful aids to enable it to survive, but since it cannot survive by its own efforts these aids are directed at other human beings.

The infant's cry

One primary aid present at birth is the cry. In common with many, perhaps most, other species of mammals in which the young are dependent on adults for survival, the cry of the infant serves as an alerting response and may trigger off behaviour in the adult that enhances the infant's survival chances. The cry of the baby rhesus monkey instantly alerts its mother, who runs to it and gathers it into her arms; it also alerts the adult males of the group who have occasionally been observed to rescue a fallen infant in the wild, and of other females and sub-adults as well. It may go further than this. In both captive rhesus monkeys and captive chimpanzees living in a social setting I have observed attacks made on an individual who had caused an infant to cry out. In each of two cases I have observed, the attacking animal was a senior female in the group, and the animal attacked was the dominant adult male, an animal who is normally immune from attack. This male had, on the occasions in question, chased and frightened a youngster whose fear call led to what struck me on each occasion as a courageous defence by the female. Curiously, in neither of the above cases was the female who responded the mother of the juvenile involved. In both cases it was a relatively old, socially mature female who responded.

A recent study of the cry of the newborn human infant is that of Wolff (1969). Wolff worked in both hospital and home settings, observing 18 infants for 30 hours a week for 1 month; then 12 of these for 12 hours a week for a further 2 months, then 5 of these for 12 hours a week up to the age of 6 months. Their cries were tape-recorded and analysed on sound spectrographs. As a result three types of cry could be distinguished, the 'basic' cry, the 'mad' or 'angry' cry and the 'pain' cry.

The 'basic' cry has also been called the 'hunger' cry. It is rhythmic, consisting on average of a cry lasting 6 s, a pause lasting 0·08 s, a high-frequency inspiration 'whistle' lasting 0·03 s, a second pause lasting 0·17 s followed by another cry, etc. (Fig. 10.1). This type of cry occurs from half an hour after birth to the end of the second month, after which it continues but in a somewhat more variable form.

The 'mad' or 'angry' cry differs from the basic cry not in its rhythmicity but in its constitution: it is a more rasping sound. The spectrograph shows this turbulence or paraphonation (Fig. 10.2). Others were able to distinguish this cry from the basic cry and reported that it expressed exasperation or anger.

F I G. 10.1. Sequence of 'basic' cries; 4-day-old healthy full-term male infant. Fundamental frequency, 350–450 Hz. (For this and Figs. 10.2 and 10.3, spectrograms were written at twice the normal speed. Vertical axis: frequency range from 0 Hz to 7000 Hz; horizontal axis: time, 4·8 s of recorded vocalization.) (Redrawn from Wolff (1969).)

The third type of cry distinguished by Wolff has quite distinct characteristics. This is the 'pain' cry and was recorded just after the newborn infants in the hospital group had been given the routine pin-prick in the heel that is standard practice for the obtaining of a blood sample. This was a *prolonged* cry (4 s in the case illustrated (Fig. 10.3) followed by a *prolonged* silence with breath expired (∼ 7 s), followed by inspiration and then more crying, also prolonged but changing to the rhythmic type. The function of this sudden, long, loud cry is clearly to alert the mother to an emergency situation; Wolff conducted an experiment in homes and played a tape-recording of the pain cry when mothers were away from their infants in another part of the house; the response of mothers was that they immediately rushed into the infant's room looking worried.

FIG. 10.2. Sequence of 'mad' (angry) cries, in a normal full-term 4-day-old female after crying for 10 min and becoming increasingly excited. The black, fuzzy background reflects turbulence produced by excess air forced through the vocal chords. (Redrawn from Wolff (1969).)

The basic and angry cries are probably signals from the infant indicating a need for food or attention such as comforting or cuddling, and these were probably the normal maternal responses in bygone times, although today they tend to be affected by maternal attitudes such as whether mothers believe in feeding on demand or not. Unable to move to the mother by its own efforts, and unlike the monkey unable to cling to the mother, the neonate's cry probably had and has great significance in co-ordinating the infant's nutritional and emotional needs with the mother's activities. However, it is not at all certain that the amount of crying in earlier times or in other cultures is as great as it now is in Western societies. Konner (1972) reports that among the bushmen, infants' needs are mostly met before they begin to cry—in that society women carry their infants close to their bodies wherever they go, and are intimately aware of their needs and quickly responsive to them. We do not know whether Australopithecine mothers carried their infants around with them, e.g. when out food gathering, or left them at a base camp, tended perhaps by older females or juveniles. It seems unlikely that infants were left alone, however, because of the danger of predators.

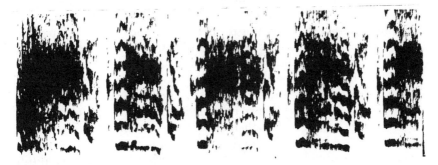

FIG. 10.3. Initial vocal response to pain, followed by a 7-s period of silence in expiration. (Redrawn from Wolff (1969).)

Human infants whose mothers stay close to them, especially if they are in physical contact with their mothers, do not cry much, judging from the data from other cultures. In our own society we create areas such as baby rooms in hospitals or nurseries in our homes where infants, well wrapped up in woolly clothes and placed in high-sided cots, can cry their hearts out. Thomas, Chess and Birch (1968) in a study of 100 children in New York found considerable individual differences in regard to crying (using a maternal-interview technique). They found clear evidence that whereas some infants cried readily and frequently, earning themselves the name of 'mother killers', others were much more placid and cried very little. These differences were not clearly attributable to any of the environmental factors studied and were regarded by the authors as largely of constitutional origin. Ainsworth (1967) has stressed the part played by rapid and consistent response by the mother in reducing the extent of crying by infants. In so far as environmental factors are concerned it does seem that spatial separation of the infant from the mother is a factor tending to increase both the amount of time spent crying and the intensity of the crying.

Curiously, there are a number of societies that practised or still practise forms of quite severe restraint and separation of infants from mothers. For instance some of the North American Indian tribes such as the Navaho strap their infants ('papooses') into cradle boards and then hang them from the walls of the dwelling house. Do such early practices have predictable effects on the development of personality? Wilhelm Reich was extremely emphatic about the effects of separation practices. In his interview with Dr. Eissler on 18 October 1952 (reported in Higgins and Raphael 1967) he made it quite clear that in his view the taking of the infant from its mother and its subjection to various medical or religious insults was a device of both Eastern and Western civilizations to 'break the will' of the child. Other psychiatrists concerned with the formation of human character (Fromm, Laing, Bowlby, not to mention Freud) have pointed towards early life experiences and the family or mother–infant context. In the meantime it remains scientifically unclear how far early childhood experiences shape the subsequent long-term development of what is called 'personality' in humans. There is as far as I know no adequately established theory relating adult personality to early infantile experiences, although inadequately established theories on the subject are legion. Two major considerations in formulating any such theory would be (a) the extent of underlying constitutional differences and (b) the extent of impact of post-early-childhood influences, in particular the impact of the socio-cultural world in giving rise to personal constructs including the self concept. Since we know very little about the former and the latter is arguably very important indeed, any case for a clear-cut cause-effect relationship between early childhood experience and later personality would have to be a very tentative one.†

Primate comparisons

It seems essential at this stage to make an excursion into the subject of primate development. It is from that quarter, notably the work of Harlow, that one psychiatrist in particular, John Bowlby, has drawn support for a theory of early childhood experience and subsequent personality development.

Harlow and his research team (including his wife) have made a series of vitally important studies concerning the postnatal behavioural development of the rhesus monkey (Harlow and Harlow 1965). Harlow started from the observation that baby monkeys in his laboratory, kept apart from their mothers, often clung tenaciously to a piece of cloth, carrying it wherever they went; indeed it was laboratory practice to give such infants a piece of cloth since this appeared to comfort them. Harlow decided to investigate this phenomenon, which raised one question in particular: if the cloth was some kind of mother substitute, did this mean that the infant monkey had a primary tendency to cling to a soft object which was quite unrelated to the need for food? He designed the now well-known experiment in which baby monkeys removed from their mothers at birth and kept in isolation were put in a situation in which they could choose to cling either to a wire 'mother-surrogate' with milk freely available from a rubber teat, or to a soft mother-surrogate made of towelling but containing no milk. The babies spent nearly all their time clinging to the latter and if disturbed or frightened they fled to it, visiting the wire mother only when wanting milk, and even occasionally getting the best of both worlds by clinging to the soft mother-surrogate and reaching across to the nipple on the wire one.

---

† An enlightening discussion of the issues raised in this context is the chapter by Harré (1974). Harré points out that adult society is not made up of emotional bonds: 'social glue is of an altogether different stuff' (p. 247). In his view, as argued here, society is a construct of individuals—'the presence in our cognitive resources of an image of a larger order with the help of which we create and explain certain actions, and give meaning to certain acts ... Provided there are certain minimal homologies between the images of a certain number of us ... a larger society can be said to exist' (p. 253). Harré's theory of adult interactions, personality and relationships is thus sociogenic, not psychogenic. He explicitly rejects the idea that child–mother attachment patterns lead on to developments in the adult world: 'I want to make the radical proposal that the mode of world ordering ("attachment"), which characterizes the autonomous world, must perish before adulthood is possible. The intermediate world of the schoolchild comes into being as the proper precursor of adulthood' (p. 261).

Having established that baby monkeys cling to a soft medium and run to it and cling tightly when alarmed, Harlow next turned to the problem of establishing whether this phenomenon was an essential part of infantile development, enabling further behavioural development to take place, or whether it was a stage that could be dispensed with without detriment to subsequent development. He found the former to be the case. The experiments consisted of isolating infants, without mother or mother-substitute materials, for various lengths of time and then exposing them to situations to test their 'normality'. (It has frequently been argued that none of Harlow's monkeys, including the ones reared by their mothers, were normal, because a laboratory-cage environment is very restrictive of development as compared with the rich and complex social and ecological conditions of the wild. With this argument I am in full agreement. However, if by 'normal' we mean, for present purposes, normal for a laboratory-reared monkey, we can use the word.)

Infants were reared apart from their mothers for various lengths of time, e.g. 3 months, 6 months, etc., and at different stages, e.g. from 3 to 6 months etc. They were then given tasks involving intellectual skills and were introduced to other monkeys for the first time. Whereas their intellectual abilities appeared unimpaired by isolation, their social skills were seriously affected, in particular their ability to play with age-mates and later on to interact successfully with other adults and especially to mate with them. Harlow concluded that there was a critical period between the third and sixth month of life during which physical contacts with either mother or peers must occur if further development of behaviour was to be normal. The monkeys totally isolated during this period would suffer some behavioural ill-effects, and so would those with nothing but a cloth mother-surrogate to interact with, though in this case the effects were less striking. Interestingly, the absence of a mother was fully compensated by the presence of peers to interact with later on, whereas infants raised with their mothers but with no opportunity to interact with peers were decidedly retarded with respect to their play and sexual development. In the extreme cases of isolation for a full 6 months or more, behavioural development was so seriously impaired that there was no subsequent play with peers, no sexual behaviour at all and a strong tendency towards self-aggression when disturbed, e.g. by an approaching human (Fig. 10.4). Subsequently a number of isolation-reared non-social females were impregnated (by use of what Harlow himself called the 'rape-rack') and all these females showed a complete absence of maternal responsiveness; they rejected their infants forcibly and refused them both milk and ventral clinging. These infants indeed *had* to be removed from their mothers in order to save their lives.

What conclusions of relevance to man can be drawn from the Harlow data? Is there a 'critical period' for the human infant during which warm friendly contact must occur if subsequent development is to lead to social competence? There are many difficulties in the way of answering such a question. First and foremost it is to be hoped that the conditions needed to settle this question will never occur. Such conditions would involve the *total* isolation, for various periods, of human infants, followed up by systematic observation of their social and sexual behaviour. Very probably the effects on humans

Experimental condition	Present age	Behaviour				
		None	Low	Almost normal	Probably normal	Normal
Raised in isolation						
Total Cage-raised for 2 years	4 years	■□▨				
Total Cage-raised for 6 months	14 months	□▨	■			
Cage-raised for 80 days	10½ months			■□▨		
Partial Cage-raised for 6 months	5–8 years	■ ▨	□			
Partial Surrogate-raised for 6 months	3–5 years	■ ▨	□			
Raised with mother						
Normal mother; no play with peers	1 year	▨	■			□
Motherless mother; play in playpen	14 months			□	▨	■□▨
Normal mother; play in playpen	2 years					■□▨
Raised with peers						
Four raised in one cage; play in playroom	1 year				■	□▨
Surrogate-raised; play in playpen	2 years				▨	■□
Surrogate-raised; play in playroom	21 months					□▨

■ Play
□ Defence
▨ Sex

F IG. 10.4. Results of experiments are summarized. The monkeys' capacity to develop normally appears to be determined by the seventh month of life. Animals isolated for 6 months are aberrant in every respect. Play with peers seems even more necessary than mothering to the development of effective social relations. (From Harlow and Harlow (1962). Copyright © 1962 by Scientific American, Inc. All rights reserved.)

would be as great as or greater than on rhesus monkeys. Isolation-reared chimpanzees show total behavioural inadequacy, self-isolation and self-aggression, and stereotyped rocking movements of a kind seen also in seriously ill human schizophrenics. One might well expect isolation-reared humans to be similarly handicapped if not more so, and the prospect of putting it to the test is too appalling to contemplate.

Separation and attachment

A few well-documented cases of isolation are on record, however. Two cases are reliably reported by Davis (1947) and they are of special interest since they are presented from a non-biological point of view and yet tend to confirm the Harlow thesis. The cases concern Anna and Isobelle.

Anna was illegitimate, her grandfather, who controlled the household, strongly disapproved of her existence and refused to have her in the house. After 2 weeks with her mother Anna went to friends, then to the local vicar, then, aged 3 weeks, to an adoption agency, where she stayed for 8 weeks. Thence she went to an adoptive couple, but at 4 months she was back in another agency where she stayed for 3 weeks, when she was transferred to yet another agency. At $5\frac{1}{2}$ months she was returned to her grandfather's house where she was kept by her mother in an attic. Her mother appeared to have lost interest in her and kept her alive on milk but did not go close to the child. Anna lived alone in the attic until she was discovered at the age of nearly 6 years. She was unable to walk, talk or do anything. Given therapy and attention she had learned by the age of 7 to walk and feed herself but could not speak. She made slight progress after this, but died at the age of 10 years when her mental age was $2\frac{1}{2}$ years.

Isobelle was born 1 month after Anna and discovered 9 months after Anna was discovered. She too was illegitimate, the daughter of a deaf-mute mother, and in this case both mother and daughter were shut off from the family. When found, Isobelle had no speech, her behaviour was fearful and her general behaviour was infantile though she was approaching 7 years old. However, she responded well to therapy and education and within an amazingly short time had caught up with her age-mates. Her later development was normal.

The author of this study, a prominent sociologist, suggested that the reasons for Anna's failure and Isobelle's success were (a) that Anna was congenitally mentally deficient, and (b) that Isobelle had a more effective post-discovery training programme. However, this case-study clearly permits of an alternative interpretation in terms of severe maternal deprivation of the Harlow type for Anna, while Isobelle was spared this.

Bowlby in 1952 distinguished severe maternal deprivation from partial deprivation. The former could occur in institutions if no person was providing care and security for the child; the latter was likely to occur if the mother was present but not giving care. The ill-effects of deprivation he listed as anxiety, revenge, guilt, depression, neurosis, instability of character, inability to make relationships. Undoubtedly many of his ideas were derived from his earlier study of juvenile thieves (1946) in which he isolated what he called the 'affectionless character' and related it to early maternal deprivation. In 1962 Ainsworth, reviewing the subject, distinguished three types of maternal deprivation: insufficiency, distortion, and discontinuity of maternal care. Retrospective studies have pointed to specific ill-effects of maternal deprivation. Bender (1947) traced language defects and inability to make friends to this cause and called the result 'psychopathic behaviour disorder'. Lewis (1954) found seven features that were positively correlated with maladjustment in children, one of which was long separation from mother.

The whole field of maternal deprivation has been reassessed again by M. Rutter (1972), who concludes as follows:

> Perhaps the most important recent development in 'maternal deprivation' research has been the emphasis on individual differences in children's responses to 'deprivation'. That some children are damaged and some escape damage has long been observed, but the differences in vulnerability have been regarded as largely inexplicable (Ainsworth, 1962). At last, some reasons are emerging for research. In the field of animal research, Hinde's studies of separation experiences in rhesus monkeys are most important in this respect. He has clearly shown that the mother–infant relationship *prior* to separation influences the infant's response to separation. This relationship is a reciprocal one and is influenced both by variables in the mother and variables in the child. The importance of child variables as determinants of mother–child interaction in humans has been emphasized by Bell (1968, 1971), and Graham and George's (1972) work examining differences in children's responses to parental illness has made an important beginning to the study of temperamental differences in children's reactions to stressful experiences. Much remains to be done, but what has been achieved so far shows that this is a fruitful field for study.

In view of the extent of individual differences both of the constitutional 'temperament' of the child and the mother–child relationship, this whole area is presumably one where we should not expect to find it easy or even possible to make general statements about 'the effects of deprivation'. Existing studies have already been evaluated and re-evaluated in the light of new interpretative ideas. A further case of interest is the one reported by Koluchova (1972) in which twin boys were isolated socially and ill-treated from 11 months to 7 years of age by a stepmother. When found their mental age was 3 years, they could barely speak and could not walk owing to severe rickets. However, after treatment in good conditions they were able to stage a remarkably rapid recovery and were performing adequately at school by the age of 9. This is a clear case of the 'cognitive catch-up' we saw with Isobelle above, but we must note that for the first 11 months of life these twin boys received normal care, albeit in a children's home, and we have no idea how important these early months were in laying the basis for subsequent recovery.

There remain a large number of problems concerning the effects of early short-term separation of human infants from the mother. Research is currently in progress to discover whether incubator-reared premature infants suffer behaviourally; there is some indication that they may be slow to develop speech. Young children undergoing hospitalization involving separation from the mother have been shown to regress behaviourally, losing bowel control and becoming much more dependent on the mother. It has not, however, been shown that such regressions cannot be made up given suitable environmental conditions, and there is good evidence that *cognitive* 'catch-up' can and does occur in all but the most severe cases of isolation (for a discussion of the relevant issues, see Clarke (1965)).

The person who has most consistently and influentially emphasized the positive value of maternal love for healthy development and the ill-effects of maternal deprivation is John Bowlby, and he has drawn heavily in recent years on the behavioural findings of Harlow, Hinde and others on rhesus monkeys and other non-human primates. In his book *Attachment* (1969) he presents a carefully reasoned case for the comparative approach. In his own words:†

Man is neither a monkey nor a white rat, let alone a canary or a cichlid fish. Man is a species in his own right with certain unusual characteristics. It may be therefore that none of the ideas stemming from studies of lower species is relevant. Yet this seems improbable. In the fields of infant-feeding, of reproduction, and of excretion we share anatomical and physiological features with lower species, and it would be odd were we to share none of the behavioural features that go with them. Furthermore, it is in early childhood, especially the preverbal period, that we might expect to find these features in least-modified form. May it not be that some at least of the neurotic tendencies and personality deviations that stem from the early years are to be understood as due to disturbance in the development of bio-psychological processes? Whether the answer proves to be 'yes' or 'no' it is only common sense to explore the possibility.

Bowlby is too wise and too experienced in psychoanalysis to jump overboard into animal ethology, and he makes a strong case for maintaining a Freudian approach alongside an ethological one. Indeed, he wishes to integrate ethological methods into psychoanalysis rather than the reverse. He argues that the known facts of non-human developmental upsets caused by abnormalities in early infancy, especially, in the case of higher mammals, removal from the mother, provide an *a priori* case for believing that like processes can

† Reprinted from *Attachment* by Dr. John Bowlby. Grateful acknowledgement is made to the author and The Hogarth Press.

and do occur in man. The great value of ethological studies is that they provide a working method that has been tried and tested: a method based on observation in detail of ongoing behaviour in context as the basis for all further analysis. He argues that Freud and ethology are saying one and the same thing but their approaches and terminology are very different. Freud argued that the central event underlying a person's neurosis or other pathological disturbance was a trauma in early childhood, during the first 5 or 6 years, but especially between the ages of 2 and 4. Trauma itself is composed of two sets of factors—the nature of the events, and the constitution of the individual. Translated into ethological terms Bowlby sees the central trauma as mother–child separation, the neuroses as behaviour disorders. Freud had much sympathy with studies of animals and he regretted that there were in fact none specifically on the problems that interested him; had he continued to live through the twentieth century he would have integrated the new data into his theories; this Bowlby seeks to do.

The empirical findings with regard to human infants are summarized in Bowlby's second chapter (Bowlby 1969). They relate predominantly to children in their second and third years of life who for one reason or another are separated from their mother. Workers such as Robertson and Schaffer have observed and in some cases filmed such children in their unfamiliar setting and on return home. The three-stage reaction process of the child that arises in these circumstances is summarized by Bowlby as follows:

In the setting described (e.g. a residential nursery or hospital ward) a child of fifteen to thirty months who has had a reasonably secure relationship with his mother and has not previously been parted from her will commonly show a predictable sequence of behaviour. This can be broken into three phases according to what attitude to his mother is dominant. We describe these phases as those of Protest, Despair, and Detachment. Though in presenting them it is convenient to differentiate them sharply, it is to be understood that each merges into the next, so that a child may be for days or weeks in a state of transition from one phase to another, or of alternation between two phases.

The initial phase, that of protest, may begin immediately or may be delayed; it lasts from a few hours to a week or more. During it the young child appears acutely distressed at having lost his mother and seeks to recapture her by the full exercise of his limited resources. He will often cry loudly, shake his cot, throw himself about, and look eagerly towards any sight or sound which might prove to be his missing mother. All his behaviour suggests strong expectation that she will return. Meantime he is apt to reject all alternative figures who offer to do things for him, though some children will cling desperately to a nurse.

During the phase of despair, which succeeds protest, the child's preoccupation with his missing mother is still evident, though his behaviour suggests increasing hopelessness. The active physical movements diminish or come to an end, and he may cry monotonously or intermittently. He is withdrawn and inactive, makes no demands on people in the environment, and appears to be in a state of deep mourning. This is a quiet stage, and sometimes, clearly erroneously, is presumed to indicate a diminution of distress.

Because the child shows more interest in his surroundings, the phase of detachment which sooner or later succeeds protest and despair is often welcomed as a sign of recovery. The child no longer rejects the nurses; he accepts their care and the food and toys they bring, and may even smile and be sociable. To some this change seems satisfactory. When his mother visits, however, it can be seen that all is not well, for there is a striking absence of the behaviour characteristic of the strong attachment normal at this age. So far from greeting his mother he may seem hardly to know her; so far from clinging to her he may remain remote and apathetic; instead of tears there is a listless turning away. He seems to have lost all interest in her.

Should his stay in hospital or residential nursery be prolonged and should he, as is usual, have the experience of becoming transiently attached to a series of nurses each of whom leaves and so repeats for him the experience of the original loss of his mother, he will in time act as if neither mothering nor contact with humans had much significance for him. After a series of upsets at losing several mother-figures to whom in turn he has given some trust and affection, he will gradually commit himself less and less to succeeding figures and in time will stop altogether attaching himself to anyone. He will become increasingly self-centred and, instead of directing his desires and feelings towards people, will become preoccupied with material things such as sweets, toys, and food. A child living in an institution or hospital who has reached this state will no longer be upset when nurses change or leave. He will cease to show feelings when his parents come and go on visiting day; and it may cause them pain when they realize that, although he has an avid interest in the presents they bring, he has little interest in them as special people. He will appear cheerful and adapted to his unusual situation and apparently easy and unafraid of anyone. But this sociability is superficial: he appears no longer to care for anyone.

Factors reducing the intensity of the child's reactions are: being in the care of one mother-substitute (rather than many), presence of a sibling, and short separation. Against the argument that it is not separation from the mother but the total change of environment that has these effects, Bowlby argues (a) that the same effects have been reported for children whose mothers have left them at home and (b) that if a child is hospitalized with its mother present in the hospital few or none of the effects are seen.

The reactions described by Bowlby do seem well established. But there is at least one major cloudy issue: the extent to which constitutional factors may be involved in determining the response to separation. Bowlby lays constant emphasis on the external environmental variables. We are thus left in the dark about one side of the problem. The reason is clear enough: we have few or no normative data on constitutional aspects of the children studied. Indeed one can ask what kind of data on constitution ought one to study here? Genetic data (e.g. ABO blood-groups) could be obtained from hospitalized children, but in view of the causal 'distance' between genes and the responses described there seems little or no likelihood of a meaningful finding. Sheldonian 'somatotype' might provide a clue. A possibly useful constitutional lead would be adrenal responsiveness or some other measure of endocrine functioning. We know all too little about individual differences in relation to this particular problem. In particular we do not know how or when the inter-individual endocrine differences that exist in adults (see Chapter 6) arise. Differences in emotional volatility are reported to occur from birth (Thomas, Chess and Birch 1968) and Bowlby reports that 'Moss (1967) has shown the great variations from one infant to another in time spent sleeping and crying during the early months, and how this affects the way the mother behaves' (p. 339). His discussion of this point (pp. 339–41) indicates that the infant's level of responsiveness has effects on the mother's ability to cope and her behaviour then feeds back to the infant. Thus infantile constitutional factors affect maternal action, maternal action is itself in part the output of ongoing constitutional factors in the mother, her action affects the development of the infant's action and constitution. It would seem that until our knowledge of the physiology of mother–infant interaction is more advanced we shall have difficulty in progressing beyond the stage of descriptions of ongoing interactions in particular cases and efforts to generalize on the basis of these.

We have already looked at one kind of interaction—the infant's cry and the mother's nurturative or protective response. We can now consider some of the other programmed behaviours that the infant brings with it or develops after birth, and mothers' typical reactions.

Early in life, infants show a tendency to look at something moving in preference to a static object. To do this they need to be able first to fixate the object and second to track it. It has been shown that the young infant is able to focus clearly on objects that are 8–9 in. from his eyes, and it thus seems that his visual faculties are programmed to enable him to fixate his mother's face during breast feeding. By 4 weeks of age he already shows a preference for looking at a human face rather than any other kind of object, and especially a face which is moving, or which has moving parts. A preference for the mother's face rather than any other face is reported by Ainsworth (1964) from the age of 14 weeks on, in Ganda children of East Africa. This orientation towards the mother's face is not just concerned with food-seeking. It also reinforces the mother's affection for her baby and induces her to talk or sing to him, pat him, hug him, smile at him, etc. These actions are by no means neutral from the infant's standpoint in that most of them have been shown to reduce the incidence of crying, i.e. to relax the infant or comfort him.

The smile

So far in this chapter we have said nothing of smiling. Smiling, like crying, can be seen as one of the infant's major aids in his struggle for attention (and thereby survival). Curiously, perhaps, this programme has a later onset than the cry. During the first 4 weeks of life hints of the smile pass across the baby's face from time to time but they are not elicited by clear-cut stimuli. During the fifth week smiles clearly recognizable as such do occur and are mostly elicited by the human voice and face. This process continues after 5 weeks and up to about 7 months, during which time infants develop a

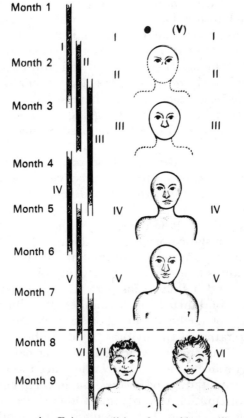

FIG. 10.5. Necessary and sufficient conditions for evoking smiling in infants up to 8 months. (Redrawn from Ahrens (1953) *Z. exptl. angew. Psychol.* **2**, 445. By permission of the journal.)

strong social smile to the configuration of the human face, be it the mother's, someone else's or a face-like picture or mask. During this period smiles may be more prolonged and 'dazzling' to the mother or caretaker than to strangers, but the latter are nevertheless greeted with smiles. After 7 months, however, this gives way to a 'fear of strangers' phase, in which smiles are not given to strange faces and indeed a stranger may be greeted with fear and crying.

Regarding the stimuli that elicit smiling, experimental work (e.g. Ahrens (1953)—see Fig. 10.5) has emphasized that during the second month two black dots on a white card will elicit smiling, but six black dots will elicit even more smiling than two—the same kind of phenomenon as has been demonstrated for animal responses to supernormal stimuli (see, for example, Tinbergen 1951). At subsequent ages the mask needs to be more face-like to elicit a smile, however, until by 8 months nothing short of a human face will do. During the time from 2 to 8 months, even though masks, etc., will elicit smiling, the biggest smiles are none the less reserved for human faces, and the mother's in particular, especially if the infant can in addition hear her voice.

Ambrose (1961) has studied institution-reared infants as compared with normals in regard to time of onset of smiling. He used his own face as the stimulus, presenting it motionless over the infants in their cots, some 4 feet away, without himself smiling. He noted the latency of the first smile and number of smiles over half a minute, repeating his experiment four times for each infant with half-minute breaks between exposures. He found a significant difference in the time of onset of smiling and the peak period of smiling between the two groups, as follows:

	Home-reared	*Institution-reared*
Onset	6–10 weeks	9–14 weeks
Peak	11–14 weeks	16–20 weeks

The later development of smiling in the institution-reared group is in line with a body of other data indicating slower early development in infants that lack the benefits of a single, devoted, well-adjusted mother in a problem-free home. What tends to be overlooked in such studies is the extent to which children in ordinary homes are battered, or left to cry themselves to sleep, or inadequately fed, cleaned and dressed. The existence and functions of organizations such as the National Society for the Prevention of Cruelty to Children are sufficient testimony to the scale of breakdown of so-called normal processes in normal homes in modern society. All too often it seems that studies of normal mother–infant relationships are made on a select group of 'adequate' families, whatever their social class. The comparison between institution-reared and home-reared infants probably disguises that end of the home-reared variance that contains those mothers who are inadequate. Nor have any long-term effects on personality or behaviour been unequivocally associated with institution-rearing as opposed to family-rearing. Indeed, there is a school within psychiatry that holds that tensions and stresses *within the family* are a predominant cause of mental illness.

Nowadays, with more than a decade of studies in sociology and social psychology of deviance and maladjustment behind us, one is reluctant to accept maternal deprivation as a sufficient cause of anything, though it must remain a definite possibility that it is a contributory cause to characteristics of human actions that come under headings such as pathology, delinquency, deviance, etc. Interference with the intimate yet robust mother–child relationship is common enough in modern society. The fact that a mother goes out to work and her young child aged 3 or 4 goes to a play group for 3 hours during the morning is something most people accept. And yet it would seem strange indeed to the majority of mothers in the unindustrialized countries of the world that a mother would put her infant in a strange place for several hours a day before it was old enough to want to be independent. In our culture we do this routinely and some countries are considering an expansion of nursery 'education' to increase the scale on which this is possible. It is well known that infants aged 3–5 years often cry and become upset and disturbed when left at nursery school. The teachers develop skill at distracting and comforting them. 'They quickly get used to it' is the comment. And so they do—some less quickly than others. If any damage is done then this would appear to be 'normative' damage since most people suffer it. What is 'normative damage'? We are back to Reich's critique (see above), or Tinbergen's (1974) complaints about our whole culture and civilization, about its norms and expectations. But how does one validate such critiques? These problems are discussed further in the final Part of the book.

CHAPTER 11

Interaction with peers

WE HAVE LOOKED at some aspects of infantile development and of mother–infant interaction in the preceding chapter. This has enabled us to see something of the developmental programme involved in our species as it unfolds during the earliest part of life, and its relation to the cultural context.

Following on the period of intimate reliance on the mother for food, comfort and social interaction there develops in the infant a new phase of wider sociability, which the Harlows (1965) on the basis of their monkey studies regard as the outcome of the development of a new affectional system, the peer-affectional system. The human infant, having passed through a phase during the second half of the first year in which it is afraid of strangers, having developed during its second year considerable linguistic skills, familiarity with its environment, manipulative skills and having achieved the ability to walk and run about, develops a keen interest in other children of its own age.

Quite when this new interest develops is not well documented. There is clearly a big difference between the situation with siblings at home and the situation where there are no siblings. Siblings, however, may be regarded with friendship or hostility, they may be friendly or hostile, they may be of closely similar age and the same sex or otherwise, there may be many of them or few. Parental attitudes to their different children may be different. By and large, these home situations in the infant's second and third years await adequate study.

What very often occurs in our own culture is that at the age of 3 the child is taken off one day to a room where he or she is suddenly faced with up to 20 (or even more) children of his own age or older, unfamiliar adult women whom he does not know, and after a few minutes, to cap it all, his mother disappears completely for 2 or 3 hours. This is the somewhat abrupt start of school life, a part-time involvement with a relatively large group of peers, that constitutes for most people in our society a large part of childhood and adolescence.

The nursery school

One naturally wonders whether any 'damage' results from the early and sudden confrontation with such a strange situation. What data are relevant to an answer? On the non-human primate side, monkeys such as macaques play in peer-groups and Harlow's data suggest this is important for development. Most other species of monkeys studied also play with peers. Among the apes, chimpanzees and gorillas do, but gibbon infants do not form like-aged peer-groups and likewise in the rather solitary orang-utan peer-play is unusual. In all cases of non-human primate play the mother is close at hand, and intervenes in quarrels or is available. In the nursery school, the child is faced, especially at the outset, with a situation in which the one reliable source of comfort is absent, just when it is most needed. Nursery teachers are of course anxious to avoid trouble and upsets and they assign themselves the role of mother-substitute; providing the child accepts one of them as such this solves the problem. But can a child make such a rapid transference? Often the child lacks a clear sense of time and studies such as McGrew's (see below) have reported a keen expectancy of the mother's return in some cases. In other cases children make the adjustment instantly and with enthusiasm, perhaps because they have been looking forward to nursery school and it is just what they hoped it would be. The whole nursery-school situation is a very complex one: a variety of infants with their individual characteristics, a variety of teachers or nurses with theirs, a physical arrangement with a certain spatial density, a certain social density, a certain richness or poverty of play materials (varying in this respect as seen by individuals on the basis of their home situations and expectations of the nursery). Besides, there are the educational purposes of the nursery school, the attitudes of staff to the question of intervention in children's activities and so on. My own observation of nursery schools (and schools further along the line) is that they all differ from each other in complex ways (especially as regards the extent of teacher confidence and control); and internally of course each school differs over time as members of staff and children come and go. In such a situation can there be any generalizations? It seems preferable to make studies of particular schools. But what method should be adopted? This depends upon the aims of the study. Studies with an educational orientation have emphasized the advantages and disadvantages of structured v. unstructured situations. Studies of psychological development have emphasized the growth of cognitive awareness and intellectual ability. In all this, what actually goes on in the school setting, on a moment-to-moment, child-to-child basis, has in many past studies been neglected. From the perspective of a student of human development who is interested in how action proceeds in the peer-group situation these are important data, though to say this does not imply any lessening of the importance of the data derived from studies of cognitive awareness, linguistic ability or the growth of internal representations of social situations and appropriateness.

Some early studies (e.g. Loomis 1931) used observational methods and appropriate statistical procedures to document the ongoing sequences of behaviour in young children. Subsequently there has been a revival of interest in such studies in the 1960s and at the present, mainly because a number of zoologists, psychologists and others have become interested in the application of ethological methods derived from animal studies to human beings. This was a natural development, in part related to the upsurge of ethological studies of non-human primates, and I would number myself among those who, having studied primate behaviour using ethological methods, subsequently turned to the study of man, selecting young children for a number of mundane reasons, e.g. they are relatively easy to observe and occur in ready-made groups in standard situations, as well as a number of more theoretical ones (Reynolds and Guest, in press).

An early study of nursery-school children by an ethologist was that of Blurton Jones (1967). This was a study of 4–5-year-old children in school, made with notebook and pencil, sitting in a corner of the room. As with all such studies the main research effort was to isolate the different types of naturally occurring behaviour and describe them, to record their frequency of occurrence in a reliable way and thus to quantify the number and types of interactions that occurred between individuals or selected groups. Questions about the evolutionary origins, the immediate causation, the form and the functions of the behaviour units observed were of the greatest interest, as they are in all ethological studies. Questions about the cultural meanings, the linguistic correlates, the attitudes and internal representations and the norms and expectations of the social context were not considered; nor have they been in subsequent ethological studies since the method of study, based as it is on observation, does not permit of any answers to these questions. This restriction of interest, seen clearly in Blurton-Jones's work, is perhaps as distinctive of ethological studies as the degree of precision they bring to the description and analysis of behaviour.

The social environment studied by Blurton-Jones was rather a loose, unstructured one, with some friendships between children, some rather submissive children, but no clear 'hierarchy'. Children's behaviour to adults depended on who the adults were. In the case of the teacher, some children stayed near her, showed her paintings they had done, etc., and clung to her if they got hurt. Others (called 'little mothers' by McGrew (1972)) led a child who was in need of help to the teacher, often with one hand behind the led child's back. Strangers were stared at, and shown things. Responses to parents took two forms: either the child smiled, ran to the parent and touched her (it was usually the mother), or the child walked to the parent and gave her an object such as a painting. A third, less frequent variety was to ignore the parent altogether.

In their relations with each other, Blurton Jones described two types of interaction, agonistic, and rough-and-tumble play. Agonistic (i.e. fight–flight) behaviour occurred mostly over objects. A 'beating movement', bringing down the hand or fist on to a child, was common. Biting occurred, especially in the case of girls. A 'fierce' expression, with lower teeth bared and mouth corners down, was interpreted as inhibited attack. A defeated child would scream, call for help, then weep with puckered brows and a reddened face, staying immobile in one spot. There was no wrestling and punching in real quarrels.

'Rough-and-tumble play', by contrast, did include wrestling and punching, and gave the appearance of violence and assault, especially to adults. Facially it was quite different, since it went with an 'open-mouthed smile with teeth covered', an expression similar to the expression described by van Hooff (1967) and Loizos (1967) as the 'relaxed open mouth face' or play face of chimpanzees and macaques. Alternation of roles, another feature of primate play, was common in rough-and-tumble play. Some children did not join in rough-and-tumble play, some fled earnestly when approached for it, and in some cases play chasing/fleeing became 'real'. The transition from rough-and-tumble play to 'real' aggression is something I too have observed, and clearly the relation between them is a complex and tenuous one. The fact that some children are reluctant to join in perhaps indicates fear on their part, and this may be derived from a lack of interaction with peers or general fearfulness or both— such questions are not answered by observational school studies and relate to personality psychology. Rough-and-tumble play was more common in boys than in girls, a finding replicated in most studies of 'Westernized' human children and in studies of rhesus macaques as well.

Whether hormonal (androgenic) factors are involved, including hormonal sex differences during prenatal life, is undecided in the case of man (see Money and Ehrhardt 1968); in rats it has been shown that experimental manipulation of early androgen levels does affect subsequent aggressivity regardless of sex (Beach 1965), and Young, Goy and Phoenix (1964) have shown relations between hormone levels and rough-and-tumble play in rhesus monkeys. But Karsh, Dierschke and Knobil (1973) have shown that there are major differences between primates and rodents in the brain control systems underlying hormone secretion, so that generalizations from one species to another need to be treated cautiously.

We have tended in earlier chapters (e.g. Chapter 6) to emphasize the extent of inter-individual differences in all species, including man, at the genetic and biochemical level. Blurton Jones, in his discussion of this point, stresses that such differences do not make ethological work on children impossible, nor do they prevent the occurrence of regularities in behaviour according to sex. Further studies have tended to confirm this; every individual has his style but overall male–female differences do occur. Other regular differences that have been found are dependent on age, or birth order. All such differences would, of course, be the outcome of multiple causation involving cultural and organic developmental factors. Besides regular differences, there is a considerable measure of agreement between child-observers, despite terminological and classificatory differences, on the standard types of behaviour into which children's behaviour falls. Behaviourally then it would seem that all children are potentially unique, but in practice great regularities occur in the things children do, the social interactions they perform and the non-verbal signals they use in given situations.

We should remember the extent to which this apparent congruity is an outcome of the method used, and of the communication between child ethologists. Individual 'oddities' of behaviour are 'noise' in the system as far as much of ethological analysis is concerned. Ethologists, whatever 'their' species, are often more interested in discovering any regularities in development or response to given situations. The first aim is often to produce an 'ethogram' or behaviour catalogue for the species as a whole, based on the most regularly seen acts. Secondly, one can produce a flow diagram showing how certain units of behaviour sequentially relate to others, and from this one can draw motivational conclusions. Both these aims, as well as many others, involve the use of methods that analyse data to ascertain whether statistically significant regularities are or are not present. If they are not, the ethologist looks elsewhere, for his science, like all science, is based on the isolation of regularities and, having found them, a quest for underlying processes. If his method were otherwise, if for instance he collected a lot of retrospective data on each child, its previous experiences, its imaginings and fantasies, hopes and fears, its loves and hates, the rules of the situation as it perceived them (as a child psychiatrist might), then regularities would perhaps not appear, nor even be sought for or considered important. Each method produces its own kind of data and its own kind of explanations.

Further work in child ethology, mainly on nursery-school children, has been done by a number of people—Grant (1969), Clark, Wyon and Richards (1969), Smith and Connolly (1972), Brannigan and Humphries (1972), Oldman (1973) and a number of others (see review by P. K. Smith (1974)). Of these the only published book-length study is that of McGrew (1972) and, as it would be impossible in this chapter to cover all the available studies, I shall now briefly examine some of the results of that study.

McGrew observed children aged 3–5 in two nursery schools, one in Oxford and one in Edinburgh. In his book he compares his findings with those hitherto published on behaviour in this age group, and with relevant comparative data on non-human primates.

He found that, overall, most child–child interactions were dyadic and short-lived. Boys formed all-male groups with a frequency greater than could be attributed to chance, while this was not true of girls. Roughly one-third of all interactions involved the transmission or manipulation of inanimate objects.

McGrew, unlike Blurton Jones, was able to rank his children into a dominance rank order, on the basis of predictable wins/losses in fights, especially over objects. The dominant boys were significantly older, heavier and more nursery-experienced than the subordinates, but were not taller or more intelligent.

Among the most valuable contributions of McGrew's study was his close analysis of the first 7 days' experience of eight children in one of his nursery schools. They were observed from the moment they entered school, usually with their mothers; all of the newcomers were aged 3, and there were in addition five nursery-experienced children, aged 4, in the group. McGrew observed the whole group at once for this study.

At the very outset the newcomers' behaviour was characterized by crying, slow locomotion and an orientation towards the teacher. Indications of 'social stress' or 'anxiety' such as digit sucking and auto-manipulation were greatest at the outset but declined during the 7-day period. In contrast, there was an increase in object struggles, and in aggressive acts such as 'push', the latter being more common in boys than girls.

Aggression among children

This increase in aggression from a very low level at the outset is discussed by McGrew in the context of the findings from studies on
non-human primates. In studies bringing a number of macaques
together the result is usually an immediate outburst of aggressive
behaviour, with considerable fighting until, fairly rapidly, a dominance rank order is established, whereafter the level of aggression
declines to a low level. McGrew's finding, by contrast, was that
aggression was absent at the outset, the children reacting to the new
situation with 'nervous caution'. As time went by aggression grew,
and in McGrew's words children seemed to be 'seeing how far a
quarrel could be pushed before tears resulted...adults' reactions
were also monitored' (p. 145).

Several reasons are suggested for the difference between the
human and monkey situations. The first and perhaps most important
is an age difference, as the humans were very young whereas the
monkeys in the studies quoted were, though not adult, at any rate
developmentally older. Secondly, there are phylogenetic differences
in social responsiveness between humans and primate species.
Thirdly, there is the possibility that the human children were all
more or less deprived of social interaction with a large peer-group—
their cautious immobility was rather like the first behaviours of socially isolated dogs or monkeys on being liberated into a new environment. A reason not considered by McGrew, mainly because of the
absence of a sociological dimension to his study, is the normative
dimension, i.e. the effects of prior instruction by the parent and
others. It seems entirely possible that children had been trained from
infancy in any number of ways to be cautious and circumspect about
new situations and new people. While this would not necessarily
account for all the difference, it might explain a part of it.

Further newcomers to the Scottish nursery group were studied as
they came in, one by one (six boys and six girls in all), over the course
of the study, with a number of interesting findings. The events on
nursery entry were as follows:

A 'new' child usually walked into the nursery with his mother (although Tommy,
Carrie, and Ian were exceptions who entered with older siblings). The child usually
walked with short, slow steps, held his mother's hand with one hand, and either
carried a snack in the other or sucked his thumb or fingers. After being greeted
by the nursery nurse and handing his snack to her, the child often clung to his
mother, leaned away from the nursery nurse, and avoided her gaze.

The mother then usually stooped beside her child to caress and verbally encourage
him. Several mothers took their children in hand and walked about the play room
pointing out toys and handing them to the children. Sometimes the nursery nurse
did this while the mother looked on. As soon as the child was involved in some

play activity or was interacting with the nursery nurse, the mother usually said goodbye and left quietly. A mother's failure to take leave properly initiated the worst disruption seen on a child's first day: Teresa's mother sneaked away while her daughter's attention was diverted, but within seconds Teresa glanced towards her mother's former location. A few seconds of agitated searching followed, and then Teresa ran from the play room screaming for her mother.

New children's reactions at entry varied greatly. Four of 16 cried when their mothers said goodbye or soon after they left, and two had to be restrained by the nurse from running after them. However, other new children quickly entered into play activities and ignored their mothers, who usually left within two or three minutes of arrival. One new boy, Edward, 'walked' on his knees into the nursery with a friend, both singing the 'Diddy men' song, on his first morning. His mother didn't bother to enter the play room. Children with older siblings also attending the nursery seemed less upset with the mother's departure, as did some children who knew nursery members from outside the nursery. The numbers of such children were too small to warrant conclusions, however, and other children, for example, Kathy, who knew none of the nursery children prior to entry, behaved similarly.

The reaction of nursery group members to a newcomer's entry ranged from neutrality to nonagonistic approach; no aggressive responses were seen. Children paid considerable attention to the morning's arrivals between 9:15 and 9:30, and sometimes spontaneously congregated at the play room door to greet arriving children. This insured that a new face was obvious. Upon initially noticing a new child, a group member visually fixated him; the visual inspection ranged from a brief glance (e.g., by a seated child engaged in manipulative activity) to staring while immobile (e.g., by standing children unengaged in activity). The observing child's facial expression usually remained neutral, but some slight frowning (not 'low frown', see Blurton Jones, 1967) occurred.

Some group members then walked slowly toward a new child, maintaining visual inspection focused on his face. The visual inspection did not seem 'hostile,' and aggressive behaviour patterns did not accompany it. If the new child were interacting with the nursery nurse, they often glanced back and forth between the two. Although they approached within touching distance, group members usually avoided touching a new child at this point; instead they sidled around him and leaned sideways keeping his face in view. A few group members exhibited patterns resembling those of the newcomers, for example, automanipulation, step, silence. This sometimes involved a 'regression': at nursery entry Heidi had shown the peculiar pattern of sucking her two middle fingers, and this sometimes recurred on days when new children were introduced. Similarly, Marcia, an older, 'well-adjusted' girl, rarely thumb-sucked except when newcomers entered, and the pattern was identical to that exhibited at her entry 18 months before.

This fascinating description gives one a good idea of the scrutinizing to which a new child is subjected—a terrifying event for a shy child! As McGrew points out, children with older siblings in the group tended to escape all this and be 'taken over' by the sibling straight away.

Newcomers' behaviour after arrival was characteristically to suck objects or their fingers, to look away from other children and avoid eye contact, to move around with a sidling, shuffling, hesitant gait.

They observed the activities of others intently, but declined offers to engage in social interaction or kept it brief. They avoided all boisterous activity and any kind of competition. In most cases the voice was quiet or silent but three children (all girls) were garrulous. In the case of the silent majority, verbalization increased subsequently, whereas in the case of the three noisy girls it declined.

Some resident girls displayed maternal attentiveness—a soothing tone of voice when talking to a newcomer, tactile comforting, e.g. holding hands, or putting a hand on the back or an arm round the shoulders, or patting or kissing. These were the 'little mothers', one of whom was aged 3, who made efforts to cheer up sad newcomers. Boys, by contrast, seemed for the most part indifferent to newcomers' tears or questions like 'when's mummy coming back?' It has been found in studies of rhesus monkeys that juvenile females are more responsive to infants than juvenile males. Is the human situation homologous? How would one demonstrate that it was not the cultural process of maternal role-taking (Flavell 1968) that underlay the actions of the 'little mothers'? The question is not tackled by McGrew and seems to remain unanswered or unanswerable in terms of ethological analysis. Will cross-cultural studies provide the answer? It seems unlikely, though for the present we do need more such studies as food for thought. But the demonstration of cross-cultural universals is not in itself adequate for, or even indicative of, a need for a resort to biological explanation. For, as Malcolm Crick has recently put it, 'there is no point in hastily handing over problems to new disciplines and speaking of "social biogrammars" ... if invariants can be located at the social level itself' (Crick 1975).

CHAPTER 12

The growth of cognitive abilities

As was stressed in Chapter 11, ethological studies of human children, by virtue of their emphasis on direct observation as a primary method of study, are unable to explore the inner workings and development of the human mind except in so far as it is manifest in behaviour. To study the mind itself, its structures and its progress towards the making of a coherent world-view from an initial stage of infantile sensori-motor awareness, has been the work of many developmental psychologists† but in particular of Jean Piaget and his co-workers. What is particularly interesting about Piaget's work is the extent to which it has succeeded in formulating in abstract terms some of the complex operations of the developing mind and knowledge systems of the child, while being at the same time grounded in experimental procedures that provide a substantive basis for the abstractions. Behind the experiments and the theory of how knowledge develops lies a view of the human mind as an organic entity with a certain predetermined sequence of normal development, divided into three main stages: sensori-motor, semiotic, and formal thought. By passing through these stages the infant acquires and re-interprets the thoughts, world-view and the logical possibilities for innovation characteristic of his culture or subculture. An understanding of Piaget is helpful in bridging the concepts derived from biological studies of child development and those derived from the social anthropology of, say, Lévi-Strauss or the sociology of symbolic interaction. In this respect Piaget is more relevant and useful than Freud, whose id, ego and super-ego are relatively crude concepts by comparison with the refined analysis of mental operations to be found in Piaget. Piaget, with the benefit of more

† And others, of course. Many of the most perceptive studies of children's thinking have been made by authors such as, for example, Jean-Jacques Rousseau (*Émile*) or Jean-Paul Sartre (*Words*). Other studies have shed light on children's thinking by study of their games (Opie and Opie 1959), a line of inquiry recently followed up by, among others, a social anthropologist (Hardman 1974).

recent work in the fields of linguistics, sociology and philosophy to draw on, not to mention developments in psychology itself, has produced a highly relevant description of mental development (see Piaget and Inhelder 1969). This I shall now attempt to summarize, keeping largely to the authors' own terminology, but including also from time to time comments based on the research of others, especially the ethologists.

'Sensori-motor intelligence'

The first stage in the development of the infantile mind is the stage of 'sensori-motor intelligence'. This is a pre-verbal stage, from birth to 18 months or so (ages are always very approximate in Piaget), during which the child 'constructs all the cognitive substructures . . . for his later perceptive and intellectual development' (p. 3). This he does by a two-way process of interaction with his social and physical environment. It is not the case that the infant, at any stage, simply responds to stimuli coming in from the outside world on a stimulus–response basis. The child as such has from the earliest days a brain with a certain organizing capacity, a brain that is already to some extent structured at birth and that becomes further structured in cognitive ways during life. The existing mental structures at any point in time take in new experiences, integrate the new data with the old, and in so doing both modify the incoming data to match the pre-existing structures, and modify the existing structures in the light of new. The first part of this, the filtering of experience, is called assimilation, and the second part, the changing of internal structures of thought, is called accommodation.† As the process of accommodation goes on it leads to a steady enrichment of the mental thought structures or action-scheme structures so that on the cognitive side development consists from the start of building up an ever more comprehensive pattern of mental constructs relating to experience of the outside world, and interpreting that world in terms of these.

Six stages or phases of the sensori-motor period are distinguishable: first a reflex stage (the earliest postnatal stage characterized by the rooting response and other such neonatal responses); second the stage characterized by the formation of habits; third, at about $4\frac{1}{2}$ months, a period of increasing co-ordination of activities; then a time when ends are separate from means—the baby wants something but does not yet have the degree of integration to find ways

---

† These terms have been criticized for their excessive generality and consequent lack of usefulness in generating testable hypotheses or experimental research. Such a criticism is submerged for present purposes in an effort simply to describe Piaget's work.

of getting it; fifth, at about a year of age, the adoption by the baby of new means to achieve ends; and last the stage of 'insight', when problems are solved in novel ways without trial and error.

Throughout this time, we should remember, there is no developed speech or linguistic thought as such; the child is not constructing sentences or using other forms of symbolic communication. As we know from ethological studies, the first year is a time in which a great deal of intercommunication, visual, auditory and verbal, goes on between mother and infant. None of this is mentioned by Piaget, which seems a grave deficiency. However, there is nothing in the ethological findings that cannot be integrated with Piaget's notions of structure, assimilation and accommodation. The biological programming that gives form to infantile actions, the biological responsiveness to certain stimuli such as the nipple or the mother's face, is the matrix within which or out of which cognitive structuring occurs. There seems to be no reason why a new framework of theory should not be able to relate the neonatal behaviour programme as seen by ethologists with the cognitive structurations of Piaget; indeed they *are* integrated in the infant. Presumably the main feature of an integrated theory is that it will include a dialectic in which the cognitive structuring process, in the course of its interaction with the internally programmed responses, begins in a weak position and ends in a strong one (see Gardner 1973).

Cognitive structuring and affectivity

During the second year of life the child embarks more and more on the construction of reality. This involves in the first place the loss of the total egocentrism of the first year and comprehension of a practical world beyond, made up of a number of permanent objects. We see the beginnings of comprehension of spatial and temporal organization of the universe of the child. This structuring process is the cognitive aspect of development. Alongside it proceeds what Piaget and Inhelder call the affective aspect. In their view cognitive and affective development proceed side by side, the former giving structure, the latter providing the 'energetics' for action. Affectivity is at first self-centred since the self has not as yet been differentiated from other people and things. With the process of decentring or decentralization of the self goes differentiation of persons and choice of affective objects—certain persons are selectively responded to on a warm emotional basis and others are not, or may induce fear. The selection is made on the basis of prior experience and the cognitive structures so far created.

In a rare reference to ethology Piaget and Inhelder seem unduly dismissive. Regarding the smile they write 'certain writers, such as J. Bowlby, regard these stimuli [masks that have been used experimentally to induce smiling—see p. 164] as hereditary triggers (IRM). But Spitz and Wolf see the smile simply as a sign of the recognition of a complex of stimuli in a context of need satisfaction, and we tend to agree with their position' (p. 23). As we saw in Chapter 10, the infant does fixate the mother's face when feeding and so there would seem no way of settling the matter if seen in terms of hereditary trigger v. conditioned response. But this very set of oppositions seems to show a lack of understanding of human ethology. Certainly the infant's smile is not a response automatically and only triggered off by a face-like pattern, be it a real face or a mask. This is clear from the fact that blind children develop a smile similar to that of sighted children, although it is said to atrophy somewhat in the absence of visual feed-back (Eibl-Eibesfeldt 1970, p. 404). But neither is it true to say that smiling occurs only in a context of need satisfaction, for it will occur in the full-fed child in response to various kinds of attention from the mother or even to the sound of her voice. It does not seem necessary to discard the idea that smiling is a natural evolved component of infantile behaviour towards the mother's face just because one accepts that it occurs in need-satisfying situations in which the mother's face is normally present.

Thus Piaget and Inhelder are right to reject any naive theory of innate responsiveness to releasers in the development of human signals, but such is not the position of human ethologists. Likewise they attack the 'minimal thesis of empiricism' in the development of perception and conceptual thought. This thesis holds that there is nothing more in concepts than abstractions and generalizations from experience. The authors believe on the contrary that experience is enriched by 'structuration', which 'is always present and stems from action or from operations; ... from the very beginning the sensori-motor schematism goes beyond perception and is not itself perceptible' (p. 44). This view, if, as I take it, it implies that we do not mirror the outside world but re-create it, seems helpful towards an understanding of the view that all human activity, including social and scientific activity, is creative and that we cannot achieve any understanding of 'reality' other than our moment-to-moment conceptions of it. It is interesting that Piaget pushes the etiology of this perplexing fact back into early infancy.

Signs and symbols

The second major stage of mental development is the semiotic or symbolic stage. At 1½–2 years the child is using signifiers to represent things. It uses linguistic words, it has mental images, and it uses gestures in symbolic ways. It names or signifies things that are present and also things that are not present. It imitates and pretends; also it commences drawing. Now too we see the development of play. Play signifies something quite different for Piaget than it does for ethologists. For the latter, play is a natural time of experimentation with objects and socialization with peers. From the standpoint of comparative primatology, play with peers is an important part of normal development, and can even, according to Harlow, substitute for maternal care in ensuring that adequate social responsiveness develops. For Piaget the significance of play is that it 'transforms reality by assimilation to the needs of the self'. It is essentially a retreat from an adult-dominated world where the controls are external to the child, into a world in which he is in control and reality can be made to meet his needs. In the words of Piaget and Inhelder (1969):

Obliged to adapt himself constantly to a social world of elders whose interests and rules remain external to him, and to a physical world which he understands only slightly, the child does not succeed as we adults do in satisfying the affective and even intellectual needs of his personality through these adaptations. It is indispensable to his affective and intellectual equilibrium, therefore, that he have available to him an area of activity whose motivation is not adaption to reality but, on the contrary, assimilation of reality to the self, without coercions or sanctions. Such an area is play, which transforms reality by assimilation to the needs of the self, whereas imitation (when it constitutes an end in itself) is accommodation to external models. Intelligence constitutes an equilibration between assimilation and accommodation.

In play, as we all know, we act out mental images of imagined situations or we play imagined parts. Language may or may not be involved. Children 'become' fathers or nurses or buildings. There is freedom for fantasy, both affective and cognitive. Mental images are 'active copies' of perceptual data. There are 'reproductive' images—evocations of past perceptions. There are 'anticipatory' images—envisagement of things not previously experienced. There are 'static', 'movement' and 'transformation' images. All these get a free rein of expression in play that is mostly unobtainable in the more closely rule-bound 'real' world of adult domination.

It follows from Piaget that adults too are caught up in structured situations of their own making—the hard, real world from which the child escapes into play is not so hard and real at all. But it is hard and real enough to contain the child and adult alike in the grip of seemingly absolute necessities.

This stage of symbolic functioning is divided into two parts, the pre-operatory stage, up to age 7 or 8 years, and the operatory stage, over 7–8 years. What do these terms mean? They refer in particular to a series of experiments in what is called 'conservation' for which Piaget is well known. Conservation appears to be the ability to understand that a given *quantity* can remain unchanged, despite a change in its *form*. The traditional experiment involves pouring a given quantity of water into (a) a short, fat glass and (b) a tall, thin glass. Before the child can understand conservation, i.e. at the pre-operatory stage, it thinks there is more water in the tall, thin glass than the short, fat one. Put crudely, it is deceived by appearances. Once the child reaches the stage of operations, it replies that there is the same amount of water in each glass. What then are operations? They are manipulations not of objects but of concepts, in the mind, to resolve the relations between them. By comparing the image of short-and-fat on the one hand, and tall-and-thin on the other, the child can reach the conclusion that in terms of volume they amount to one and the same thing. Having reached this operational stage, the child can go on to anticipate how things *would* be *if* certain changes occurred, and by such anticipatory images can produce improved performance.

Memory, too, is involved in improved performance and 'schemes of action'. Two types of memory are distinguished: 'recognition' memory, in the presence of the remembered object, and 'evocation' memory, in its absence. The former kind is found not only in the young human but also in non-human species. The latter kind is more characteristic of humans and involves reconstruction, not just triggering of stored perceptions, as is shown by the existence of 'false but vivid memories'.

Linguistic development

Language development is clearly central to development of symbolic functioning, though it is interesting that Piaget makes language much less central to human mental development than many linguists, psycholinguists and linguistically inclined social anthropologists (e.g. Ardener 1971). Language, to Piaget, appears to be just one (though admittedly the most advanced) form of semiotic (sign) communication system. Deaf-mutes show that the semiotic faculty can be developed without spoken language. Their systems of gestural signs are very complex and enable them to communicate with one another in a variety of complex ways. In normal individuals, however, gestural language is rendered less necessary by spoken language.

Articulate language follows a period of spontaneous vocalization (babbling), found in all cultures from 6–10 or 11 months of age, and a phase of differentiation of phonemes by imitation at or around the end of the sensori-motor period. The first articulate language consists of 'one-word sentences' expressing desires, emotions or observations. By the end of the second year there are two-word sentences, then complete short sentences without conjugation or declension, and then the gradual acquisition of grammar. Chomsky (1968) has argued that this period of grammatical progress is not an outcome of painstakingly learned, step-by-step rules but proceeds at a pace and with a complexity not explicable without recourse to a notion of some pushing or stimulating inner process, or 'innate grammar'. He has argued that children learning to speak put together quite original constructions that have not been learnt as such, but indicate the existence of linguistic rules that have not been taught to the children concerned. Cross-cultural studies also seem to indicate a common 'deep structure' to the grammars of languages in all cultures, as if there were a species-characteristic kind of grammatical language-construction, characterized by nouns and verbs, subject and object, and other features.

The advantages of language, as seen by Piaget and Inhelder (1969), are that it enables quick representations of long event-chains, a liberation from the immediate, and simultaneous representation of different structures. It detaches thought from action and thus together with operational ability enables a progressive ability to envisage and plan. There is not as yet, in this second stage, the development of logical or formal thought, however, but perhaps rather a mastery of words and their referents, a keen interest in them, and an ever deepening and widening of the world structure that is being formed and re-formed. Language, as it comes to the child, already contains a 'system of cognitive instruments (relationships, classifications etc.) for use in the service of thought. The individual learns this system and then proceeds to enrich it' (p. 87).

Is language the source of logic? Piaget and Inhelder think not. They point out that deaf-mutes have a 1–2 year delay in the development of logic but that they subsequently catch up. Language is shown by their experiments not to be the source of logic 'but is on the contrary structured by it' (p. 90). The roots of logic itself are seen by them to be deeper, in the general co-ordination of actions that arises during the pre-verbal sensori-motor stage.

'Concrete operations'

Clearly the development of 'operations' marks a great step forward for the child. Two kinds of operations are distinguished: 'concrete' operations, that involve mental transformations of objects, and 'propositional' operations, that involve playing around with verbal hypotheses. The concrete operations develop out of the sensori-motor period of direct interaction with the outside world (up to 2 or 3 years), through a long intermediate period (from 2 or 3 to 6 or 7 years of age) to the operational stage at 6 or 7 years. During the intermediate period children show their ability to comprehend certain out-of-sight spatial relations, for example they cannot represent a short journey from A to B in picture or model form, even though they may be able to find their way from A to B in real life; they have 'motor memories', memories involving short-term guidance by a series of cues along the way rather than an overall representation of the whole route, which comes later, at the operational stage, when reality can be manipulated and transformed in mental imagery. This process also involves 'decentring' of representations, e.g. the qualities of leftness and rightness need to be reversed for objects along the route depending on the direction of travel, and this the pre-operational child cannot do.

The operations that make these things possible are of a number of basic kinds: seriation, classification, number, space, time and speed; the universe is both broken down and built up in these terms, and the problems of causality and chance are attacked with renewed vigour ('why?' questions having in fact been asked from the age of 3). This question of causality provides fascinating glimpses into the child's mental world. At the pre-operatory level the child has what Piaget and Inhelder call 'pre-causality': 'the subject believes he has grasped the external and objective mechanisms of reality, whereas from the observer's point of view it is clear that he is merely assimilating them to a certain number of subjective characteristics of his own action' (pp. 117–18). All who have dealt with young children will know that from their questions and statements they disclose the existence of notions of causality that we would regard as quite false—that their dolls or toys, for example, are alive and have feelings. They are also greatly interested in 'magic', which, until it is 'seen through', seems to offer an alternative and superior system of causation if only one can master the spells involved. Again, with regard to the probability that a given result will occur, e.g. that a dip into a bag of numbers will produce the 'lucky' number first time, children without clear ideas of probability will be unable to calculate the chances of winning, and will be chagrined at failure. 'Chance is at first conceived only in a negative sense, as an obstacle to deductibility'. Later, of course, the situation is reversed (though judging by the amount squandered in various forms of gambling one wonders how completely!).

In the field of social and affective relations the pre-operational–operational change is equally manifest. The difference appears to be mainly one of structuring of games and play interactions generally. Before the age of 7 or so, interactions between children are unstructured compared with subsequently. This seems to be borne out by ethological studies of nursery-school children, where long-lasting highly organized games involving collective and co-ordinated effort by a number of children do not occur. Subsequently, with operational thinking, the new interest in the movements and transformations of objects makes possible the transition from games that are fun to play but in which rules are not very important to longer games in which there is strict observance of rules and the outcome (wins and losses) is a logical necessity. Marbles is an example. A social interaction development that goes together with this is the development of role-taking (see Flavell 1968), i.e. the ability to instruct another child what to do, seeing the situation from the point of view of that child.

'Propositional operations' and 'moral autonomy'

The final stage in Piaget's schema is the stage of pre-adolescence and adolescence, characterized by the propositional operations. Whereas before, operations had to be related to the concrete, there is now a new process of freeing thought from its concrete referents, and a final decentring of the self from envisaged situations, making possible from the age of 11–12 years on a great liberation of ideas, a new world of hypotheses to be weighed against other hypotheses and a final development, depending on the experience and personality of the individual, of adult logical thinking and adult intelligence. Some of the new ways of thinking are based on the following mental operations: if–then, either–or, both, and neither. Hypotheses are further developed about proportions, e.g. the relation of weight to length around a fulcrum, about relative motion, and about probability and randomness.

Not all the advances of this time are the result of improvements in language: there is also intellectual development at the organic level, in Piaget's view; clear formulation, however, helps this development to realize its potential. During pre-adolescence there is a spontaneous development of experimental methods. The child naturally dissociates factors and analyses them one by one to discover which variable is the one responsible for the effect seen. This is an advance over the stage of concrete operations, when factors were less systematically analysed but were all varied together so that no clear results could be obtained. Now this is avoided because the properties of objects are kept separate in the mind and the mind weighs one against the other on a systematic basis. To take an example:

... the subject is presented with a number of metal rods which he can fasten at one end, the problem being to account for their differences in flexibility. The factors involved in this experiment are the length of the rods, their thickness, their cross-section, and the material they are made of.... At the level of concrete operations, the subject does not attempt to make a preliminary inventory of the factors but proceeds directly to action ... From eleven or twelve onward, subjects, after a little groping, make a list of factors by way of hypothesis and then study them one by one ... This method ... is all the more remarkable in that none of the subjects we interviewed had received instruction in this method in school [Piaget and Inhelder 1969, pp. 146–7].

The final development treated by Piaget and Inhelder as characteristic of the third stage of mental development is the emergence, alongside the formal thought of the propositional operations, of a new era of moral autonomy. From the primitive morality of the young child, very much a black–white, good–evil morality, there now emerges a system of ideal values, an ideal person with ideal qualities, and notions of social justice of great clarity. These gain strong affective value at adolescence; there is a devotion to ideals. Such ideals now very much take over and guide the life-style. They show once again the close relation between the affective or emotional and the cognitive sides of development, and as at all ages the affective developments provide the energetics that power the cognitive notions into actions. Adolescence is perhaps the greatest time of crises and struggles in the mind, the final great push to establish coherence of the self.

A comment on Piaget's work: it is an impressive effort to establish the first principles that govern the growth and development of thought. The basis of this development is conceived by Piaget as an *organic* process, so that the forms of thought are not finally explicable in terms of abstract logic or mathematics but in terms of biological organic development. This point is discussed further in Piaget's later works, *Biology and Knowledge* (1971) and *Structuralism* (1972).

Where Piaget is perhaps weakest is on the 'affective' side, to which he frequently appeals as the source of energy for action, but which he makes no effort to analyse. We are thus not given any clues about emotional development. And yet every one of us who can remember knows that childhood is full of hopes and fears, loves and hates, and that these can be very extreme at times in childhood. If we now contrast Piaget with the child ethologists, we can see that the latter do in some sense get closer to the affective side of childhood in their studies of laughing and crying, holding hands and fighting. Yet, by their emphasis on observation, ethologists must also miss much of the real force of subjective experience, which depends very largely on our interpretations of external events rather than the events themselves.

CHAPTER 13

Non-verbal communication and linguistic development

THE MANNER in which action develops remains, at the present time, very much a mystery. There are many relevant theories and empirical data, some of which we have looked at or shall look at in the ensuing pages, but the fact remains that in this area we are still groping for methods and concepts that will enable progress to be made. Let us start by re-formulating the problem; this will clarify the difficulties we are up against.

In the earlier chapters we have seen something of the basis of infant–mother interaction, and we noted elements of this interaction—such as the cry and the smile—that were clearly of fundamental importance in the ontogeny of action. But we know too that our developing individual is moving towards an ever-increasingly cultural *interpretation of his environment*, including his social environment and including the cry, the smile and all other such elements of communication. This interpretative process is what makes him a human being; it is the brain-based process whose evolution we discussed in Chapter 5. A part of this process consists of the mastery of language, but we should not mistake this for the whole process, which involves a progressive structuring of the external universe within the developing mind of the child. Language no doubt mirrors that process, to some extent guides it and to some extent follows it. The problem is how to describe and analyse the process by which humans acquire a world-view.

In one sense this matter has always been with us—it has always been the case that people acquired world-views; there is absolutely nothing new about *doing* it. But, curiously, it is actually only in recent years that the matter seems no longer to have been taken for granted, and to have emerged as one of the knottiest problems psychologists and other interested parties have had to face. There have been reasons for this—mainly developments in child ethology and social anthropology/sociology. The findings of child ethologists and others interested in the observation of early behaviour have given us a clearer awareness of the nature and structure of the human non-verbal interaction process during early life. The social anthropologists and sociologists have given us a clearer insight into the infinitely ramifying ways our thought is structured by the categories and concepts of our cultural environment. It is out of this pair of oppositions that the new problem has so clearly emerged, primarily as a problem for the psychologists.

Reflexive interaction

There have, of course, been psychologists and others who have given aspects of the problem a great deal of attention in the past. G. H. Mead (1934), rejecting both Watson's behaviourism and Darwin's evolutionary appeal to inbuilt 'emotions' as ways of understanding human communicative interaction, resorted to the concept of 'significant gestures'—signals that signify something in the culture concerned and are taken up by individuals in the course of their interactions with others. In his own words, when two people engage in a 'conversation of significant gestures it is not a case of moment to moment responses to signals such as is found in animal communication but is a much more adequate and effective mechanism of mutual adjustment with the social act involving, as it does, the taking by each of the individuals carrying it on of the attitudes of the others towards himself' (p. 46).

This formulation just quoted is very typical of Mead and contains the essence of his idea of the reflexive nature of human interaction. It is not, according to Mead, possible to understand human interaction on the basis of mutual responses by the interactants to each other. One has in addition to take into account the fact that any one individual is putting himself into the place of the other or others as well as just being himself. Thus a child acts differently at school and at home; a man is a 'different person' at the office and at home; and the explanation is not just a matter of 'conditioning' but involves the envisaging by the child or the man of how he is being seen by the others. This quality of human thought makes human interaction very different from that of other species. †

On the question of how our thinking develops, Mead emphasized the importance of early social interaction and the communication between the child and others as the essential matrix for development

† To be precise, we have no evidence of the existence of such a process in animals, and every reason to doubt it. Whereas in man we know of its existence and can demonstrate it.

of thought, anticipating to a certain extent the more recent research of psychologists such as Bruner or Richards.

But Mead, though in advance of his time in *describing* the human interaction process, did not explain *how* this interaction process might develop out of or alongside a non-verbal matrix, simply because at that time neither child ethology nor observational studies of other kinds on human non-verbal interaction were in existence as organized bodies of thought. Those early observational studies of child interaction that did exist (for a good summary and discussion of these see Smith and Connolly 1972) mainly concerned themselves with documenting interactions as expressive of underlying emotions or motivations, and Mead was clearly unhappy about such an approach. Thus, apart from *contrasting* man and animals, Mead did not greatly concern himself with non-verbal elements of communication.

Non-verbal elements in communication

Let us now turn to the work of those who in more recent times have tended to emphasize the importance of non-verbal elements in human communication. (I shall not here include the child ethologists whose work on mother–infant and peer–peer interaction was discussed in Chapters 10 and 11.) Among the best known are two anthropologists, a psychiatrist and a psychologist. The anthropologists are E. T. Hall and R. Birdwhistell. Hall (1959, 1966) was concerned to show how there are hidden, implicit rules of comportment underlying the processes of social (including verbal) communication in different cultures. In particular these involve the matter of spacing and Hall called the study of spacing 'proxemics'. In any given culture there are rules about how closely one should approach another person and these rules are dependent on the context of the interaction and the relationship between the persons involved. Within this basic framework of rules, verbal interaction takes place. Hall did not study the development of rule-consciousness in childhood but described its expressions in adulthood.

Birdwhistell (1949) likewise has been very concerned to document the implicit rules of non-verbal interaction, only in his case he has been more concerned with the relation between these and speech utterances, seeing the non-verbal aspects of the communication process very often as accompaniments and markers emphasizing the type, beginning and ending of verbal statements. He has also shown the existence of different non-verbal styles in single individuals depending on the setting, a theme explored by Goffman and others.

Scheflen (1964), in the course of psychiatric work with patients, interviewed them in the context of their parents and made interesting observations about the extent to which the ways in which they sat, crossed their legs, and used their bodies generally, indicated the 'power structure' or the underlying mental struggles between them.

Argyle (1967) has made extensive studies of eye contact and has constantly emphasized this as a predominant non-verbal communicative mechanism. The extent of cultural variance in patterns of eye contact is as yet unknown, but it seems certain that in those cultures studied successful interaction involves some degree of eye contact, the amount and distribution depending on both the pattern of speech interaction and the rules governing the total setting—rules relating to seniority, intimacy, etc. Argyle argues that the non-verbal elements of interaction are as integral in the composition of messages as the verbal elements. Thus it is not the case that the non-verbal patterns operate as a backcloth to the 'essential' verbal message, but rather that the non-verbal ingredients are essential parts of the total message.

Brief reference was made above to Goffman, and perhaps a word more should be said about his work, which has had much impact in micro- or small-group sociology. In his first book, *Presentation of Self in Everyday Life* (1956), he documented some of the details of posture, expression, tone of voice, etc., that people showed in interaction, and saw these as 'fronts'—culturally accepted, context-specific styles and mannerisms. He used a lot of stage terminology in his descriptions and his approach has been described as 'dramaturgical', but we need to consider carefully the sense in which it is so. For it is not so in any naïve sense. The sense in which Goffman's approach is dramaturgical is the sense in which life is a drama and *nothing but* a drama. Thus there is no opting-out of one dramaturgical style except into another, and in this respect the term 'dramaturgical' and the analogy with the theatre loses most of its force. For if 'all the world's a stage' then what takes place in the theatre must be some kind of meta-drama and so the terminology begins to fall apart. But, criticisms aside, Goffman's strength lies in the point he makes about the massive encroachment of the rules prescribed by our culture and its institutions on our manner of interaction.

In none of the cases cited above, however, do we have any adequate *developmental* theory, mainly because this has not been the problem to which the authors have addressed themselves. By 'developmental' I mean a theory that begins with the neonate and looks at the acquisition of culture in ontogenetic terms. It seems to have been quite convincingly demonstrated by the above authors and others that we do eventually come to interact in context-specific verbal/non-verbal ways. But how do words and meanings enter into a mould that is in the first place composed of wholly non-verbal, pre-cultural, neonatal activities? A number of arguments can be adduced, for instance that the infant learns by imitation. In that case we are just faced by a whole set of problems. How does imitation proceed? Why should the infant imitate? Are words imitated first and meanings attached afterwards? Answers to such obvious questions are very easy to formulate and very hard to demonstrate. What is the role of rewards from the child's 'significant others' in structuring his actions? Is it the mother's smile, her tone of voice and pleasant body-contacts that reward 'correct' words and actions? What is the significance of infantile babbling? How much does the *infant* bring to the acculturation process?

Biological aspects of language

In respect of the last question the names of two psycho-linguists come to mind: Chomsky and Lenneberg. The latter (1967) was concerned primarily to document those essential biological attributes that predispose, prepare or make possible speech communication in man. Lenneberg proceeded by making point-by-point comparisons between man on the one hand and non-human primates on the other. He also compared normal individuals with mentally deficient individuals and with aphasic individuals (those with damage to the speech areas of the brain). The work provides a useful biological basis for the discussion of speech development but does not take us far into the mechanics or processes of what can crudely be called 'world-view acquisition'.

Chomsky (1968) produced an intriguing and potentially very fruitful line of inquiry with his suggestion of an 'innate grammar' in the developing child's mind. This suggestion has many of the needed ingredients. It relates to the developmental question, focuses on the child, and combines organic ingredients (brain structures) with cultural ones (language structures). According to Chomsky, the way in which children pick up and use language utterances and the speed and readiness with which they do so, not only repeating what they hear but formulating new phrases, forces us to accept that there must be underlying predisposing brain structures that facilitate their efforts. Otherwise, Chomsky said, they simply could not do it. Analysis of children's *mistakes* as they learned to speak indicated that there were rules of language acquisition guiding their efforts, but these were not the rules of the *particular* grammar they were learning, which were in fact being infringed. Instead, might they be rules of a different, universal, organic grammar, written into brain structures and underlying both the ontogeny of language acquisition in individual children and the basic structure of languages everywhere; an outcome of the evolution of speech capacity?

Clearly such an argument comes closer to the requirements of a biological theory of language acquisition than most others. But it still does not relate language development back to its non-verbal antecedents, tending to treat linguistic development in its own terms, rather than in the wider context of child development. This point is made by Bruner (1975) who writes:

> If language grows from its own roots, it suffices to study the beginnings of language proper if one wishes to understand the nature of its early acquisition. The programme, in effect, was the linguists' programme: gather a corpus of speech, with due regard for context (unspecified), and subject it to grammatical analysis. Or, to add an experimental dimension, contrive experimental situations to tap the child's capacities for producing and comprehending speech in particular contexts, and draw inferences from the child's responses concerning his underlying linguistic competence.
>
> There can be little doubt that this programme has deeply enriched our understanding of early language and of the course of its early development. The work of Brown (1970, 1973) and his group, of Bloom (1970), of McNeill (1970a, 1970b), of Slobin (1973), of the Edinburgh group (e.g. Donaldson & Wales, 1970)—all attest to the enormous progress of the last decade.
>
> But the early language for which a grammar is written is the end result of psychological processes leading to its acquisition, and to write a grammar of that language at any point in its development is in no sense to explicate the nature of its acquisition. Even if it were literally true (as claimed by Chomsky) that the child, mastering a particular language, initially possesses a tacit knowledge of an alleged universal deep structure of language, we would still have to know how he managed to recognize these universal deep rules as they manifest themselves in the surface structure of a particular language. Even an innate 'language acquisition device' would require a programme to guide such recognition and it would fall to the psychologist to discover the nature of the programme by investigating the alleged recognition process.

In place of Chomsky's linguisticism Bruner advocates a much closer study of the pre-linguistic stage of the child—the long period before verbal utterances begin to occur. He and his colleagues are studying the details of infant–caretaker interaction to try to discover the nature of the significant interactions by which rapport is established and maintained, and meanings come to be attached to vocal sounds, actions and objects. Eye-to-eye contact, tone of voice changes, selective focusing of attention by both parties on particular environmental features, games like 'peekaboo'—all need to be scrutinized for clues. A continuity with adult interaction is posited by Bruner: 'In the first year of life, then, the child is mastering a convention-checking procedure not unlike that of adults—indeed, even using eye-to-eye contact for determining intent, readiness and whose 'turn' it is (Argyle & Ingham, 1972)' (Bruner, 1975).

Interesting work on the early development of the interaction process, again focusing on the infant–mother or infant–caretaker situation, has been done by Richards and his co-workers at Cambridge (see Richards 1974). As has been shown in a number of studies, very young infants selectively attend to faces; likewise they prefer speech-like sounds to other sorts of sounds. These abilities give them 'a handle on the world'. In this sense, 'the beginnings of language acquisition may fairly be said to be observable in the first days of extra-uterine life'. Richards points out that speech develops slowly. 'The outside observer is usually impressed by the steady increase in understanding that occurs from a point long before the infant produces any speech through the early stages of language acquisition' (Richards 1974, pp. 91–2).

Regarding the actual details of the early interactions, the 'first fumbling links of intersubjectivity', Richards writes as follows:

The infant looks at the caretaker's face. The caretaker looks back into the eyes of the infant. A smile moves on the infant's face. The adult responds with a vocal greeting and a smile. There is mutual social acknowledgement. The 'meaning' of this exchange does not simply depend on the action patterns employed by the two participants. Each must fit his sequence of actions with that of the other; if this is not done, the exchange may well become meaningless. An important means of knowing that a message is intended for you is that it follows an alternating sequence with yours.

After the first few weeks, the interaction sequences and their mutual timing patterns become more complex. The following is an account from an earlier study carried out in conjunction with Dr. C. Trevarthen:

'After eight weeks or so when social smiling is well established, the mother may spend long periods eliciting smiling in her infant. During such periods the infant is held on the mother's lap facing her and supported by her arms or is placed in an infant seat. The mother smiles and vocalizes to the infant and moves her head rhythmically towards and away from his face. The infant first responds by rapt attention, with a widening of his eyes and a stilling of his body movements. Then his excitement increases, body movements begin again, he may vocalize and eventually a smile spreads over his face. At this point he turns away from his mother before beginning the whole cycle once again. Throughout this sequence the mother's actions are carefully phased with those of the infant. During the infant's attention phase the mother's behaviour is restrained but as his excitement increases she vocalizes more rapidly and the pitch of her voice rises. At the point when he is about to smile her movements are suddenly reduced, as if she was allowing him time to reply. However, not all mothers behave in this way. Some subject their infants to a constant and unphased barrage of stimulation. The infant is given no pauses in which to reply and he seems totally overwhelmed by his mother. Instead of playing this game for long periods, he is quickly reduced to fussing and crying and shows sustained and prolonged turning away from the mother's face.' (Quoted from Richards, 1974, pp. 92–3.)

Thus we can see how differences in mothers' actions and reactions can affect the infants' own responses and patterns of development.

But, as Bruner acknowledges, there is a great step from non-linguistic to true linguistic interaction. We must continue to search for clues to how the child manages to 'crack the linguistic code'. He concludes that there is still probably much of value in Chomsky's ideas but that we must now fit them on to their ontogenetic base. In his own concluding words:

If there is one point that deserves emphasis, whether one is searching for syntactic, semantic, or pragmatic precursors of early language, it is that language acquisition occurs in the context of an 'active dialogue' in which joint action is being undertaken by infant and adult. The joint enterprise sets the deictic limits that govern joint reference, determines the need for a referential taxonomy, establishes the need for signalling intent, and provides a context for the development of explicit predication. The evolution of language itself, notably its universal structures, probably reflects the requirements of joint action and it is probably because of that evolutionary history that its use is mastered with such relative ease, though its theoretical explication still eludes us.

PART V

Human action in cultural context

Introduction to Part V

In the two preceding parts we examined a number of aspects of human development, physical and mental, and tried to describe the ingredients of a whole-body approach including physiological, emotional and cognitive aspects of action. In this final part we come back to the perspective stressed in Part II, to man acting in the world of his own construction. We look first at the world of ideas we inhabit and then the book ends with an effort at a synthesis that will do equal justice to the organic side of man's existence and to the fact that it is out of the concepts prevailing in his culture that, by his own interpretations, he creates himself. At the same time, it is within this cultural context that, because of his limitations, he can be destroyed.

CHAPTER 14

The biosociology of knowledge

W H A T I S human society? Of what is it constructed? The question was raised in Part II in relation to a comparison between human and non-human society. We now revert to the same problem only this time with a new orientation—that of the relation between society and the development of an integrated human self. In the ensuing discussion I shall follow the basic outlines of the arguments presented by Peter Berger and Thomas Luckmann in *The Social Construction of Reality* (1967); their post-Meadian standpoint and the clarity of their exposition make this an ideal book for present purposes.

The sociology of knowledge

The 'sociology of knowledge' is a phrase in common enough usage among sociologists but not especially meaningful to many biologists or other scientists who are more used to thinking of knowledge as the outcome of empirical, preferably experimental, procedures and hypothetico-deductive reasoning. What the phrase means is the study of the social basis for 'everyday' knowledge, i.e. the common-sense knowledge about life, what to say, how to behave, and so on. The project of the sociology of knowledge is to show that these things do have a social base, that they serve certain functions for individuals, in making their actions mesh in with those of others, and that they have other functions for society, in producing coherent institutions and social order. It starts from the assumption that there exists a fabric of shared meanings in any society and examines the distribution, manner of transmission, and effects of this fabric. It does not question the existence of such a fabric, regarding that as a philosophical issue outside the scope of the sociology of knowledge itself. But indeed there is ample evidence from social anthropology and studies of groups within our society that shared meanings and a shared body of knowledge and beliefs are characteristic of and essential to the life of social groups.

The study of human development, biological or otherwise, needs to take account of the sociology of knowledge because it is in the terms proposed by the individual's awareness and consciousness of the world around him, its dictates and prohibitions, that his entire life (except the very earliest months) is lived. There is the greatest difference between the life of an Eskimo and that of a London stockbroker, and this difference is in part (though only in part) an outcome of their different views on the kind of life project in which each feels, or 'knows', himself to be engaged. What is more, the same can be said of two Eskimos or two stockbrokers, although it is more likely to be true in the latter case than in the former.

One of the most significant features of social life as we conceive of it is that it appears to have objective existence independent of ourselves—it is simply 'there'. We know ourselves to have entered it through a certain family or in a certain sector, but we find ourselves in childhood and throughout life confronted by a continuing and in many ways (especially in industrial societies) bafflingly complex system of people, roles and institutions, whose roots lie in history. In so far as we consider society objectively, we tend to forget or even deny its fundamental existence as a human product, subject to change by the efforts of human beings. The social world—relations with kinsfolk, with other families, with the Church; religion; knowledge about school behaviour; attitudes to sex and fighting—comes across to us in childhood as a set of more or less 'givens', in which certainty is easier to handle than doubt. As we mature we modify our concepts of social groups and appropriateness of behaviour, but we need to maintain a certain assurance of what should happen and what should not happen in social situations if we are to interact coherently with others.

Each of us has his or her own 'projects' or life enterprises, not just an actual job of work but also searching for a partner, perhaps, or bringing up a family, or projecting an invention, and in the details of our projects each of us is unique and faces unique problems. But at the same time we need to interact successfully with others in order to realize our projects and in so doing we need to inhabit a common universe of shared meanings in order to communicate. That common universe is the world of shared ideas, expressed in language, which we enter during socialization and which produces us, so that we in turn can reproduce it when the time comes. Those changes that we initiate during our lives have a greater or lesser effect depending on the extent to which they spread and are incorporated into publicly accepted knowledge.

Lest it be thought that what is being propounded here is a *tabula rasa* theory of human development, let me explain why this is not so. It is clear from the arguments and data in Parts III and IV of this book that man is a biological organism and that despite individual uniqueness at the genetic level we all share many features of growth and development in common, up to and including the level of social gestures, postures, noises and facial expressions. The fact that we 'construct ourselves' does not deny this. What we in fact construct is our cognitive, conscious selves, that part of ourselves that knows what's what and who's who. There is a clear-cut denial in both Mead and in Berger and Luckmann of the idea that we are biologically limited to certain forms of social organization. The latter write 'there is no human nature in the sense of a biologically fixed substratum determining the variability of socio-cultural formations'. With this I agree. Arguments that there are biological determinants of 'social formations' are unacceptable. Organic inputs go so far as indicated in earlier chapters and no further. It is the inputs from social history via its ongoing institutions and via the ideas and knowledge systems they perpetuate, reaching our neurones via significant others with whom we interact, that very largely make us the people we are, doing the things we do and making the social arrangements we make, not our bodies or the organic construction of our brains. Of course, there are physiological inputs into the system—the increase of sex hormones at puberty contributes to new social arrangements at that time. But 'dating' is a rule-governed activity whether in the U.S.A. or New Guinea and it is those rules and the associated ideas that underlie the *forms* of the institutions of courtship and marriage.

Roles and legitimation

Institutions are the constructions in society within which co-ordinated activity is carried on. Within them certain actions are considered appropriate and certain roles are in existence or are brought into existence to focus these actions. Roles are socially appropriate sets of actions. They have existence over and beyond the lives and abilities of their incumbents. They can be well or badly 'played'. They may be precisely formulated, such as the role of juror on a jury, or left very open, such as the role of conjurer or hitch-hiker, to which few rules apply.

The relation between an individual and his roles in life is an interesting speculative topic. At one extreme one can argue that all an individual can do is play roles; the moment he ceases to play one role he begins to play another. Alternatively we can see an opposition between role playing and the basic non-socially active person. In both the above cases individuals can assess their roles and role-playing from an alternative vantage point. Where they feel totally involved in their roles, we can say the attributes and actions involved have been thoroughly internalized so that an identification has occurred between the person and his role or roles. Thus a business-man may come to believe in the importance of hard work and the absolute necessity for making more profits, while the committed layabout cannot keep a job for more than a week and cannot ever save a penny of what he earns. If a person has a certain role but does not like it or plays it reluctantly, constantly standing apart and surveying 'himself' from the vantage point of some other and 'truer' self outside, we can say he is 'role-distancing'. His reasons for not giving up his disliked role are possibly due to economic con-siderations or perhaps just lethargy. 'Alienation' generally refers to the condition in which a person not only role-distances but in addi-tion feels powerless to do anything about the predicament in which he finds himself—it is a term most often applied in Marxist analysis of the situation of industrial workers who hate their jobs and the whole system of factory production but feel there is no alternative for them but to take part; they thus lose their sense of purpose and the ability to act to change the system.

There is a third position with regard to roles, the opposite of the first, in which emphasis is placed on the individual's powers of choice and not on the role itself as a determining factor in human social life. This is an attractive theory and may have much to offer along a moral dimension. For at what point, morally, should an individual refuse to play a role he has been allocated? It is the Eichmann ques-tion. Sociology suffers from an amorality with regard to such ques-tions. Morality is not a subdivision of sociology. Individual social schemes give rise to their own moralities, but there is a further sense in which a society's moral notions can be seen from the standpoint of one or more individuals within that society as immoral, and such individuals may well, in some non-sociological sense, be 'right'. (Sociologically they cannot be 'right' if they stand alone or represent a tiny minority—they are 'deviant' or in breach of norms. The word 'right' has no meaning outside of a conformist context in sociology.) A major exposition of the moral basis of individual choice and the necessity for constant vigilance and doubt about social decisions and actions is to be found in the work of Sartre (see Introduction and Appendix 3).

Given that society is a human product, it is also clear that in most cases it involves very unequal distribution of resources and very con-siderable sacrifices by some of its members. How is the permanence of these conditions assured? By what means is the *status quo* but-tressed? The answer is of some interest in the present context, because it involves a process that makes the intolerable tolerable to individuals—'legitimation'. Legitimation refers to any conventionally acceptable explanation for why things are as they are. Generally it has a positive aspect, the *explanation*, and *sanctions* to ensure conformity. Thus in all societies some forms of incest are tabooed. The explanation given may be that incest prevents rainfall by angering the gods, or that it causes genetic defects in the child. The sanction may be severe—offenders may be ostracized to the point where one commits suicide, or they may be killed or imprisoned or merely chastised. Thus the world of social reality arms itself with teeth.

Language is a subtle servant of legitimation. A walk-out by industrial workers may be described as a 'wildcat strike engineered by communist saboteurs' in one newspaper, or the 'refusal of decent men to be treated like animals by high-handed management' in another. Thus individual sectors of society attempt to bolster their claims to legitimacy. The two 'classes' of classical Marxist analysis are seen locked in struggle, each side with its own world-view and consequent solidarity. On each side, as far as individuals are concerned, the struggle gives coherence and substance to notions of the self. There is legitimation on both sides: private education, wealth and Galtonian notions of superiority and survival for the top group; a feeling of good, plain, fun-loving and unprivileged honesty for the masses. The man in the middle is in a dilemma, as Huw Beynon's book *Working for Ford* shows. He tends to go mad. That is highly relevant to our theme. Society legitimates its structures; individuals are the agents of and believers in these legitimations; by so being and doing they attain solidarity and sanity. Authors such as Simmel (1955) and Coser (1956) have argued that social conflict has positive functions. The giving of mental coherence may be numbered among them. It is the person who has no clear idea who he is and where he fits, or who has divided loyalties, who suffers and may become institutionalized as a psychotic.

Normative self-construction

Thus we return to our theme—in truth we never left it—of individual development. If society is so constructed as to fill minds with self-assurance and meaning, how is it that in our own industrial society such a high proportion of people suffer from mental disturbances? Such a question raises many awkward problems. On the one hand writers such as Szasz (1971) regard mental illness as a social category, and claim that it is the increasing trend towards conformity arising out of ever more crowded and competitive conditions that has led to the growth of both people labelled (by themselves and others) 'mentally ill', and of specialists to 'cure' them. According to him the medical terminology and treatments applied in most cases are unfounded, because what we have is a problem of deviance, not of sickness, and were it not for the intolerance and conformity of others such people would not need treatment. On the other hand mental illness in some sense is real enough, and is often, in our society, a collapse of normal mental *integration* resulting from an inability to cope with aspects of what is often seen as a competitive, individualistic, unfriendly world. Thirdly it can be pointed out that owing to an increase in diagnosis and treatment, personnel and facilities, as well as population, we really do not know whether there is more mental 'sickness' now than at any past time; also that patterns of mental illness change from time to time; also that today some mental illness is known to have organic causes and that society is more enlightened in its attitudes than it was in the days when village idiots were given a ducking for fun.

Certainly Szasz would seem to have a point when he says that a person's mental state is to some extent the outcome of the decisions of others about his sanity. This fits with the whole of the argument of this chapter, that the self is a social product. If a person does surprising things this may or may not be considered insane, depending on how social life is affected. If a person goes out with a gun and shoots half a dozen pedestrians he is considered, at least temporarily, insane. If a person does not reply appropriately to questions but talks nonsense the same conclusion is reached. But if a person sits on a pole for twelve hours in the cause of charity that is a very sane and humanitarian thing to do. If Clement Freud, M.P., does dog-food commercials on television that is rather *infra dig.* but not insane because the profit motive is regarded as very sane indeed. Certain unfortunate people alive today believe themselves to be Jesus, or to be unrecognized geniuses or universally hated when they are not. Such people have an internalized social reality and a self-concept that makes it impossible for others to tolerate them. How such mental states arise is a question not answerable at present. To some extent they are a response to mental crisis, but a non-viable response in our society.

There are viable responses to such crises. Religious conversion is one described by Berger and Luckmann, who take the example of St. Paul. In these cases there is 'a problem of dismantling, disintegrating the preceding nomic structure of subjective reality. How can this be done? A "recipe" for successful alternation has to include both social and conceptual conditions, the social, of course, serving as the matrix of the conceptual.' In other words, the new way of thinking and seeing is given endurance and strength by a social matrix. Perhaps it is when the individual is forced too far into his or her own rationalizations and interpretations rather than into those of others that 'mental sickness' such as paranoia or schizophrenia develops. But if a legitimate social context is located where a new approach to life and a new set of social contacts can develop and flourish, the old anxieties and fears can die down and mental stability be reached.

Integration of mind and body

How are these processes—the processes of normative integration, of deviance and of insanity—related to the internal functioning of the body? That is the core question for a biosociology of knowledge. The most fruitful way to obtain some relevant answers is through an increasingly close study of the working of the physiological mechanisms of the body in social contexts.

Recapitulating on the arguments so far, we began by a critique of those who would explain adult action on the basis of organic, 'biogrammatic' predispositions of man. We speculated that at some point man must have evolved what was called 'conceptual thought' and that this radically transformed his life to the extent that he came to live in a physical and mental world of his own (and his ancestors') construction. We saw what could legitimately be said about human physical and mental development from a biological standpoint. And then we mounted an answer to the 'naïve evolutionists' based on the sociology of knowledge but in a form modified by the acceptance of an organic development whose exact nature remains at the present time poorly understood. We noted the 'developmental' school of Piaget and the 'structuralist' school of Lévi-Strauss. Also we noted the emergence of a body of writers such as Bruner, Richards, Harré and others who are attacking this problem of the nature of the transition from infant–mother communication at birth to the fully developed, autonomously thinking later child and adult.

If we are to continue to try and achieve an ever more integrated understanding of how the mind and its concepts (i.e. knowledge) become actions, we need an ever-increasing understanding of the intermediary processes—we need to think in terms of currently non-existent borderline areas such as social physiology.† Of course it can be argued that such 'subjects' do not exist because they represent nothing: there is society and there is physiology and the two are separate. This book clearly disputes that argument and states its

---

† Cf. Mair (1975), who uses the same phrase in the context of face-to-face interaction.

opposite: that both in animals and man there is social physiology, although it works rather differently in the two cases.

Before continuing, let us bear in mind a distortion caused by the current state of knowledge in this field. In seeking for a social physiology, or for the biology of action, there is a danger which the present work faces of *reducing* human life to a series of autonomic or adrenal functions. This has not been my intention, yet inevitably such an impression may be left with the reader because the available evidence linking knowledge with action comes largely from studies in those areas. But one cannot be other than aware that to study a few physiological sub-systems is a travesty of the beautifully integrated working of the body as a whole.

Let us try and progress from the point reached so far. It seems that according to the world-construct of the individual, including his self-construct within it, so his nervous and other body systems will be more or less responsive to life-situations and in consequence he will become more or less susceptible to certain kinds of emotional upsets. Can we now put this into a social frame of reference?

Social anthropologists have pointed out that ritualized methods exist in most societies for dealing with life-crises and emotional difficulties: for example there are taboos and special forms of dress or self-denial for people in distress caused by death. Thus we can begin a thesis linking up the social rituals that accompany and mark life crises with the ability not only to cope psychologically with those crises but also to cope *physiologically*, i.e. to continue to function as a physiologically normal individual.† But how might such rituals work? If we look at them we often find that they give expression to or even demand quite extreme kinds of behaviour—loud weeping and wailing, plus waving of body and hands in socially accepted ways at the funeral itself, followed by a slow but rule-governed way back to normal living. The surrounding context is *public*, the community knows and sympathizes and there may be ritualized, even paid, co-wailers and mourners. The ceremonies of burial or cremation are attended by socially appointed, senior dignitaries, especially those who mediate the individual's contact with God or spirits of the after-life.

Why, we can ask, are such ceremonies designed to be *physically* as well as socially arousing? Is it that we have to deal with upsets in physiological processes and that advantages accrue to individuals who can handle these changes in socially accepted ways? For *some* rituals at least, something on these lines may be taking place. It is by the study of the mechanisms of action of the human body

† The same point is made by Chapple (1970, pp. 317–18).

in social contexts that we may be able to advance our understanding of these rituals and perhaps of other aspects of social structures. Conversely we can perhaps throw light on body functioning by looking at it in the context of the rule-bound, ritualizing events accompanying life-crises.

Apart from the more dramatic cases of physically arousing rituals, there is the whole question of the *raison d'être* of religious and magical beliefs and practices. Granted that in every case the explanation of the forms they take is to be found in the history of the society and its structures, we still can ask *why* they are there and, though perhaps changing over time, persist? Nadel (1954) and others have emphasized functional aspects of religions, but no one to date, as far as I know, has given them a thorough analysis as sanity-promoting institutions. We saw in Chapter 9 that men going into battle, and parents facing the loss of a child, were subject to less physiological upset if they had firm beliefs to account for their predicament than if not. Other data could be adduced. G. Jahoda, A. Harrison and E. Maple have all written about the part played by superstition in people's lives. Jahoda (1969) describes the fixed ritual order found in soldiers making their pre-battle preparations. They jealously guard those items of clothing and equipment associated with past escapes from danger, pinning on these and other inanimate objects hopes for their own invincibility. Among such people, and other groups such as footballers and fishermen, superstitions are legion (Harrison 1972). Maple (1971) generalizes as follows: 'every superstitious action is a clearly defined protective device to offset psychic attack and to attract influences that are favourable to life'. Jahoda (1969) writes 'where chance and circumstances are not fully controlled by knowledge, man is more likely to resort to magic'—i.e. superstition is relative to scientific knowledge. (In the above sense, 'knowledge' is opposed to 'superstition'. In the anthropologist's sense, and the sense in which the word is being used in the present context, knowledge is more inclusive, meaning all that passes for knowledge in a community.)

But just because firm belief structures have a calming effect on individuals at times of crisis, can we conceivably jump to an explanation of social institutions without falling into the pitfalls of biological or psychological reductionism and naïve functionalism that we have been accusing others of in Part I of this book? Is it not just as erroneous to say 'religions exist to calm human bodies by giving structure to their minds and answers to their dilemmas' as to say 'hierarchical structures exist to give vent to people's innate aggressiveness by providing it with legitimate outlets'? The two statements look similar, but I think they are in fact very different. The difference is that whereas the latter implies the existence of an inner force that must emerge and results in a social outcome by its emergence, the former implies no such one-way process. On the contrary, it is based on a sociogenic model, for it is only in the context of the norms and values prevailing in a society that the 'upsets' religion is supposed to 'calm' exist.

This is not to say that death is not physiologically upsetting in non-human species. I have observed a rhesus monkey with her dead infant, to which she clung for weeks until it was a mere scrap of skin (Reynolds 1962) and Jane Goodall (1967) has described the plight of an infant chimpanzee whose mother died. The case is that of Merlin. Though accompanied after his mother's death by his brother Pepe and his sister Miff, he became less mischievous, his growth was stunted, his interactions with peers were reduced, and he sat alone for long periods rocking from side to side. There is clearly a massive psycho-physiological upheaval in such cases. But the upset to which I refer is the upsetting of a specifically human world-view, an established comprehension, and this I take to be the uniquely human trauma with which religion and associated institutions have to deal. (Of course, that is not their sole, nor maybe their most important *raison d'être*. Durkheim and others have seen in religions a much more general function—the representation of the 'conscience collective'. We are looking here at one aspect only.)

Besides their calming relation to life-crises, religions may indeed *induce* fear as part of their 'programme'. I am thinking here of the awful threats of hell-fire in the world to come that were incorporated in medieval Christianity. Dante's *Inferno*, the ghastly scenes of Hieronymus Bosch, the sermons of doomsday clerics up and down the land, can hardly be described as 'calming'. In these cases what is happening is that religion is setting up a fear-inducing context alongside a conformist programme for avoiding it. Such is the nature of our social life that we invent for ourselves all kinds of imaginary evils and miseries together with the means, often very arduous, of avoiding them! Not just religion but all human social life is of this kind. It is because the norms of social life are taken by people as *givens* that they react to them, whether by conformity or deviance, in such powerful ways. Once their arbitrariness is grasped they lose their power, and the individual is 'free'. Once the 'implicit' becomes 'explicit' we see it for what it is—an idea, a construct in the minds of those around us that earlier on we shared.

But, in de Musset's words, *'qui s'élève, s'isole'*. The price for standing apart, for observing, for ceasing to be *engagé* is the very price of freedom—a falling apart of the security structures of the mind, a frightening look into the unknown. Those who have experienced this will know what I mean. One flees from it in horror, back to a world of meaning, any world rather than that abyss.

We have already seen some evidence pertaining to the function of beliefs in terms of psychological and physiological calming processes. A third line of evidence relates to causes of death. Comstock (1970), in a study on the relation of fatal arteriosclerotic heart disease in relation to water-hardness, collected data on the socio-economic and other personal characteristics of the individuals studied. For present purposes, it was an accidental finding of his that is of most interest:

> A surprising finding was the strong negative association of frequency of religious attendance with fatal arteriosclerotic heart disease. It is premature to speculate on the meaning of this association other than to note that it is obvious that regular church attenders differ in many ways from those who rarely or never go to church. It is also possible that church attendance may produce a favorable psychic or emotional response. Because frequency of attendance is an aspect of religious experience that is very easily determined, it is hoped that future investigations will include information on church attendance to confirm or deny its importance as a risk factor for arteriosclerotic heart disease. If confirmed, the implications of this finding raise intriguing questions for future research.

Following this finding he and a colleague made a special study of the relation between church attendance and health (Comstock and Partridge (1972). In a review of the literature they found a number of studies of relevance (For references to the various studies see Comstock and Partridge 1972.)

> In the field of mental health, religious attendance has been found to be positively correlated with personal adjustment in old age, and with reduced anxiety and apprehension about death ... Hypertension among Zulu women was most common among those who did not attend church frequently, while the opposite was true for men. In Zulu society, women were expected to attend church, while men who did so were considered peculiar ... Preliminary findings from the Israel Ischemic Heart Disease project indicated a two-fold increase in risk of first myocardial infarction among the non-religious vs. the very religious when religiosity was measured by frequency of attendance at the synagogue.

The findings of Comstock and Partridge (1972) in Washington County, made on a large sample, showed that if comparison was made between people who went to church once a week or more, and those who went less than once weekly, the second group had twice as high a death rate from arteriosclerotic heart disease, pulmonary emphysema, and suicide as the first group. For cirrhosis of the liver the second group had a relative risk of 3·9 as compared with the first group. For two kinds of cancer the two groups did not differ.

In the present context, the suicide and heart-disease differences are of interest. The authors are duly cautious in their own interpretations. They emphasize the need for closer investigation of dietary and life-style factors—smoking and drinking habits, for instance—and also the possibility that people who are sick will not be able to attend church frequently. But they add:

> Does this association [between church attendance and arteriosclerotic heart disease] merely reflect the 'good guy' or 'Leo Durocher syndrome' ('Nice guys finish last')? Is it related to the sense of identification with a supportive group? Are churchgoers likely to have Type B personalities? Or is the effect mediated through peace of mind and release of tensions? Recent studies on the effect of the mind on pulse and blood pressure make this last question more pertinent than it might have seemed some years ago [Comstock and Partridge 1972, p. 671.]

In the above, the reference to Type B personalities is to the work first reported by Friedman and Rosenman (1959) and subsequently widely followed up and confirmed. They first reported a high incidence of clinical coronary artery disease in a group of 83 men chosen as manifesting 'an intense, sustained drive for achievement, being continually involved in competition and deadlines' as against a much lower rate in 83 men who 'manifested the opposite sort of behavior'. The former group were the 'A' group, the latter the 'B' group.

The reference to 'recent studies on the effect of the mind on pulse and blood pressure' is to a paper by Dicara (1971); this relates to the work of Miller, Dicara and others already described (Chapter 9) on the voluntary control of the 'autonomic' functions. Recent work in this field has shown, for instance, that blood-pressure can be reduced both by instrumentation—the individual seeks to relax sufficiently to lower a tone produced by level of blood-pressure—or simply by the art of meditation.

Biological functions of knowledge

At the greatest level of generality, it seems possible that all knowledge—as we humans perceive or 'know' it and in so far as we incorporate it into our everyday thinking and everyday lives, arising out of our social world and derived from the thinking of our ancestors, mediated to us by our families, by educational institutions and by non-institutional contacts with others, validated and legitimated in various ways—serves to give us the wherewithal to keep not only our social but our physiological house in order. This neglected aspect is of great significance because that house can be in disorder and if it is so then not only do grave and distressing mental breakdowns occur for individuals but social life itself becomes distorted or ceases to exist.

Many consequences follow from this approach. What sociologists have called 'reification' of social forms and situations, i.e. the process by which the individual comes to believe in the reality and fixity of social forms, can be seen as a sanity-promoting process. 'Anomie', by contrast, in which there is a loss of contact between individuals and social forms, can be seen as a failure of knowledge to grip the individual in its vice, leaving him not defenceless but unable to cope and thus physiologically vulnerable and liable to 'depression' or some other labelled body condition in this well-ordered world, and eventually, as Durkheim (1952) described, to suicide.

This highly functionalist interpretation can also be turned on its head. The extent of orderliness of individual minds, and in consequence the orderliness of their whole physiological apparatus, can enable them to co-ordinate their activities and produce wonderfully well-ordered social systems such as armies or national sports teams. Such organizations are characterized by high 'morale', a high degree, that is, of psycho-physical integration both of and between members. But in such cases (as in armies in retreat or sports teams losing badly) there can be consequent disaster. Flexibility of the kind described by Bateson (1973, pp. 472–9) is doubtless best. This flexibility applies to whole cultures and civilizations as well as individuals and other biological systems. It is defined as 'uncommitted potentiality for change'—a kind of hidden reserve of resourcefulness with which to adapt to new conditions. But Bateson does not tell us anything of the mechanisms by which it is to be achieved; perhaps it is precisely the discovery of ways of inculcating the young with the array of ideas needed for adjustment to new circumstances that can lead to abilities in later life to cope with problems at the individual and social levels. As Fromm (1946), among others, has pointed out, modern man just cannot cope with his giant states and their lego-political machinery: he yearns to love yet finds himself hating; he seeks freedom yet finds himself in a uniform under orders; he eventually gives up and wants only to be told what to do, and finds that there are those who are only too ready to tell him.

Our concluding hypothesis is thus that knowledge enters the mind and gives 'contour' to the world, thus making physiological functioning smooth or erratic: belief enters to deal with physiological problems; certain rituals enter to establish points of controlled physiological release in difficult conditions. Lack of social controls seems in theory excellent, but individuals can fail to 'cope' and then, instead of releasing the necessary sympathetic and endocrine activity to deal with life-situations, people collapse and we 'sane' ones institutionalize them. Their adaptation or adjustment is no longer ours; we label them 'maladjusted' and give them therapy because their adjustment is inappropriate to social norms, yet it is their way of dealing with the strains of their particular lives.

The physiological 'problem' for a civilization such as ours, based on a competitive ethos underlying capitalism, is how to harness the body's physiological systems to the quest for ever more socially acceptable effort. To do this it is necessary firmly to implant a set of values and a knowledge system in the minds of individuals so that they will consistently act according to its dictates. Its enemy is the relapsing into apathy and those 'defences' that ensue from failure at the psychological and the physical levels to 'cope'. It fights this enemy by making us *expect* to work and making us feel *guilty* if we do not.

Theories of repression and liberation

This hypothesis is an alternative intended to replace the 'naïve' school of biologistic theories of society analysed in Part I. It is also seen as an alternative to the theory of civilization advanced by Freud in *Civilization and its Discontents* (1963), which was based on the notion that civilization proceeds by 'repressing' certain 'natural' 'pleasure-seeking drives' in the individual and by so doing (a) brings social order out of individual quests for pleasure, and (b) makes for unhappiness because of the loss of pleasure and freedom involved. The implications of this theory led Wilhelm Reich to break away from Freud because he did not approve of the efforts at therapy made by Freud to re-integrate people who had broken down, to return them into the society, because in turn he did not agree with the set of values that places repression over and above individual freedom or liberty. Instead he wanted to return to a libertarian, and finally in his later years, an orgasm-based society. Marcuse (1969, 1970, see also MacIntyre 1970) has worked with the same fundamental premises about civilization, although he has differed from Reich in important respects. He finds Reich's 'sweeping primitivism', especially his appeal for sexual liberation, too naïve, and points out that one can end up with 'repressive de-sublimation', i.e. a pseudo-libertarian, pseudo-permissive situation which is again just another form of repression (not 'you *must* sublimate your desires!' but 'you *must* liberate yourself!'). Some of the relevant points in this debate are discussed by Young (1974, pp. 250–3).

But Freud, Reich and Marcuse could be wrong in their basic premises. It is not just that there is not necessarily any such organic or neural 'id', 'ego' and 'super-ego' as the Freudian scheme calls for—a criticism often made. The critique presented here is more sweeping than that. It argues that the whole notion of repression v. libertarianism is a false way into the understanding of civilization. Instead it is argued that we need to think of a knowledge-producing/ knowledge-imbibing system which can and does lead to coherence of action, the intervening variable being the physiological mechanisms of the body that have the job of 'coping'. Mental breakdown is often failure to cope normatively with the social knowledge schemes and is a resort to independent adaptation to situational stresses—it is labelled deviant or maladjusted by those who are able to cope normatively, and institutions exist for the so-called 'failures'. For those who 'succeed' the social world is well provided with legitimate institutions—at work (offices, bureaucratic institutions, factories) and at leisure (pubs and clubs).

The 'problem' for any individual-achievement-based civilization or society is to *maintain* a system whereby people struggle to get ahead of each other, to legitimate ways in which they can do so and supply rationalizations for failure. The answers are normally to be found in their *educational systems*. Class-based educational systems, whereby sponsored mobility is made possible and sanctioned, arise at one end of the social spectrum; examination failure is utilized at the other; dialects, used as social devices perpetuated through upper- or lower-class educational establishments, are the road to the unequal society. Recent work in Britain has shown that by the age of 7 children are already well stratified with regard to reading ability, comprehension, or I.Q., and the reasons are partly to be found in the types of education offered by different schools and how these types relate to the mastery of socially relevant knowledge.

The other part of the answer is of course provided by the home background and its influence on children's achievement-orientation. This influence is often said, even, and indeed especially, by educationists, to exceed that of the school. Where the home negates, undervalues or even rejects as disadvantageous the achievement of good results in school terms, the child has a dilemma which it normally solves in favour of parental aspirations. A strong mediating agency here is the linguistic code in operation—if mastery of language just makes the parents laugh ironically, children can soon be brought to heel and their future as factory workers assured. Relevant studies have been made in the field of class differences in Britain, especially by John and Elizabeth Newson (1968*a*, *b*) and Basil Bernstein (1965), and some of the issues are discussed by Douglas (1964) and Floud, Halsey and Martin (1957).

Thus we can return to the starting point of the book only to find we have to some extent reversed the arguments presented there. We are now arguing against the idea that there is something within man's nature or 'biogrammar' that in some way structures his social dimensions. That may have been so up to the time when the species *Homo* first emerged, but now a very different and rather opposite situation prevails, namely that there is something in social structures and structures of thought that provides a more or less workable matrix for the physiology of the human nervous systems and the other systems of the body.

CHAPTER 15

The limits of flexibility

'As long as a man feels healthy and happy he tends to take his condition for granted. It does not occur to him that living is like a tightrope act—that there are infinitely more ways in which one can fail than the narrow road that leads to success.' (N. Tinbergen 1972, p. 385.)

'The nature of modern society imposes innumerable quantitatively and qualitatively new demands on human behavioural plasticity.' (G. A. Harrison 1973, p. 222.)

'The future evolutionary and ecological success of the species in the face of an ever-accelerating rate of environmental change, associated with growing urbanization and industrialization, will depend entirely on the extent to which cultural adaptation continues to be effective. The success of cultural adaptation, in turn, will depend on the level of understanding in society of the increasingly complex interactions between natural processes on the one hand and cultural processes on the other.' (S. V. Boyden 1972, p. 436.)

These three statements, and there are many others in the same vein, can serve to introduce an important corollary to the hypothesis with which we ended the last chapter. Even if a highly structured social thought-world provides the matrix for adequate social action and physiological functioning, this still does not tell us whether there might not be possible social conditions that were *un*workable, i.e. that did not permit of or bring about a coherent world-view and thus with which the body could not cope. Indeed, the very existence of people who cannot cope with the demands of everyday social life, and suffer mental and physical breakdowns in consequence, forces us to accept that our very own social system, for many of those born into it, is unworkable in just this way.

Natural selection in society
To admit this is to take a crucial step in the analysis here presented, for it means that the physiological house is not simply the dependent variable, adjusting itself to the social matrix, but has its own *limits of flexibility* beyond which it cannot be pushed without breaking down. This is not to say that there is any kind of predisposing 'bio-

grammar' of society. Nor is it to say that all individuals have equal limits: rather, the reverse is seen to be the case since only a proportion of us break under the social strain. In any case we would expect, judging from the mere fact of biological variation, that individuals would vary just as much in this respect as they do in others. Those who break down must be seen as among the victims of natural selection. For though society is a human construct, it is nevertheless, as we have seen, an outcome of evolutionary processes and a part of life and of nature (cf. Harrison 1973, p. 226).

These considerations lead us to see the biology of human action as part of a set of variables forming a *system*. It will be a system full of homeostatic mechanisms. A change in the social world, say a major economic change from an agricultural to an urban–commercial–industrial way of life, will upset and re-order the world of knowledge about how to live. The adjustment will involve not just the mind but the whole body. Studies in developing countries of newly urbanized ex-agriculturalists (e.g. Southall and Gutkind's *Townsmen in the Making* (1957)) show the great stresses on individuals of adjusting to a new life. Cut off from the family in a strange world with new and perplexing rules they often fail. The result can often be mental breakdown, or a retreat into alcoholism or other drugs. The body succumbs.

Of course not all changes are so far-reaching and yet even quite minor ones in comparison with the above can have equally or more far-reaching effects on individuals, altering their mental balance and their disease susceptibility. Rahe (1972) has developed a 'life-change' index, based on a study of naval personnel, which shows that sickness is more frequent in individuals who have had major changes in their social circumstances than in those who have not. Such circumstances were even quantified by Rahe with regard to their impact on health (see Table 15.1). Interesting though the findings of Rahe undoubtedly are for the present analysis, one cannot but be struck by the crudity of such an analysis. In particular we must note the absence of any intervening 'coping-ability' factor which, in actual life, would be the crucial variable determining whether or not any particular person was or was not physically upset by a life-change. The implication one might—quite falsely—draw from the index is that certain experiences have, for one and all, an impact that can be readily measured, quantified and even predicted. Certainly Rahe himself would not intend this. The 'count' figures in the index are average points relating to a particular all-male, all-military sample within a narrow age range, belonging to a particular culture at a given point in time. Other studies might, and doubtless would, show different counts for the same events, and of course different events could be scored and might be more relevant in other situations.

TABLE 15.1

Life event	Count
Death of spouse	100
Divorce	73
Marital separation	65
Jail term	63
Death of close family member	63
Personal injury or illness	53
Marriage	50
Fired at work	47
Marital reconciliation	45
Retirement	45
Change in health of family member	44
Pregnancy	40
Sex difficulties	39
Gain of new family member	39
Business merger, reorganization or bankruptcy	39
Change in financial state	38
Death of close friend	37
Change to different line of work	36
Change in number of arguments with spouse	35
Mortgage over £4000	31
Foreclosure of mortgage or loan	30
Change in responsibilities at work	29
Son or daughter leaving home	29
Trouble with in-laws	29
Outstanding personal achievement	28
Wife begins or stops work	26
Begin or end school	26
Change in living conditions	25
Revision of personal habits (dress, manners, etc.)	24
Trouble with boss	23
Change in work hours or conditions	20
Change in residence or school	20
Change in recreation or social activities	19
Mortgage or loan less than £4000	17
Change in sleeping or eating habits	16
Change in number of family get-togethers	15
Vacation	13
Christmas	12
Minor violations of the law	11

Again, the figures in Rahe's index are *averages*. They apply to that grey person—the composite man in the middle of everything. Such an individual has no real existence; he is a statistical construct. Real people have greater or lesser susceptibilities to life's upsets depending on psycho-physical constitution and cognitive coping ability. This may in fact be especially true of children and as a next step we can consider a puzzling and distressing phenomenon of great current psychiatric interest—the occurrence of what is called 'autism' in certain children. What is of interest here, apart from the actual nature and causes of the disease, are the arguments that have been used in explanations of autism.

The example of autism

The first major description of the autistic syndrome was that of Kanner (1943), who described 11 children who were characterized by an inability to relate themselves to other people, had problems acquiring speech, an excellent rote memory and an obsessive desire for maintenance of sameness. At first Kanner attributed this to an inborn disturbance of affective control; later (Kanner and Eisenberg 1955; Eisenberg and Kanner 1956) he placed greater emphasis on the emotional coldness and obsessive qualities that he saw in the parents, though maintaining the earlier view as well. Subsequently the psychogenic view has gained many adherents, especially as no organic deficiency or damage has been conclusively shown to exist. A recent list of symptoms, given by MacCulloch and Williams (1971) is as follows:

1. The U-shaped relationship between incidence and ordinal birth position (Wing 1966; Rutter 1967).
2. The high male to female ratio (Creak and Ini 1960).
3. Early onset (Kanner 1943; Rutter 1968b).
4. Wide inter-subject variation in intelligence (Mittler 1968).
5. Social withdrawal (Kanner 1943; Creak 1963).
6. Stereotypi (Rachman and Berger 1967).
7. Learning difficulties (Hermelin and O'Connor 1964, 1965 and 1967).
8. Abnormalities of sensory preference (Hermelin and O'Connor 1964).
9. Lack of dominant alpha rhythm in the EEG (Hutt *et al.* 1965; Creak and Pampiglione 1969).
10. Speech disorder (Rutter 1968a).
11. Abnormalities of auditory threshold (Creak 1961a; Wing 1966).
12. Evidence of neurological deficit including epilepsy in one-sixth of the children (Rutter *et al.* 1967; Creak and Pampiglione 1969).
13. Early and slight impairment of motor power and co-ordination (Rimland 1965; Wing 1966).
14. Significant spontaneous fluctuation in galvanic skin resistance activity (Angus 1970).

Ethologists, notably N. and E. Tinbergen (1972), have contributed to the search for understanding. N. Tinbergen, in his Nobel lecture given at Stockholm in 1973 (Tinbergen 1974), summarized his views as follows: †

> I can sum up in a few sentences the gist of what the ethological approach to early childhood autism has produced so far.
>
> 1) There are strong indications that many autists suffer primarily from an emotional disturbance, from a form of anxiety neurosis, which prevents or retards normal affiliation and subsequent socialization, and this in its turn hampers or suppresses the development of overt speech, of reading, of exploration, and of other learning processes, based on these three behaviors.
>
> 2) More often than has so far been assumed these aberrations are not due to either genetic abnormalities or to gross brain damage, but to early environmental influences. The majority of autists, as well as their parents, seem to be genuine victims of environmental stress. And our work on normal children has convinced us not only that this type of stress disease is actually on the increase in Western and Westernized countries, but also that very many children must be regarded as semi-autistic, and even more as being seriously at risk.
>
> 3) Those therapies that aim at the reduction of anxiety and at a restarting of proper socialization seem to be far more effective than, for instance, speech therapy per se and enforced social instruction, which seem to be at best symptom treatments, and to have only limited success. Time and again treatment at the emotional level has produced an explosive emergence of speech and other skills.

Against the reproach that he overlooks or pays insufficient attention to the organic side of autistic malfunctioning, Tinbergen defends himself in a footnote, as follows:

> Time and again we receive the comment that we overlook the 'hard' evidence of internal malfunctioning in autists as well as in other categories of the mentally ill. I assure my readers that we do not *overlook* such evidence (such as that on blood platelets, on lead contents, and on electroencephalogram patterns). The erroneous assumption underlying most of the arguments in which such facts are used for the purpose of throwing light on the causation of the behavioral deviation is almost invariably due to *the confusion between correlations and cause–effect relations*. With some exceptions (such as the deleterious effect of lead) the physiological or biochemical evidence is considered, without any ground whatsoever, to indicate causes, whereas the correlations found could just as well point to consequences or side effects. It is just as nonsensical to say that retarded bone growth, or abnormalities in the blood platelet picture (or for that matter speech defects, or high overall arousal), are causes of autism as it is to say that a high temperature is the cause of typhoid or pneumonia. Unless there is evidence, clinical and ultimately experimental, indicating what is cause and what is effect the opinions based on hard evidence are in fact worthless.

Towards the end of the lecture he says 'a little more attention to the body as a whole and to the unity of body and mind could substantially enrich the field of medical research'.

With Tinbergen's lecture I want to compare a very different approach to the explanation of autism, this time coming down on

---

† Reprinted from *Science*, **185**, 20–27. Copyright 1974 by the American Association for the Advancement of Science.

the side of brain damage as the main and original cause. M. J. Mac-Culloch and C. Williams (1971) reported their own findings on heart-rate variability in a group of 19 autistic children. Their basic finding was that while the mean heart-rate of these children was similar to that of normal children, there was 'a clear difference in the range of fluctuation of heart rate between the two samples' with the autistic children showing the greater fluctuation. Statistical analysis showed this difference to be highly significant ($p < 0.001$). Thus, in this study, heart-rate, often taken as a general measure of autonomic arousal, showed greater lability, a greater tendency to speed up and slow down, in the autists than in the normal children.

Reviewing the literature, MacCulloch and Williams eventually conclude as follows:

In our view the probability is infinitely small that any psycho-dynamic formulation of the causation of autism is correct. Instead a search must be made for organic pathology [p. 309].

We suggest that the abnormal cardiac rate variability described earlier is evidence of disordered nervous system control. The mean heart rates in the autistic and normal control groups are similar, which suggests a central imbalance probably mediated via the vagus nerve ... The central process of the visceral afferent pathways are known to alter heart rate ... We suggest that such damage is in part or wholly responsible for the phenomena displayed by at least a number of children who display the syndrome known as autism [pp. 310–11].

This damage, the authors think, most likely occurs during the birth process.

In the results of our current research at Oxford my colleagues and I have found some evidence in a small sample of autistic children that, compared with a normal control group, there is a significant difference in the variability of the excretion rate of the adrenal medullary hormone adrenalin, with greater variability in the autists. This variability is most apparent when the low night-resting values are compared with the higher day values, the autists showing a greater increase than the normal children (Helevuo, Reynolds and Carruthers 1975). In earlier work on the EEG patterns of autistic children, Hutt, Hutt, Lee and Ounsted (1965) found that 8 out of 10 autistic children 'had waking EEG rhythms characterized by low voltage irregular activity without any established rhythms' and suggested that such children suffered from a 'chronically high state of physiological arousal'. The irregularities were most characteristic of children showing stereotyped behaviour patterns. In addition, Hutt, Forrest and Richer (1975) have described a significantly greater extent of cardiac arrhythmia (variability of heart-rate) in autistic than in normal children, and have shown that this is greatest when the children are performing stereotyped behaviour patterns and least when they are involved in doing tasks. Stereotypies are most frequent when autistic children are failing at doing a task. Thus one can see that in some way both the physiological variability and the aberrant behaviour are the outcome of failure to 'cope'.

So, at the present time, we have a number of lines of circumstantial evidence. There is the suggestion that *external* environmental factors are involved, namely stress-inducing aspects of the wider society, the family, and the immediate context. There is the suggestion that the autistic child is, emotionally, in a state of chronic high arousal or anxiety. There is the evidence that the child's heart-rate, brain activity, and adrenalin output are unusually irregular. There is the suggestion that some physical insult at birth has caused brain damage. None of these lines of evidence entirely excludes the others—indeed, except for the last one the other three are highly compatible with each other. The fact that some autistic children can stage a recovery with suitable psycho-social treatment (Clancy and McBride 1969) tends to discount the brain-damage explanation unless it is seen as a reversible condition. It may, however, be true that some autists are brain-damaged; it is too early yet to say.

What can be learned from the example of autism? First, this does not seem to be a condition with a simple, uni-causal, basis just waiting to be discovered. We are forced not only to consider but to accept a wide variety of external environmental as well as inner psychological and physiological factors in the aetiology of this extremely distressing condition. Part of its great interest is the language impairment involved. Without adequate language there can be no adequate structuring of the environment. One individual who recovered from autism said that the worst thing about being autistic was that he never knew from one moment to the next what was going to happen. In other words, he was 'defending' all the time against the unfamiliar. This fear may well lie at the root of the physiological fluctuations described above, and help explain the compulsive sticking to routines characteristic of autists. Behaviourally, their isolation from others and retreat into solitude, with, in some cases, occasional aggressive outbursts, could likewise arise from anxiety about social relations. The Tinbergens' work and their ideas, together with those of others, and the physiological results described above, can all be integrated. If we have to pin-point a single original cause then it must be something that has *both* psychogenic and organic correlates, but the extent to which psychological 'insults' cause organic malfunction or vice versa could easily vary from case to case.

We can now leave the prolonged excursion into the nature and explanation of autism and return to our general theme. What remains to be done is to formulate a little more clearly the parts of the system described above and how they relate to one another.

Physiology in a social context

A recent paper by Kiritz and Moos (1974) has already made use of a very interesting model. Their paper is entitled 'Physiological effects of social environments' and in it they review much of the psychosomatic and other literature to which reference was made in Chapter 9. They are concerned with 'individual differences in defences and coping strategies' (p. 98), with the psychological conditions they refer to as 'support', 'cohesion' and 'involvement' as bases for effective physiological functioning. They also write about 'responsibility', 'Type A and Type B personality', and a phenomenon referred to as 'clarity': the quality of the psycho-social environment that determines whether future courses of action are clear-cut or doubtful and indeterminate. The effects of variations in all the above on physiological (mainly hormonal and autonomic) functioning are briefly described on the basis of the available evidence.

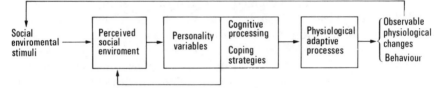

FIG. 15.1. Conceptual model for the relationship between social environmental stimuli and observable physiological changes. (Redrawn from Kiritz and Moos (1974).)

These authors go on to formulate a model, as shown in Fig. 15.1. Quite clearly this model has most of the features discussed in our own inquiry, and has been arrived at by consideration of largely the same empirical findings.

The authors' own comment on their model is as follows:

We believe that the social environment can be seen as a system of interpersonal stimuli exerting influences on the individuals within that environment. These influences or presses can be categorized as relationship dimensions, personal development dimensions, and system maintenance and system change dimensions. Although individuals are sufficiently similar and environmental stimuli sufficiently potent that the individuals within a given environment can make reliable and consistent judgements about the magnitude of a given dimension, the social stimuli do not act directly on the individual. Rather, it is his *perception* of the social environment, as mediated by personality variables, role and status relationships, and his behavior within the environment, which affects him directly, and in turn affects his personality and behavior [pp. 107–8].

The steps involved in the system they outline are thus:

(a) the conversion of an 'actual' social environment into a *perceived* social environment within the mind of the individual;
(b) the sorting or evaluation process in the individual mind, which, on the basis of prior inputs, organizes the perceptions and plans for action;
(c) consequent physical changes in body processes;
(d) action;
(e) changes in the 'actual' social environment brought about by action, leading back to (a) above.

Both the model and the focus of interest of Kiritz and Moos concern, in the main, inter-individual differences. The problem they face is how to explain different responses to common situations and common responses to different situations. The answer is given in the relations between the perceived world, the 'personality' and cognitive mind, and the reactions of the body. One can ask a number of questions of the model. For instance, what evidence is there of the existence as real independent entities of the 'personality variables'? Should not physiological changes feed back into the cognitive processing box (as individuals work things out, before acting)? But to ask these questions is not the immediate objective here, which is rather to search for ways of expressing the relation between human physiology and the social environment. Obviously, this has also been the objective of Kiritz and Moos.

To what extent are comparable processes of physiological adjustment involved in individuals' adaptations to new socio-economic circumstances? A recent study of a situation especially selected because of the occurrence of a major upset to a people's way of life is Lumsden's study of the Volta River Project in Ghana (Lumsden 1975). The constuction of the Akosombo Dam to create Lake Volta necessitated the resettlement of 80,000 people from 740 villages. They were rehoused away from their ancestral lands in a new type of dwelling, subject to an increased amount of government scrutiny and constraints. Lumsden's description of their upheaval indicates clearly the strategies developed by individuals in their efforts to cope with the new situations. No actual physiological data seem to have been collected, but Lumsden emphasizes their relevance for a deeper understanding of the process of a people's social and psychological adaptation to a major stress of this kind. His accompanying model (Fig. 15.2) summarizes the way in which he envisages the workings of the complex adaptive system involved in such a situation.

Clearly one important task is that of further 'culture shock' studies. But here we are concerned mainly with our own culture, which has been portrayed as one founded on competitive individual-

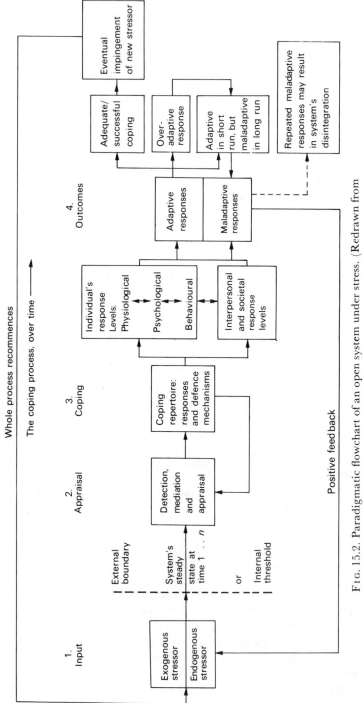

FIG. 15.2. Paradigmatic flowchart of an open system under stress. (Redrawn from Lumsden (1975). Copyright © 1975 by Hemisphere Publishing Corporation.)

ism. Within this structure of ideas the life-chances of individuals exist. During development we grasp or fail to grasp what is required in each situation to achieve the essential competence needed for conventional recognition and conventional success or conventional failure. Behind convention and its façades lies the no man's land of the eccentric. Behind that lies the area of social condemnation, fully equipped with institutions for those incompetents who have lost their way.

Let us return here to the dictum of Sartre: '*l'existence précède l'essence*'. How does such a statement, bound as it is to command respect, fit together with the findings of biology? Let us say for the moment that social structures, mediated by knowledge, coded in linguistic form, give structure and meaning to our lives and thus enable co-ordinated physiological functioning and psychological coping. Let us grant that where there is confusion of knowledge there is a retreat into defensive psychological reactions and excessive or inadequate physiological functioning with the possibility of exhaustion, either short- or long-term, at both levels. Let us add that society is equipped with services, institutions and personnel both to promote particular forms of approved action and to deal with those who fail to conform. Then what of Sartre's '*existence*'? In a very crucial sense, by '*existence*' Sartre does *not* mean social conformity but rather its opposite, individual choice and individual responsibility. As he makes abundantly clear, it is *not* the uncritical acceptance of social knowledge or socially sanctioned actions that constitutes humanistic or humanitarian '*existence*' but rather the choosing between alternative possibilities of action, conceived by each one of us in his or her own way.

Interestingly, for the present analysis, he uses the word '*angoisse*' over and over again to describe the state of mind involved in making these decisions. This 'anguish' is precisely the state of mind of the person who is for some reason striving to 'cope' in our functional sense. Sartre, seeing all the dangers of an unthinking conformist society, argues that individuals must confront their lives and decisions, daily, on first principles, with the aims of humanitarianism at the forefront of their minds, not the dictates of social norms. He expects us to tolerate the anguish of choice. He does not examine the mechanisms of action as we have done; he is not a biologist, but a moral philosopher.

What has the biologist to say about all this? Perhaps this: Sartre is right in principle in what he expects, but he is wrong in thinking that we have all got the mental and physical resources to draw on. If we had been brought up to work out our problems in this way all might be different. But most of us have been reared in starkly authoritarian, institution-oriented, conformist ways that have in the last analysis to do with the power structure of modern states. To go back to individual choice-making of the real kind advocated by Sartre must remain an object the means to which we can dimly perceive on the horizon but which, except for a few, must remain a distant prospect. There have been Schweitzer and Russell and Bonhoffer; there are Solzhenitsyn and a goodly number of lesser-known others who have succeeded in choosing according to the qualms of conscience and against the pressures of conformity. They might, in a better world, represent the seeds of social change; but against them in this one stands the formidable weaponry of bureaucracy and technology, uncontrolled by those who are caught up in it, moving forward through time by a giant, uncomprehending consensus.

Biology and social policy

In its apparent obsession with physiological mechanisms this book has focused on the need for new thinking about the *biological* impact of developments in modern society. Society imposes a great coping load, and pushes down those who fail. Yet we ourselves have constructed it. We have constructed those stresses by which we are now, in many cases, overwhelmed. It is our own creation that now creates and destroys us. Further discussions on this issue need to be *legitimated* by all available means if they are to achieve success. Individuals must be able to understand what their physical and mental well-being depends on and be encouraged to seek stability and coherence in their lives, whereas at present they are too often encouraged to forsake such things in the quest for 'success', or simply given no chance to achieve them. Enlightened governmental and educational policies must likewise revolve around improving the quality of life, rather than their current preoccupation with economic, political and military themes. There is much scope for social improvement and an enlightened biology has much to contribute, but only when we have got our priorities right. At present there is no legitimation behind any planning for a new 'relaxed' society in most post-industrial states. In the absence of such legitimation people cannot be blamed for looking after their own physiological and mental survival by adopting the strategies that, in an increasingly complex and difficult world, are advantageous for their own survival.

Doubtless there are good historical reasons for our preoccupation with economic viability, political strength, military preparedness. It would be foolish to blind oneself to these. But historical thinking is not necessarily the best thinking, or the only thinking. For our planning of the future and in the future we can, perhaps for the first time in history, begin to think in terms of ourselves as biological entities. We have already begun to realize that there are limits to the resources of our planet, as world shortages of food and raw materials have hit the treasuries of states and the pockets of individuals. We now need, in addition, to begin to ask questions about our own inner resources as human beings.

In the past we have tended to regard our inner resources as flexible enough to meet any social situation that could be contrived. And we have regarded our minds as capable of contriving anything. With that latter view there is no quarrel: one can conceive of anything. To take an example, David Cooper's book *Death of the Family* (1971) sketches a brave new world in which children are left to their own devices from the age of 6, people live in communes and cohabit with one another as and when they wish, people currently regarded as sane become the insane ones, and vice versa, law-enforcement agents are regarded as 'pigs', etc. The book, which begins as a critique of the tense, closed, schizogenic little families of modern times—a critique that has much to commend it—meanders into worlds of pure fantasy in its devastating attacks on modern society, and ends up largely destroying itself.

Still, one can ask: why not have a Cooperian society? If it would not work, why not? The answer must be in terms of psychological stresses, of the non-viability of the mind and the body in the world Cooper has portrayed. We need to aim not at freedom *from* rules but at freedom *within* rules, and we need to devise rules that are just and egalitarian to start with. Again we must stress the neutrality of biology with regard to the ethics of the rules and structures of society. Biology must not be used as a validation for unjust rule systems: health is not worth so high a price. But within a just society efforts can and should now be made to bring our increasingly sophisticated knowledge of the body and its functioning into the planning of life-styles, settlement patterns, arrangements for residence and work, the demands of work as against the rights and needs of families, especially children, to share their parents' time and lives. True biological health and well-being depend on an adequate reconciliation of many different factors and we need to think long and hard about these, both as individuals planning our own lives and as governmental agencies responsible for national welfare and the planning of national growth.

Sweden seems to be ahead of most countries in planning for a better future. In Sweden representatives of the government, the trades unions, and the scientific community can and do meet together and discuss future developments in their country, bringing into line both the needs of individuals for a fair quality of home life, the needs of industry for consistent, high-quality production, the needs of working men for improved factory conditions, and the resultant obligations of government agencies in the fields of health, welfare and education. Sweden's prosperity is neither entirely fortuitous nor a result of historical antecedents but very largely a result of rational planning and co-operation, including co-operation with psychologists and physiologists. Again, it is no accident that much of the most socially relevant biological research reported earlier in Chapter 9 was done in Sweden, for it has been there that such research has been policy-orientated whereas elsewhere it has, by comparison, lacked direction.

Let us take a slightly closer look at the kind of thinking we are advocating here. In a contribution to the United Nations conference on the Human Environment, Stockholm 1971, Drs. Gösta Carlestam and Lennart Levi prepared a report on psycho-social stress factors which can occur in urban conglomerates. The thinking in this report was based on the theoretical model propounded in earlier work reported in *Society, Stress and Disease* (Levi 1971) and discussed in Chapter 9. We are not concerned here with the substantive documentation of the evidence for disease resulting from urban stress so much as the results of this kind of thinking in policy formulation. They conclude that in cases where there is some suspicion of detrimental effects on health or well-being resulting from urbanization, planning and building should be accompanied by research so as to evaluate the physical and mental effects on those who subsequently occupy the buildings concerned. 'This has a scientific and a social purpose. The former is to establish knowledge. The social purpose is to protect individuals from danger, and the community (and other communities) from unnecessary expense.' In this latter respect, if for no other reason, the policy should appeal to ministers and others who can act to bring a biological awareness into future planning!

It seemed necessary to mention the matter of biology and social policy simply because it is crucial to future developments in the field: without an awareness of its significance, the research needed will not be envisaged, research proposals will not be formulated, research will not be financed, and the relevant knowledge will not be forthcoming. However, this book is not a policy document but has had an academic aim: to explore and establish the true nature of the links between social phenomena and biological functioning. The emphasis on which we have ended is one of mechanisms: biological mechanisms that respond to and feed back to social actions, via the intervening variable of conceptual thought. We have ended, too, by concluding that our own society is, for some (perhaps many) individuals, an unpleasant or even non-viable environment and in answering the question of why this should be so we have become involved in the nature of *limitations* to the human being's capacity to adjust to prevailing social conditions.

Future research

With regard to the extent of these limitations, research is still at an early stage. We know of the breakdown of mental competence, the relation of neuro-endocrine mechanisms to psycho-social stress, and the existence of metabolic pathways linking the sedentary/high-stress life-style, and its accompanying dietary and personality components, with early death from heart disease. What other limitations can already be described and to what extent can they be documented?

Marianne Frankenhaeuser (1974) has written about some of these, and has discussed the 'tolerance limits' of man in modern society. One such limit she saw as resulting from over-stimulation in relation to the rate of change of the surrounding environment:

The cumulative effects of repeated adjustment to new life conditions may manifest themselves in lowered resistance to somatic diseases and in severely upsetting changes in the individual's norm system . . . Another example of the risks due to over-stimulation involves our reactions to the information flow [cf. Lipowski 1973]. Man's ability to receive and handle information is much more limited than one would generally imagine. Experimental studies of decision-making show that increasing the number of information units tends to impair the ability to reach a decision.

This effect she calls 'cognitive saturation', and she points out the increasing danger of this effect with the current increase in communications technology. Another limitation she sees is on emotional reactivity: 'emotional saturation . . . may supervene whenever great demands are imposed on our capacity for emotional involvement', and she writes as follows:

In the long run, perhaps the gravest consequence of straining human tolerance lies on the emotional level, in the process of habituation which is our most effective means of coping with overstimulation. When we are bombarded with excessively many, excessively strong or all too frequent stimuli, the response of the nervous system gradually weakens—the stimuli lose their impact and the reactions are toned down. The physiological stress effects become less intense and feelings of aversion and discomfort fade. But so do feelings such as involvement, understanding, consideration and sympathy. This attrition of feeling comes about stealthily, without warning signals, because the mechanism of habituation involves a blunting of emotions, a reduction of sensitivity and reactivity. Consequently overstimulation may form part of a general process towards passivity.

One seems in these words to hear echoes of Fromm's complaint about the weakness of the modern personality and its willingness to be led (Fromm 1946). One also hears echoes of Lorenz's complaint about the lily-livered character of modern youth (Lorenz 1970). Is Frankenhaeuser closer to the realities of what is going on than the psychiatrist or the ethologist? Her data are certainly 'harder' in that she has measured the 'physiological stress effects' in terms of bio-chemical substances. This would seem to be a distinct advantage from the scientific point of view over the largely psychoanalytic inter-pretations of Lorenz. Despite the latter's occasional appeals to the hypothalamus, much of his interpretation of the modern condition is phrased in terms of a wholly notional 'pleasure–displeasure equi-librium', which is thrown off balance because of a lack of obstacles to overcome (see Appendix 1). The physiology of this equilibrium is never described by Lorenz and we are left in the dark about it. But there is, besides this lack of detail on Lorenz's part, a serious difference between him and Frankenhaeuser or Lipowski (see below) with regard to the causation of the human unresponsiveness they all describe. In Lorenz's view this is caused by a *lack of goals*, but in the view of Frankenhaeuser and Lipowski it is caused by cognitive *saturation*, i.e. *too much* input. Whether and how these two aspects are related remains to be elucidated by further study, but it seems quite possible that the latter might lead to the former.

With regard to Lipowski's ideas, mentioned above, Franken-haeuser (1974) summarizes as follows:

In an attempt to integrate data from empirical studies and draw a complete picture of the causes and effects of overstimulation, Lipowski [1971] has proposed a theory of surfeit stress. The central thesis is that a highly technological society presents a surfeit of attractive offers to consume. Commercial forces, advertising and mass media interact to build up expectations and demands in all areas of human endeavour. The consumer is offered a multitude of material and symbolic objects, e.g. educational facilities, leisure activities, travel, social contacts and life styles. The pressure to consume harmonizes with and is reinforced by the general ideology of growth and achievement. Seizing as many chances as possible, utilizing every oppor-tunity, is made to seem exemplary and desirable.

Inherent restrictions, financial limits and lack of time prevent people from exploit-ing more than part of the supply. Different groups in society are affected in different ways. The poor are exposed to the same offers as the rich, but their freedom of choice is severely circumscribed. Being excluded from the possibilities presented so stridently may generate feelings of impotence, failure or anger.

The well situated face a purely psychological problem, a choice between equally attractive but mutually exclusive alternatives. Those who cannot cope with the 'de-cision stress' find themselves in the position of Buridan's ass between two piles of hay. It is suggested that this theory may help to explain manifestations of discontent, apathy, flight from reality and violence in the affluent society.

Again, this seems a useful synthesis of the ideas, already examined, of cognitive saturation and the prevailing ethos of the consumption-oriented society.

What then are we to conclude about human limitations? First, a primary conclusion, that such limitations as may exist are limitations on the extent to which man can cope with social forms and inputs he has himself devised and set in motion. Such limitations, being essentially biological in nature, must ultimately be grounded in our genetic make-up, even if very remotely, since all our organic aspects are so grounded. This is clearly not to accept that biological predispositions shape our social actions—the argument criticized in Part I. It is to argue that *our social forms and structures, the world of ideas and its technological outgrowths, that we have created as an environment to live in, can get the better of us*, and the limitations of which we speak are the limits of the flexibility of the mental and physical machinery within each one of us.

Being variable, as all life is, from one to another we each have our tolerance limits—and thresholds of response—to environmental inputs. Some of us are highly responsive to noise, or emotional upset, or information input: our level of coping is rapidly reached and we pass rapidly into defensive strategies and perhaps, if these fail, into one or another kind of nervous breakdown or physiological pathology or both. Behind these individual differences lie our different rearing and socialization patterns and behind these our organic constitution and, behind these again, our genetic potentials. But this is not an echo of Ardrey, for in the present analysis there is no assumption that individuals with greater genetic potentials achieve or maintain higher status than those with lesser ones.

Thus we can end this effort at a synthesis of biological functioning and sociological context. The structure that we have built is of a man whose body and mind are inseparable and both locked within society. We have explored some of the ways in which the three are interdependent. Perhaps, if anything, one is impressed with the vast extent of our ignorance in this important field. There are so few well-documented studies to draw on in which the three necessary dimensions are included. But data of relevance to our theme are in far greater abundance than they were a decade ago. It is to be hoped that there will be more research on the impact of society on the human organism in the near future so that we can see what we are doing to ourselves, how we are doing it, and eventually develop a more sophisticated and better-documented biology of human action.

CHAPTER 16

Summary, conclusions, and a look ahead

BRIEF SUMMARIES of each part of the book and how it relates to the whole have been presented at the beginning of each part. I shall now look back over the book as a whole. In doing so I am painfully aware of its imperfections, but nevertheless some progress has hopefully been made in resolving the initial problem.

This problem was set out in the Introduction. It was the problem of how to determine the causes of human actions and the forms of human social institutions. There seemed to be two major contenders for the explanation: the 'culture–history' school and the 'evolutionary biology' school. Each school acknowledged the existence of the other and to greater or lesser extent accepted the validity of its findings, but gave prior causal status to explanations couched in its own terms. The object of this book was to examine carefully the claims of one of these, the latter; hence the book's title. I have not intended to examine the claims of the former, nor am I competent to do so.

The first part of the book was, then, a critical analysis of what have been called 'strong' theories: theories of biological determinism of human action and human society. These were found to fall short of credibility in a number of respects. Where they relied on man–animal comparisons it was never conclusively shown that such comparisons provided valid evidence of homologous processes in animals and man. Indeed, because of the invariably overlooked Weberian distinction between animal *behaviour* and human *action* it seemed quite unlikely that a truly comparable causal process underlay human and non-human social interaction (except perhaps in the case of human infants, who in many respects could still be said to 'behave'). Other problems with the 'strong' theories concerned the use of motivational terms such as 'aggression' or 'sex': the entire project of establishing whether such elementary and seemingly essential categories for the discussion of human and non-human activities were in fact applicable across the divide, and what the implications of using them for man and animals actually were, was omitted by the authors in question. They therefore fell into a variety of semantic traps left lying around by the language. Such problems, incidentally, remain largely unstudied even now, though a few starts have been made, e.g. Callan (1970). Ardener (1973) has made a fascinating and highly relevant analysis of the word 'behaviour' itself and has begun to pull back the heavy door of language that shuts off, for most of us, the unknown events behind our conventional categories and structures of thought.

We then left the land of 'strong' theories, concluding it was something of a metaphorical dream-world of easy explanations. In Part II an effort was made to draw an outline of a particular change that has occurred in the course of human evolution, the change from a signal-based social communication system, heavily pre-programmed by heredity and leading in most cases to a rather limited number of possible social structures, to a breakthrough occasioned by the evolution of conceptual thought, from which there arose all sorts of new possibilities: linguistic communication based on arbitrary symbols, definitions of social relationships, evaluations and prescriptions of ongoing social processes, non-hereditary transmission of information from generation to generation. The outcome of these changes was the emergence of cultures acting as screens between man and the environment: man saw, and still sees, only what his conceptual world allows him to see—the version of reality that his culture (to be more precise the part of it he encounters) displays to him. But of course cultures are human products and so we see only what our ancestors have produced; at the same time by acting out our lives we re-affirm and re-create the past as the present and offer it as reality to our children and the future in general. Novelty enters as a result of culture-contact, discovery, inventiveness, and changes in the surrounding non-social environment. Part II offered, then, a perspective on human affairs that would make it difficult to accept more than a minor element of 'strong' evolutionary determinism in the causation of human actions, interactions or social forms.

But a problem remained: had the baby been lost with the bathwater? Was it not still as true as ever that man is composed of flesh and blood? Even if they were not directly relevant to the causation of action, was one justified in forgetting all about the body? Might there not be senses in which the organic side of man, closely programmed by our genetic inheritance and its physical developmental environment, might set limits to what cultures can achieve, or give form to what they provide? What is a culture without actual people? Why are cultures *there*? What is it cultures have to work on?

A naïve question perhaps, but one which nevertheless crops up in some of the most erudite writings of our time. Take, for instance, Timpanaro's (1974) formulation of it in his *Considerations on Materialism*:

The historicist polemic against 'man in general', which is completely correct as long as it denies that certain historical and social forms such as private property or class divisions are inherent in humanity in general, errs when it overlooks the fact that man as a biological being, endowed with a certain (not unlimited) adaptability to his external environment, and with certain impulses towards activity and the pursuit of happiness, subject to old age and death, is not an abstract construction, nor one of our prehistoric ancestors, a species of pithecanthropus now superseded by historical and social man, but still exists in each of us and in all probability will still exist in the future. It is certainly true that the development of society changes man's ways of feeling pain, pleasure and other elementary psycho-physical reactions, and that there is hardly anything that is 'purely natural' left in contemporary man, that has not been enriched and remoulded by the social and cultural environment. But the general aspects of the 'human condition' still remain, and the specific characteristics introduced into it by the various forms of associated life have not been such as to overthrow them completely. To maintain that, since the 'biological' is always presented to us as mediated by the 'social', the 'biological' is nothing and the 'social' is everything would . . . be idealist sophistry. If we make it ours, how are we to defend ourselves from those who will in turn maintain that, since all reality (including economic and social reality) is knowable only through language (or through the thinking mind), language (or the thinking mind) is the sole reality, and all the rest is abstraction?

. . . Humanity is not made up of individuals who are all equal in psycho-physical constitution, differentiated only by the social environment in which they happen to find themselves. As well as differences in socio-cultural formation (differences which should in turn be translatable into determinate 'acquired characteristics' of the brain and nervous system), 'constitutional differences' derived from a multiplicity of other biological factors come into play [Timpanaro 1974, pp. 15–16].

It is a problem that reproaches us the more we wander into the wilderness of political or economic theory, the more we philosophize about forms of society or the nature of liberty. A man may avoid contemplating others as flesh and blood and regard them as the purest and most unrestrained spirit, but others will in various ways redress the balance and emphasize the flesh. But how, in any meaningful scientific sense, are flesh and spirit to be reconciled? There is no holistic science of man. Instead there are many human sciences. There are human palaeontology, human genetics, human evolution, physical anthropology, social anthropology, sociology, social psychology, experimental psychology, human geography, ethnology, archaeology, not to mention the study of history, linguistics, politics and so on. What, in such circumstances, is a holistic approach to the study of man going to look like?

It was because of the almost universal neglect of human biology in the study of action that I thought Part III necessary to this book. Having saved the baby it was necessary at the outset to give it a thorough physical examination. What were its properties as an organic body developing through time? What kinds of information were available concerning these properties and how could such information be integrated into a theory of action? Much remains to be done in this latter respect, but it seems clear that progress towards scientific understanding of the mind–body problem, which is at the root of the action–behaviour problem and the man–animal problem, must include more than a passing reference to our knowledge about the human body and its physical properties. The problem raised by Timpanaro was in no sense solved or answered by him, but just left in the air.

Part III was thus a series of first steps in the biology of man, but a series chosen to emphasize the developmental process. There was no intention to make a systematic survey of all aspects of human anatomy and physiology—such would have been ridiculous. Rather, I wanted to look at certain features of man developing from his first genetic beginnings, through the highly programmed stages of embryonic life, into childhood and adolescence and finally maturity. A dynamic, forwards-moving approach was adopted because it seemed the only one appropriate to the general theme of the book. A piecemeal or functional approach such as most anatomy books provide would not have helped. But hopefully, by seeing the human organism as a constantly changing entity, expressing at all times the interplay of its inner programmes with their environments, something was done towards providing a backcloth for the data and arguments that followed in later sections of the book. Much, however, remains to be thought out *from scratch* before an integrated picture of human physical development will emerge.

What were the major points that arose in Part III? First, perhaps, the awe-inspiring biochemistry of the 'genetic code', simple in its outlines yet complex in its outcome. This led to the point that each individual person must be organically unique, a point validated by subsequent biochemical work on adults. The uniqueness of individuals led in two directions. First, it was clear that uniqueness had its limits, beyond which the organism was not viable. Secondly, we saw that, developmentally, the uniqueness of individuals consisted of a carefully patterned genetic–environmental interaction, complex biochemical substances seeking out matching partners, derived either from other genetic sources or from metabolism of dietary elements or environmental inputs of other sorts.

From birth on we traced the growth of the body in gross terms such as height and weight changes, and bone and tooth development. The conclusion was that individual development was all of a piece, that individuals whose 'developmental age' was advanced relative to their chronological age tended to mature earlier in all respects. Looking next at the factors underlying growth rates, it became clear that diet was especially relevant, as also were family size and income, hygiene and medical care, judging from both small-scale studies and major cross-sectional studies illustrating the so-called 'secular trend'.

We examined some of the morphological and developmental events of puberty, adolescence and adult sexuality. For each physically normal individual puberty is marked by a set of changes in growth rates besides the better-known changes in hormone secretions and the sexual developments associated with these. Within a fairly broad band of individual variation the body follows a pattern distinctive of the sex that is written chromosomally in the nucleus of every body cell. With sex development after birth, it became essential to think in terms of *gender* rather than sex in the explanation of all the developments that had to do with action and not just physical appearance. This raised the interesting problem of the determination of action in individuals who were chromosomally abnormal and/or physically abnormal in their sex characteristics. The examples given provided a demonstration of the interplay of inner predispositions modified and interpreted by the individuals concerned in the light of prevailing notions of gender roles. These cases provided some of the best examples available of the results of the continuous interaction of organic and cultural forces in the causation of action. They demanded a closer look at other studies of psycho-social development.

In the final chapter of Part III we attempted to get a closer look, by focusing on our physiology rather than our evolutionary or genetic biology, at evidence for the role of thought in relation to individual reactivity. We did this through an analysis of the 'emotions'. We still do not know what these entities truly are, but it seems clear that they can be measured in terms of autonomic functioning, responding (in the case of man) not so much to external stimuli but to internal representations and interpretations of external stimuli. Thus the body can be shown to accelerate and reduce its nervous and hormonal functions in response to subjective interpretations of particular experimental and real-life situations, and we looked at some of the evidence bearing on this point, both in terms of brain and body mechanisms.

Part IV focused on social development. As in the previous section on physical aspects, a developmental approach was felt most appropriate in order to illustrate the interplay between organic and cultural forces in the determination of action. In the broadest sense all human development can be thought of as 'social', simply because it all takes place in a social context. In this part, however, we confined our attention to a narrower field, or rather to a particular selection of what seemed the most significant areas in the discussion of action.

First we examined the early interactions of infant and mother, in terms of a communication system in which each party brings a certain impact to bear on the other. The newborn infant cries, the mother picks him up and holds him to her, he roots innately for the nipple and she helps him find it, he sucks vigorously and if all goes well he drinks himself into a somnolent state and falls asleep. But some infants are hard to satisfy and some mothers, whether for physical or psychological reasons, have difficulty holding and breast-feeding, or even bottle-feeding and caring for their babies. Each relationship takes its own individual path and is in some respects unique.

Then we looked at peer interactions. The child, now a cultural, thinking individual, meets others with their own particular and unknown social backgrounds, in some kind of institutional setting such as home, nursery, park or school. Adults are around, guarding against accidents by imposing norms with a variety of sanctions, also monitoring social interactions with different attitudes and responses to different kinds of play.

From the observational level—the description of ongoing events between infants and mothers and between children and their peers—we then delved into the question of mental development. We examined Piaget's ideas concerning the evidence that there exist distinct stages of cognitive growth (pre-operational representations, concrete operational representations and finally propositional representations) and we looked at other ideas, some relatively new, concerning the nature and processes of cognitive development. In so doing, the object was not so much to discover the 'facts of the matter' of cognitive growth processes—an impossible task in a field which is currently undergoing intensive research and will doubtless in future lead to many new findings. Our interest was rather in the grasping of the essential idea that there *is* a cognitive process, that the mental world in which we live, stressed so often in so many places in this book, is put together in an exceedingly slow, regular and complex way. Even if the details of how this is achieved are still by no means clear we need nevertheless to appreciate that the world of objects and relations between objects in which we live is the result of a gradual build-up by accretion and re-formulation of successive layers of interpreted experience. This gives *it* coherence, but equally it gives *us* coherence.

Finally, In Part V, an effort was made to see man as a biological entity in a cultural context. The context chosen was that of ourselves—people living in modern 'Western' industrial societies, among whom the vast majority of relevant research has been carried out. The change of emphasis from the preceding chapter at the end of Part IV was as follows. There it was sufficient to show how the structure of meanings in individuals' minds was slowly and laboriously achieved during childhood. Here we were beginning to move away from the individual to the societal level, and this raised interesting questions about the relation of physiology to knowledge. Physiological mechanisms can in certain ways show us the relation of individuals' knowledge to their actions. Knowledge, however, is part of society. Society is the provider of the structure of knowledge that individuals draw from in deriving their ideas for action. *Our* society's knowledge is derived from *its* history and is deeply imbued with ideas of competition and achievement. Thus we developed the idea of the biosociology of knowledge: the idea of social knowledge as the matrix for biological functioning.

So we returned to the book's initial question, to the problem that preoccupied in particular Konrad Lorenz but also to greater or lesser extent the other authors reviewed in Part I: how to formulate a biology of social action. We rejected their explanations in terms of biological *predispositions* because (a) they were unprovable, (b) the study of human biology had not convincingly demonstrated them, (c) the study of psychology and the findings of social anthropology and sociology lent them no real support.

Instead we came down on the side of biological *limitations*. The human body is a highly flexible and adaptable system. But it has limits. In some respects it has narrow limits—in its ability to adjust to high temperature and/or water shortage, for example. But in other respects its limits are extremely wide, and this includes the ability to incorporate different social arrangements, accept them as normal, and live by them. We rejected the idea that the body could impose patterns on the social institutions and structures of society. That was putting the cart before the horse. On the contrary, the structures of society, mediated to the individual through language and thought, were seen to impose patterns on the biology of the individual, by subjecting him to characteristic physiological stresses and strains.

Much of what was posited towards the end of the final chapter lies at the forefront of modern psychosomatic research. These are the new directions research is beginning to take in the study of the biology of human action. There is no longer a one-way determinist viewpoint: a systems approach is beginning to prevail. The mind : body dichotomy, so deeply entrenched for so long, so central in the work of philosophers such as Kant, will ultimately vanish as an outmoded dichotomy, and become a pair of logical oppositions instead ('mind' is to 'body' as 'island' is to 'water'). Biologists concerned with human existence in the round will no longer need to adopt an organic-determinist position in which 'mind' is largely written off as an epiphenomenon, but will feel free to incorporate the mind and its structure of ideas as a vital part of the system that makes up every human being.

For such a perspective to emerge and become universal a much closer *rapprochement* will be needed than exists at the present time between the biological and the social sciences. This is not to argue against specialization, for it is only by specialized research that new knowledge comes into being. But it is an argument against the compartmentalization of knowledge, against the all-too-often closedness of academic departments and faculties, and the suspicion and hostility that tend to characterize their relationships.

This book is not, however, about the structure of the knowledge industry. It is about the very real place of biology in the understanding of the human condition and about the equally real place of all studies that emphasize conceptual awareness and the structure of thought in the control of body processes. The importance of such studies is twofold. On the one hand, in terms of individual well-being, health and the quality of life, we in the 'Western' post-industrial world need to understand these things if we are to thrive and lead satisfying lives. Secondly, we need, with the help of governing agencies, trades unions and others, to reform our society, to re-think its order of priorities. We need to legitimate more co-operative and relaxed ways of living. The competitive ethic today runs right through from primary school to the international struggle for maximum *per capita* production. The losses in terms of human health, happiness and dignity are incalculable. Given our resourcefulness something better should surely be possible. For present purposes, though, it will have been enough if it has been shown that our society, its strengths and its aberrations, is not the outcome of biological predispositions lurking within us, but that, given our biology, much can be done and should still be done in the social world, and not only the material one, to increase the sum total of human health and well-being.

APPENDIX 1 : Quotations from Konrad Lorenz's *The Enmity between Generations*†

From Section 7, 'The disequilibrium of pleasure–displeasure economy'

I begin with the description of some symptoms which I believe to be caused by the disturbance of pleasure–displeasure equilibrium. Perhaps the most telling of these symptoms is the *urge for instant gratification* [p. 394].

Although it is not clear which is cause and which is effect, there is certainly a close connection between the current loss of patience and a general *inability to endure any kind of pain or displeasure.* [p. 394]

A third symptom, closely allied to the two already mentioned, is a general *unwillingness to move* [p. 394]

It was Kurt Hahn who called attention to the disquieting fact that this type of physical laziness is very often correlated with an accompanying *sluggishness of emotion.* A weakness of ability to feel *compassion* is, according to the great expert, a frequent concomitant of the typical laziness of blasé adolescents [p. 395].

The inability to wait, the inability to bear displeasure, the unwillingness to move and the weakness of compassionate emotion are all caused by a disturbance of the mechanism achieving the balanced equilibrium of pleasure–displeasure–economy [p. 397].

The normal rhythm of eating with enjoyment, after having got really hungry, the enjoyment of any consummation after having strenuously striven for it, the joy in achieving success after toiling for it in near-despair, in short the whole glorious amplitude of the waves of human emotion, all that makes life worth living, is dampened down to a hardly perceptible oscillation between hardly perceptible tiny displeasures and pleasures. The result is an immeasurable *boredom.*

If you have eyes to see, you will perceive this boredom in a truly frightening multitude of young faces. Have you ever watched young people courting, kissing, petting and all-but-copulating in public? You need not be a peeping Tom to do it, you cannot help observing if you walk in the evening through Hyde Park or ride on the Underground in London. In these unfortunates, the fire of love and the thrill of sex are toned-down to the intensity of emotion to be observed in a pampered baby half-disgustedly sucking an unwanted lollipop. The bored juvenile is in a particular hell of his own, he must be an object of sincere pity and we must

† Grateful acknowledgement is made to Professor Lorenz for permission to reprint these extracts.

not be deterred from our commiseration by the fact that he hates us more than anything in the world [p. 400].

To sum up: the cause of the symptoms hitherto discussed is, at least to a great part, to be found in the fact that the mechanisms equilibrating pleasure and displeasure are thrown off balance because civilized man lacks obstacles which force him to accept a healthy amount of painful, toilsome displeasure or alternatively perish.

From Section 8, 'Disequilibration of mechanisms preserving and adapting culture'
If only in parenthesis, I must here mention an old hypothesis of mine which contends that some of the phenomena under discussion have a *genetic* basis. In all these alarming symptoms I cannot help feeling a strong undercurrent of *infantilism*. Diligence, long-term striving for future goals, patient bearing up with hard labour, the courage to take the responsibility for calculated risk and, above all, the faculty of compassion are all characteristic of the *adult*, in fact they are so uncharacteristic of children that, in them, we all are gladly ready to condone their absence.

We know from the work of Bolck and others that man owes some of his specifically human properties to what he has called 'retardation', in terms of common biological parlance to neoteny. In my contribution to Heberer's book on evolution, I myself have tried to show that this permanent retention of infantile characters in man has its parallel in many domesticated animals, also that one of these characters retained, infantile *curiosity*, has been one of the essential prerequisites for the genesis of man. I have a shrewd suspicion that mankind has to pay for this gift of heaven by incurring the danger that a further process of progressive self-domestication might procedure [*sic*; is 'produce' meant?] a type of man whose genetic constitution renders him incapable of full maturation and who, therefore, plays the same role in the context of human society which immature cells, by their infiltrating proliferation, play in the organization of the body. It is a nightmare to think that disintegration of society may be caused by the genetic disintegration of its elements, because education, which is our hope otherwise, would be powerless against it [p. 404].

Still I believe that the bulk of the disintegration phenomena here under discussion are 'only' cultural. A culture, however, is nothing but a living system and a highly complicated and vulnerable one at that! [p. 405].

The essence of the disturbance indubitably lies in the fact that the process of *identification* by which the younger generation normally accepts and makes its own the greatest part of the rites and norms of social behaviour characteristic of the older, is seriously impeded or entirely obstructed [p. 406].

However, it must be emphasized that this failure to identify with the social norms of the parental culture is the direct cause of truly pathological phenomena. The urge to embrace some sort of cause, to pledge allegiance to some sort of ideal, in short to *belong* to some sort of human group, is as strong as that of any other instinct. Like any other creature which, under the imperative drive of an instinct, cannot find its adequate object, the deracinated adolescent searches for and invariably finds a *substitute object* [pp. 406–7].

The Hamburg rockers who declare open war on older people, represent the most clear-cut paradigm, but even the most emphatically non-violent groups are constituted as surrogates to assuage the burning need of adolescents who, by the processes described, are deprived of a natural group whose causes they can embrace and for whose values they can fight [p. 407].

There are several circumstances which tend to raise our hope that there is an element of intelligent rationality in the rebellion of youth. One is its ubiquity: the youthful protest against Stalinistic orthodoxy in communist countries, against race discrimination in Berkeley, against the utilitarianistic and commercial 'American way of life' all over the United States, against antiquated tyranny of professors at German universities etc. Another reason for optimism is that never, as far as I know, have the youthful exerted their powers in the wrong direction, never have they demanded a more effective commercial system, better armament, or a more nationalistic attitude of their government. In other words, they seem to know—or at least feel— quite correctly what is wrong with the world. A third reason for assuming that there is a considerable rational element in the rebellion of youth is a very special one: rebelling students of biology are far more accessible to intelligent communication than are those of philosophy, philology and (I am sorry to say) of sociology.

We do not know how great a part of the rebellion of youth is motivated by rational and intelligent considerations. I must confess that it is only a very small part, even with those young people who profess—and honestly believe—that they are fighting for purely rational reasons. The main roots of the rebellion of youth are to be found in wholly irrational, ethological causes, as I hope to demonstrate. Many adults have found, to their cost, that it is useless to try reasoning with rebellious young people [p. 408].

Anyone familiar with ethological facts needs only to observe the hate-distorted faces of the more primitive type of rebel student in order to realize that they are not only unwilling, but quite unable to come to an understanding with their antagonists. In people wearing that kind of facial expression the hypothalamus is at the helm and the cortex completely inhibited. If a crowd of them approaches you, you have the choice of either to run, or to fight, as your temperament and the situation may demand. In order to avoid bloodshed, a responsible man may be forced to do the first—and be accused of cowardice in consequence. If he sees fit to fight, he will be accused of brutality, so whatever he does will be considered wrong. Yet it seems nearly hopeless to argue, as it appears impossible to reach the cortex across the smoke screen of hypothalamic excitation [p. 409].

When rebelling students resort to defecating, urinating and masturbating publicly in the lecture theaters of the university, as they have been known to do in Vienna, it becomes all too clear that this is not a reasoned protest against the war in Vietnam or against social injustice, but an entirely unconscious and deeply infantile revolt against all parental precepts in general, right down to those of early toilet training. This type of behaviour can only be explained on the basis of a genuine regression causing the recrudescence of ontogenetic phases of earliest infancy, or, from the historical viewpoint, precultural states of affairs far below those of palaeolithic times [p. 409].

The indispensable process of *identification* is severely hindered by the *lack of contact* between the generations. Lack of parent–child contact even during the first months can cause inconspicuous but lasting damage: we know, by the work of René Spitz, that it is in earliest infancy that the faculty to develop human contacts passes through its most critical period [p. 410].

Today's children are literally 'uneducated', they do not 'know the first things'. How should they, as nobody takes the time to tell them? So the basis for later phenomena of dehumanization is laid down at an early age, by diminishing the readiness for contact and compassion as well as by dampening the natural curiosity of man.

I am aware that the precept that all young mothers should spend most or all of their time with their babies is one that cannot be followed. The scarcity of mother–child contact is a consequence of the scarcity of time which, in turn, is caused by intraspecific competition and ultimately by crowding and other effects of overpopulation. The same fundamental evils have, with equally disastrous results, wrought profound changes in the sociological structure of the family [p. 411].

APPENDIX 2: Quotations from Max Weber's *The Theory of Social and Economic Organization*†

In 'action' is included all human behaviour when and in so far as the acting individual attaches a subjective meaning to it. Action in this sense may be either overt or purely inward or subjective; it may consist of positive intervention in a situation, or of deliberately refraining from such intervention or passively acquiescing in the situation. Action is social in so far as, by virtue of the subjective meaning attached to it by the acting individual (or individuals), it takes account of the behaviour of others and is thereby oriented in its course [p. 88].

As to questions concerning knowledge of and verifiability of the subjective meanings underlying behaviour, Weber is carefully non-commital, as the following shows:

The line between meaningful action and merely reactive behaviour to which no subjective meaning is attached, cannot be sharply drawn empirically. A very considerable part of all sociologically relevant behaviour, especially purely traditional behaviour, is marginal between the two. In the case of many psychophysical processes, meaningful, i.e. subjectively understandable, action is not to be found at all; in others it is discernible only by the expert psychologist [p. 90].

Obviously, much work has been done and much has been accomplished since Weber wrote on the subject of the uniformities underlying both non-human and human behaviour. It is precisely with the latter that many sections of this book are concerned. It is thus of interest that Weber, writing before studies of human non-verbal interaction (whether ethological or social–psychological) had got started, was able to envisage the form they might take. He wrote:

It is altogether possible that future research may be able to discover non-understandable uniformities underlying what has appeared to be specifically meaningful action, though little has been accomplished in this direction thus far. Thus, for example, differences in hereditary biological constitution, as of 'races', would have to be treated by sociology as given data in the same way as the physiological facts of the need of nutrition or the effect of senescence on action. This would be the case if, and in so far as, we had statistically conclusive proof of their influence on sociologically relevant behaviour [p. 94].

† Reprinted from Weber, M. (1947). *The Theory of Social and Economic Organization.* By permission of Macmillan Publishing Co., Inc.

In the following two quotations Weber actively concerns himself with animal interaction, functional analysis, and the starting points for an understanding of human social processes:

It would lead too far afield even to attempt to discuss how far the behaviour of animals is subjectively understandable to us and vice versa; in both cases the meaning of the term understanding and its extent of application would be highly problematical. But in so far as such understanding existed it would be theoretically possible to formulate a sociology of the relations of men to animals, both domestic and wild ... Unfortunately we either do not have any reliable means of determining the subjective state of mind of an animal or what we have is at best very unsatisfactory. It is well known that the problems of animal psychology, however interesting, are very thorny ones. There are in particular various forms of social organization among animals: 'monogamous and polygamous families,' herds, flocks, and finally 'state,' with a functional division of labour. The extent of functional differentiation found in these animal societies is by no means, however, entirely a matter of the degree of organic or morphological differentiation of the individual members of the species [pp. 104–5].

In the last analysis, however, Weber expresses himself doubtful as to the usefulness of work on animals for an understanding of human action, but his discussion of the relation between the two fields is worth close scrutiny:

A verifiable conception of the state of mind of these social animals accessible to meaningful understanding, would seem to be attainable even as an ideal goal only within narrow limits. However that may be, a contribution to the understanding of human social action is hardly to be expected from this quarter. On the contrary, in the field of animal psychology, human analogies are and must be continually employed. The most that can be hoped for is, then, that these biological analogies may some day be useful in suggesting significant problems. For instance they may throw light on the question of the relative role in the early stages of human social differentiation of mechanical and instinctive factors, as compared with that of the factors which are accessible to subjective interpretation generally, and more particularly to the role of consciously rational action. It is necessary for the sociologist to be thoroughly aware of the fact that in the early stages even of human development, the first set of factors is completely predominant. Even in the later stages he must take account of their continual interaction with the others in a role which is often of decisive importance [p. 106].

APPENDIX 3: Quotations from J.-P. Sartre's
Existentialism and Humanism†

What do we mean by saying that existence precedes essence? We mean that man first of all exists, encounters himself, surges up in the world—and defines himself afterwards. If man as the existentialist sees him is not definable, it is because to begin with he is nothing. He will not be anything until later, and then he will be what he makes of himself. Thus, there is no human nature, because there is no God to have a conception of it. Man simply is. Not that he is simply what he conceives himself to be, but he is what he wills, and as he conceives himself after already existing—as he wills to be after that leap towards existence. Man is nothing else but that which he makes of himself. This is the first principle of existentialism. And this is what people call its 'subjectivity', using the word as a reproach against us. But what do we mean to say by this, but that man is of a greater dignity than a stone or a table? For we mean to say that man primarily exists—that man is, before all else, something which propels itself towards a future and is aware that it is doing so. Man is, indeed, a project which possesses a subjective life, instead of being a kind of moss, or a fungus or a cauliflower. Before that projection of the self nothing exists; not even in the heaven of intelligence: man will only attain existence when he is what he purposes to be. Not, however, what he may wish to be. For what we usually understand by wishing or willing is a conscious decision taken—much more often than not—after we have made ourselves what we are. I may wish to join a party, to write a book or to marry—but in such a case what is usually called my will is probably a manifestation of a prior and more spontaneous decision. If, however, it is true that existence is prior to essence, man is responsible for what he is. Thus, the first effect of existentialism is that it puts every man in possession of himself as he is, and places the entire responsibility for his existence squarely upon his own shoulders. And, when we say that man is responsible for himself, we do not mean that he is responsible only for his own individuality, but that he is responsible for all men. The word 'subjectivism' is to be understood in two senses, and our adversaries play upon only one of them. Subjectivism means, on the one hand, the freedom of the individual subject and, on the other, that man cannot pass beyond human subjectivity. It is the latter which is the deeper meaning of existentialism.

For if indeed existence precedes essence, one will never be able to explain one's action by reference to a given and specific human nature; in other words, there is no determinism—man is free, man *is* freedom. Nor, on the other hand, if God does not exist, are we provided with any values or commands that could legitimize our behaviour. Thus we have neither behind us, nor before us in a luminous realm of values, any means of justification or excuse. We are left alone, without excuse.

† Grateful acknowledgment is made to Eyre Methuen for permission to reprint these passages.

That is what I mean when I say that man is condemned to be free. Condemned, because he did not create himself, yet is nevertheless at liberty, and from the moment that he is thrown into this world he is responsible for everything he does. The existentialist does not believe in the power of passion. He will never regard a grand passion as a destructive torrent upon which a man is swept into certain actions as by fate, and which, therefore, is an excuse for them. He thinks that man is responsible for his passion. Neither will an existentialist think that a man can find help through some sign being vouchsafed upon earth for his orientation: for he thinks that the man himself interprets the sign as he chooses. He thinks that every man, without any support or help whatever, is condemned at every instant to invent man.

Our point of departure is, indeed, the subjectivity of the individual, and that for strictly philosophic reasons. It is not because we are bourgeois, but because we seek to base our teaching upon the truth, and not upon a collection of fine theories, full of hope but lacking real foundations. And at the point of departure there cannot be any other truth than this, *I think, therefore I am*, which is the absolute truth of consciousness as it attains to itself. Every theory which begins with man, outside of this moment of self-attainment, is a theory which thereby suppresses the truth, for outside of the Cartesian *cogito*, all objects are no more than probable, and any doctrine of probabilities which is not attached to a truth will crumble into nothing. In order to define the probable one must possess the true. Before there can be any truth whatever, then, there must be an absolute truth, and there is such a truth which is simple, easily attained and within the reach of everybody; it consists in one's immediate sense of one's self.

In the second place, this theory alone is compatible with the dignity of man, it is the only one which does not make man into an object. All kinds of materialism lead one to treat every man including oneself as an object—that is, as a set of pre-determined reactions, in no way different from the patterns of qualities and phenomena which constitute a table, or a chair or a stone. Our aim is precisely to establish the human kingdom as a pattern of values in distinction from the material world.

There is always some way of understanding an idiot, a child, a primitive man or a foreigner if one has sufficient information. In this sense we may say that there is a human universality, but it is not something given, it is being perpetually made. I make this universality in choosing myself; I also make it by understanding the purpose of any other man, of whatever epoch. This absoluteness of the act of choice does not alter the relativity of each epoch.

Since we have defined the situation of man as one of free choice, without excuse and without help, any man who takes refuge behind the excuse of his passions, or by inventing some deterministic doctrine, is a self-deceiver.

Consequently, when I recognize, as entirely authentic, that man is a being whose existence precedes his essence, and that he is a free being who cannot, in any circumstances, but will his freedom, at the same time I realize that I cannot will the freedom of others. Thus, in the name of that will to freedom which is implied in freedom itself, I can form judgements upon those who seek to hide from themselves the wholly voluntary nature of their existence and its complete freedom. Those who hide from this total freedom, in a guise of solemnity or with deterministic excuses, I shall call cowards.

Suggested further reading

It is not possible to give a definitive list of books and readings to cover the whole subject. But the following consists of works which the author has found useful and thought-provoking. The titles listed under *Theoretical background* are concerned with the basic issues around which the book revolves. Titles are then listed under the part of this book to which they are most relevant.

Theoretical background

BATESON, G. (1973). *Steps to an Ecology of Mind*. Paladin, St. Albans.

DARWIN, C. (1872). *The Expression of the Emotions in Man and Animals*. Murray, London.

DURKHEIM, E. (1952). *Suicide, a Study in Sociology*. Routledge and Kegan Paul, London.

FREUD, S. (1963). *Civilization and its Discontents* (2nd edn.). Hogarth Press, London.

FROMM, E. (1946). *The Fear of Freedom*. Routledge, London.

MARCUSE, H. (1970). *Five Lectures: Psychoanalysis, Politics and Utopia*. Allen Lane, London.

MEAD, G. H. (1934). *Mind, Self and Society*. University of Chicago Press.

SARTRE, J.-P. (1948). *Existentialism and Humanism*. Methuen, London.

WEBER, M. (1947). *The Theory of Social and Economic Organization*. Free Press, London.

Part I. Biological determinism and human action

ALLAND, A. (1972). *The Human Imperative*. Columbia University Press.

ALSBERG, P. (1970). *In Quest of Man: a biological approach to the problem of man's place in nature*. Pergamon Press, Oxford.

BENTHALL, J. (ed.) (1974). *The Limits of Human Nature*. Dutton, New York.

CALLAN, H. (1970). *Ethology and Society*. Clarendon Press, Oxford.

COUNT, E. W. (1973). *Being and Becoming Human*. Van Nostrand Reinhold, New York.

FLETCHER, R. (1968). *Instinct in Man* (2nd edn.). Allen and Unwin, London.

LEWIS, J. and TOWERS, B. (1969). *Naked Ape or Homo Sapiens?* Garnstone Press, London.

MONTAGU, M. F. A. (ed.) (1968). *Man and Aggression*. (Especially the chapter by J. H. Crook). Oxford University Press, New York.

Part II. The evolution of human action

BARKOW, J. H. (1973). Darwinian psychological anthropology: a biosocial approach. *Cur. Anthrop.* **14**, (4), 373–87.

CHAPPLE, E. D. (1970). *Culture and Biological Man*. Holt, Rinehart and Winston, New York.

D'AQUILI, E. G. (1972). *The Biopsychological Determinants of Culture*. Module 13. Addison–Wesley, New York.

EIBL-EIBESFELDT, I. (1970). *Ethology: the Biology of Behavior*. Holt, Rinehart and Winston, New York.

FRISCH, K. von (1954). *The Dancing Bees*. Methuen, London.

HOWELL, F. C. (1966). *Early Man*. Time–Life, New York.

HOWELLS, W. (1973). *Evolution of the Genus Homo*. Addison–Wesley, New York.

KLOPFER, P. H. and HAILMAN, J. P. (1967). *An Introduction to Animal Behavior*. Prentice Hall, Englewood Cliffs.

KUMMER, H. (1971). *Primate Societies*. Aldine–Atherton, Chicago.

LE GROS CLARK, W. E. (1962). *The Antecedents of Man* (2nd edn.). Edinburgh University Press.

NAPIER, J. (1971). *The Roots of Mankind*. Allen and Unwin, London.

PFEIFFER, J. (1969). *The Emergence of Man*. Harper and Row, New York.

SCHILLER, C. H. (ed.) (1957). *Instinctive Behavior*. International University Press, New York.

TINBERGEN, N. (1951). *The Study of Instinct*. Clarendon Press, Oxford.

VIAUD, G. (1960). *Intelligence, its Evolution and Forms*. Hutchinson, London.

Part III. The physical mechanisms of human action

CANNON, W. B. (1929). *Bodily Changes in Pain, Hunger, Fear and Rage* (2nd edn. 1953). Branford, Boston.

CAVALLI-SFORZA, L. L. and BODMER, W. F. (1971). *The Genetics of Human Populations*. Freeman, San Francisco.

ELEFTHERIOU, B. E. and SCOTT, J. P. (eds.) (1971). *The Physiology of Aggression and Defeat*. Plenum Press, New York.

LEVI, L. (ed.) (1971). *Society, Stress and Disease*. Oxford University Press, London.

LEVI, L. (1972). *Stress and Distress in Response to Psychosocial Stimuli*. Pergamon Press, Oxford.

MONOD, J. (1972). *Chance and Necessity*. Collins, London.

OUNSTED, C. and TAYLOR, D. C. (ed.) (1972). *Gender Differences: their Ontogeny and Significance*. Churchill Livingstone, Edinburgh.

SPIELBERGER, C. D. (ed.) (1966). *Anxiety and Behavior*. Academic Press, New York.

TANNER, J. M. (1962). *Growth at Adolescence*. Blackwell Scientific Publications, Oxford.

TOBACH, E., ARONSON, L. R. and SHAW, E. (ed.) (1971). *The Biopsychology of Development*. Academic Press, New York.

YOUNG, J. Z. (1971). *An Introduction to the Study of Man*. Clarendon Press, Oxford.

Part IV. The psycho-social development of human action

ARGYLE, M. (1969). *Social Interaction*. Methuen, London.

BANNISTER, D. and FANSELLA, F. (1971). *Inquiring Man: the theory of personal constructs*. Penguin, Harmondsworth.

BLURTON JONES, N. G. (ed.) (1972). *Ethological Studies of Child Behaviour*. Cambridge University Press.

BOWLBY, J. (1969). *Attachment*. Hogarth Press, London.

FOSS, B. (ed.) (1974). *New Perspectives in Child Development*. Penguin, Harmondsworth.

GOFFMAN, E. (1972). *Interaction Ritual*. Penguin, Harmondsworth.

HINDE, R. A. (ed.) (1972). *Non-verbal Communication*. Cambridge University Press.

PIAGET, J. and INHELDER, B. (1969). *The Psychology of the Child*. Routledge and Kegan Paul, London.

RICHARDS, M. P. M. (ed.) (1974). *The Integration of a Child into a Social World*. Cambridge University Press.

Part V. Human action in cultural context

BERGER, P. L. and LUCKMANN, T. (1966). *The Social Construction of Reality*. Penguin, Harmondsworth.

BERGER, P. L., BERGER, B. and KELLNER, H. (1974). *The Homeless Mind*. Penguin, Harmondsworth.

BOYDEN, S. V. (ed.) (1970). *The Impact of Civilization on the Biology of Man*. Australian National University, Canberra.

CARRUTHERS, M. (1974). *The Western Way of Death*. Davis–Poynter, London.

CHEIN, I. (1972). *The Science of Behaviour and the Image of Man*. Tavistock, London.

CICOUREL, A. V. (1973). *Cognitive Sociology*. Penguin, Harmondsworth.

CUZZORT, R. P. (ed.) (1969). *Humanity and Modern Sociological Thought*. Holt, Rinehart and Winston, New York.

HARRÉ, R. and SECORD, P. F. (1972). *The Explanation of Social Behaviour*. Blackwell, Oxford.

LEVI, L. and ANDERSSON, L. (1972). *Population, Environment and Quality of Life*. Royal Ministry for Foreign Affairs, Stockholm.

References

ACHESON, R. M. and HEWITT, D. (1954). Oxford Child Health Survey. Stature and skeletal maturation in the pre-school child. *Br. J. prev. soc. Med.* **8,** 59–65.

AHRENS, R. (1953). Beitrag zur Entwicklung des Physiognomie und Mimikerkennens. *Z. exptl. angew. Psychol.* **2,** 412–54.

AINSWORTH, M. D. (1962). *Deprivation of Maternal Care, a Reassessment of its Effects.* World Health Organization, Geneva.

—— (1964). Patterns of attachment behavior shown by the infant in interaction with his mother. *Merrill-Palmer Q. Behav. Devel.* **10,** 51–8.

—— (1967). *Infancy in Uganda: Infant Care and the Growth of Love.* Johns Hopkins University Press, Baltimore.

AMBROSE, J. A. (1961). Development of the smiling response in early infancy. In *Determinants of Infant Behaviour* (ed. B. M. Foss), Vol. 1. Methuen, London.

ARDENER, E. (1971). Introductory essay: social anthropology and language. *A.S.A. Monographs* **10.**

—— (1973). Behaviour: a social anthropological criticism. *J. anth. Soc. Oxford,* **4,** 152–4.

ARDREY, R. (1961). *African Genesis.* Collins, London.

—— (1966). *The Territorial Imperative.* Collins, London.

—— (1970). *The Social Contract.* Collins, London.

ARGYLE, M. (1967). *The Psychology of Interpersonal Behaviour.* Penguin, Harmondsworth.

BANTON, M. (1967). *Race Relations.* Tavistock, London.

BARCHAS, J. D., CIARANELLO, R. D., STOLK, J. M., BRODIE, H. K. H. and HAMBURG, D. A. (1972). Biogenic amines and behavior. In *Hormones and Behavior* (ed. S. Levine). Academic Press, London.

BATESON, G. (1973). Ecology and flexibility in urban civilization. In *Steps to an Ecology of Mind* (ed. G. Bateson). Paladin, St. Albans.

BAUER, H. (1954). Nephrosesyndrom and Körperwachstum. *Helv. Paediat. Acta* **9,** 127–34.

BEACH, F. A. (ed.) (1965). *Sex and Behavior.* Wiley, New York.

BECKER, H. S. (1953). Becoming a marijuana user. *Am. J. Sociol.* **59,** 235–42.

BELL, R. Q. (1968). A reinterpretation of the direction of effects in studies of socialization. *Psychol. Rev.* **75,** 81–95.

BENDER, L. (1947). Psychopathic behavior disorders in children. In *Handbook of Correctional Psychology* (ed. R. M. Lindner and R. V. Seliger). Philosophical Library, New York.

BERGER, P. L. and LUCKMANN, T. (1967). *The Social Construction of Reality.* Penguin, Harmondsworth.

BERNARD, J. (1968). The eudaemonists. In *Why Man takes Chances* (ed. S. Z. Klausner). Garden City, New York.

BERNSTEIN, B. (1965). A socio-linguistic approach to social learning. In *Penguin Survey of the Social Sciences 1965* (ed. J. Gould). Penguin, Harmondsworth.

BERNSTEIN, I. S. (1966). Analysis of a key role in a capuchin (*Cebus albifrons*) group. *Tulane Stud. Zool.* **13**, 49–54.

BEYNON, H. (1973). *Working for Ford*. Allen Lane, London.

BIRDWHISTELL, R. L. (1949). *Introduction to Kinesics*. Louisville University Press.

BISCHOF, N. (1972). The biological foundations of the incest taboo. *Soc. Sci. Inform.* **11**, (6), 7–36.

BLURTON JONES, N. G. (1967). An ethological study of some aspects of social behaviour of children in nursery school. In *Primate Ethology* (ed. D. Morris). Weidenfeld and Nicolson, London.

—— and KONNER, M. J. (1973). Sex differences in behaviour of London and Bushmen children. In *Comparative Ecology and Behaviour of Primates* (ed. R. P. Michael and J. H. Crook). Academic Press, London.

BOJLÉN, K. W., RASCH, G. and WEIS–BENTZON, M. (1954). The age incidence of the menarche in Copenhagen. *Acta Obstet. Gynec. Scand.* **33**, 405–33.

BOURNE, P. G. (1971). Altered adrenal function in two combat situations in Viet Nam. In *The Physiology of Aggression and Defeat* (ed. B. E. Eleftheriou and J. P. Scott). Plenum Press, London.

BOWLBY, J. (1946). *Forty-four Juvenile Thieves, their Characters and Home Life*. Baillière, Tindall and Cox, London.

—— (1952). *Maternal Care and Mental Health*. World Health Organization, Geneva.

—— (1969). *Attachment*. Hogarth Press, London.

BOYDEN, S. V. (ed.) (1970). *The Impact of Civilisation on the Biology of Man*. Australian National University, Canberra.

BRANNIGAN, C. R. and HUMPHRIES, D. A. (1972). Human non-verbal behaviour: a means of communication. In *Ethological Studies of Child Behaviour* (ed. N. G. Blurton Jones). Cambridge University Press.

BROWN, R. (1970). The first sentences of child and chimpanzee. *Selected Psycholinguistical Papers*. Macmillan, New York.

BRUNER, J. S. (1966). *Toward a Theory of Instruction*, Chapter 7. Harvard University Press.

—— (1975). From communication to language: a psychological perspective. *Cognition* **3**, 255–87.

BURROW, J. W. (1966). *Evolution and Society*. Cambridge University Press.

CALLAN, H. (1970). *Ethology and Society*. Clarendon Press, Oxford.

CAMPBELL, B. G. (1966). *Human Evolution: an Introduction to Man's Adaptations*. Aldine–Atherton, Chicago.

CAMPBELL, H. J. (1973). *The Pleasure Areas*. Eyre Methuen, London.

CANDLAND, D. K. (1971). The ontogeny of emotional behavior. In *The Ontogeny of Vertebrate Behavior* (ed. H. Moltz). Academic Press, New York.

CANDLAND, D. K. and LESHNER, A. I. (1974). A model of agonistic behavior: endocrine and autonomic correlates. In *Limbic and Autonomic Nervous Systems Research* (ed. L. V. DiCara). Plenum Press, New York.

CANNON, W. B. (1953). *Bodily Changes in Pain, Hunger, Fear and Rage* (2nd edn.). Branford, Boston.

CARFAGNA, M., FIGURELLI, E., MATARESE, G. and MATARESE, S. (1972). Menarcheal age of schoolgirls in the District of Naples, Italy, in 1969–70. *Hum. Biol.* **44**, 117–25.

CARLESTAM, G. and LEVI, L. (1971). *Urban Conglomerates as Psychosocial Human Stressors. General Aspects, Swedish Trends, and Psychological and Medical Implications.* Royal Ministry for Foreign Affairs, Stockholm.

CARPENTER, C. R. (1940). A field study in Siam of the behavior and social relations of the gibbon (*Hylobates lar*). *Comp. Psych. Mon.* **16**, (5), 1–212.

CARRUTHERS, M. E. (1973). Maintaining the cardiovascular fitness of pilots. *Lancet* **1,** 1048.

CATTELL, R. B. (1966). Anxiety and motivation: theory and crucial experiments. In *Anxiety and Behavior* (ed. C. D. Spielberger). Academic Press, New York.

CAVALLI-SFORZA, L. L. and BODMER, W. F. (1971). *The Genetics of Human Populations.* Freeman, San Francisco.

CHANCE, M. R. A. (1967). Attention structure as the basis of primate rank orders. *Man* **2,** 503–18.

CHOMSKY, N. (1968). *Language and Mind.* Harcourt, Brace and World, New York.

CHRISTIAN, J. J. (1964). Pathopoietic consequences of increasing population. *Proc. R. Soc. Med.* **57,** 169–74.

CLANCY, H. and McBRIDE, G. (1969). The autistic process and its treatment. *J. Child Psychol. Psychiat.* **10,** 233–44.

CLARK, A. H., WYON, S. M. and RICHARDS, M. P. M. (1969). Free-play in nursery school children. *J. Child Psychol. Psychiat.* **10,** 205–16.

CLARKE, A. D. B. (1965). Genetic and environmental studies of intelligence. In *Mental Deficiency, the Changing Outlook* (ed. A. M. Clarke and A. D. B. Clarke). Methuen, London.

COLE, S. (1963). *Races of Man.* British Museum (Natural History), London.

COMSTOCK, G. W. (1970). Fatal arteriosclerotic heart disease, water hardness at home, and socioeconomic characteristics. *Am. J. Epidemiol.* **94,** (1), 1–10.

—— and PARTRIDGE, K. B. (1972). Church attendance and health. *J. chron. Dis.* **25,** 665–72.

CONROY, R. and MILLS, J. (1970). *Human Circadian Rhythms.* Churchill, London.

COOPER, D. (1971). *The Death of the Family.* Allen Lane, London.

COSER, L. A. (1956). *The Functions of Social Conflict.* Routledge and Kegan Paul, London.

CRICK, M. (1975). Ethology, language and the study of human action. *J. anth. Soc. Oxford* **6,** (2), 106–18.

D'ANDRADE, R. G. (1966). Sex differences and cultural institutions. In *The Development of Sex Differences* (ed. E. E. Maccoby). Stanford University Press, Stanford.

DAVIS, K. (1947). Final note on a case of extreme isolation. *Am. J. Sociol.* **50,** 432–437.

DEVORE, I. and WASHBURN, S. L. (1963). Baboon ecology and human evolution. In *African Ecology and Human Evolution* (ed. F. C. Howell and F. Bourlière). Aldine, Chicago.

DICARA, L. V. (1971). Learning of cardio-vascular response: a review and description of physiological and biochemical consequence. *Trans. N.Y. Acad. Sci.* **33,** 411–22.

DOUGLAS, J. W. B. (1964). *The Home and the School.* MacGibbon and Kee, London.

DURKHEIM, E. (1952). *Suicide, a Study in Sociology.* Routledge and Kegan Paul, London.

EIBL-EIBESFELDT, I. (1970). *Ethology, the Biology of Behavior*. Holt, Rinehart and Winston, New York.

—— (1971). *Love and Hate*. Methuen, London.

—— (1973). *Der Vorprogrammierte Mensch*. Molden, Wien, München, Zürich.

EISENBERG, L. (1971). Persistent problems in the study of the biopsychology of development. In *The Biopsychology of Development* (ed. E. Tobach, L. R. Aronson and E. Shaw). Academic Press, New York.

—— and KANNER, L. (1956). Early infantile autism. *Am. J. Orthopsychiat.* **26,** 556.

EKMAN, P. and FRIESEN, W. V. (1971). Constants across cultures in the face and emotion. *J. Personality soc. Psychol.* **17,** (2), 124–9.

ELLEFSON, J. O. (1968). Territorial behavior in the common white-handed gibbon (*Hylobates lar*). In *Primates: studies in adaptation and variability* (ed. P. C. Jay). Holt, Rinehart and Winston, New York.

FLAVELL, J. H. (1968). *The Development of Role-taking and Communication Skills in Children*. Wiley, New York.

FLOUD, J. E., HALSEY, A. H. and MARTIN, F. M. (1957). *Social Class and Educational Opportunity*. Heinemann, London.

FOX, H. M., MURAWSKI, B. J., BARTHOLOMAY, A. F. and GIFFORD, S. (1961). Adrenal steroid excretion patterns in 18 healthy subjects: tentative correlations with personality structure. *Psychosom. Med.* **23,** 33–40.

FRANKENHAEUSER, M. (1971). Experimental approaches to the study of human behaviour as related to neuroendocrine functions. In *Society, Stress and Disease* (ed. L. Levi). Oxford University Press, London.

—— (1974). *Man in Technological Society: stress, adaptation, and tolerance limits*. Reports from the Psychological Laboratories, University of Stockholm, Suppl. no. 26.

FREEMAN, D. (1965). *Social Anthropology and the Scientific Study of Human Behaviour*. Institute of Advanced Studies, Australian National University, Canberra.

—— (1974). The evolutionary theories of Charles Darwin and Herbert Spencer. *Cur. Anthrop.* **15,** (3), 211–37.

FREUD, S. (1963). *Civilization and its Discontents* (2nd edn.). Hogarth Press, London.

FRIEDMAN, M. and ROSENMAN, R. H. (1959). Association of specific overt behavior pattern with blood and cardiovascular findings. *J. Am. med. Ass.* **169,** (12), 1286–1296.

FRISCH, K. VON (1954). *The Dancing Bees*. Methuen, London.

FROMM, E. (1946). *The Fear of Freedom*. Routledge and Kegan Paul, London.

GANONG, W. F. (1973). *Review of Medical Physiology* (6th edn.). Lange Medical Publications, Los Altos.

GARDNER, H. (1973). Structure and development. *Hum. Context* **5,** (1), 50–67.

GARDNER, L. I. (1972). Deprivation dwarfism. *Scient. Am.* **227,** 76–83.

GARDNER, R. A. and GARDNER, B. T. (1969). Teaching sign language to a chimpanzee. *Science, N.Y.* **165,** 664–72.

GESCHWIND, N. (1972). Language and the brain. *Scient. Am.* **226,** 76–83.

GOFFMAN, E. (1956). *The Presentation of Self in Everyday Life*. University of Edinburgh.

GOTTLIEB, G. (1971). Ontogenesis of sensory function in birds and mammals. In *The Biopsychology of Development* (ed. E. Tobach, L. R. Aronson and E. Shaw). Academic Press, New York.

GRAHAM, P. and GEORGE, S. (1972). Children's response to parental illness: individual differences. *J. Psychosom. Res.* **16,** 251–5.

GRANT, E. C. (1969). Human facial expression. *Man* **4,** 525–36.

GRAY, J. (1971). *The Psychology of Fear and Stress.* Weidenfeld and Nicolson, London.
GREENE, R. (1970). *Human Hormones.* Weidenfeld and Nicolson, London.
GREULICH, W. W. (1951). The growth and developmental status of Guamanian schoolchildren in 1947. *Am. J. phys. Anth.* **9,** 55–70.
—— (1957). A comparison of the physical growth and development of American-born and native Japanese children. *Am. J. phys. Anth.* **15,** 489–515.
——, CRISMON, C. S. and TURNER, M. L. (1953). The physical growth and development of children who survived the atomic bombing of Hiroshima or Nagasaki. *J. Pediat.* **43,** 121–45.

HALL, E. T. (1959). *The Silent Language.* Doubleday, New York.
—— (1966). *The Hidden Dimension.* Doubleday, New York.
HARDMAN, C. (1974). Fact and fantasy in the playground. *New Society* **29,** 801–3.
HARLOW, H. F. and HARLOW, M. K. (1962). Social deprivation in monkeys. *Scient. Am.* **207,** 136–46.
—— —— (1965). The affectional systems. In *Behavior of Non-Human Primates* (ed. A. M. Schrier, H. F. Harlow and F. Stollnitz), Vol. 2. Academic Press, New York.
HARRÉ, R. (1974). The conditions for a social psychology of childhood. In *The Integration of a Child into a Social World* (ed. M. P. M. Richards). Cambridge University Press.
HARRISON, A. (1972). *Superstitions.* Mason, Havant.
HARRISON, G. A. (1973). The effects of modern living. *J. biosoc. Sci.* **5,** 217–28.
HAYES, C. (1952). *The Ape in Our House.* Harper, New York.
HELEVUO, H., REYNOLDS, V. and CARRUTHERS, M. E. (1975). Intra- and inter-individual variation in catecholamine excretion rates in a sample of normal and autistic school children. *Paper read at Society for the Study of Human Biology Meeting,* 18 April 1975.
HEWES, G. W. (1973). Primate communication and the gestural origin of language. *Cur. Anthrop.* **14,** 5–24.
HEWITT, D., WESTROPP, C. K. and ACHESON, R. M. (1955). Oxford Child Health Survey: effect of childish ailments on skeletal development. *Br. J. prev. soc. Med.* **9,** 179–86.
HIERNAUX, J. (1966). Human biological diversity in Central Africa. *Man.* **1,** 287–306.
HIGGINS, M. and RAPHAEL, C. M. (ed.) (1967). *Reich speaks of Freud.* Souvenir Press, London.
HINDE, R. A. (1972). Aggression. In *Biology and the Human Sciences* (ed. J. W. S. Pringle). Clarendon Press, Oxford.
HOFER, M. A., WOLFF, C. T., FRIEDMAN, S. B. and MASON, J. W. (1972). A psychoendocrine study of bereavement. *Psychosom. Med.* **34,** (6), 481–91 and 492–504.
HOLLDÖBLER, B. (1971). Communication between ants and their guests. *Scient. Am.* **224,** 86–95.
HOLLOWAY, R. L. (1969). Culture: a *human* domain. *Cur. Anthrop.* **10,** (4), 395–412.
—— (1972). Australopithecine endocasts, brain evolution in the Hominoidea, and a model of hominid evolution. In *The Functional and Evolutionary Biology of Primates* (ed. R. Tuttle). Aldine, Chicago.
—— (1974). The casts of fossil hominid brains. *Scient. Am.* July 1974.

HOOFF, J. A. R. A. M. VAN (1967). The facial displays of the Catarrhine monkeys and apes. In *Primate Ethology* (ed. D. Morris). Weidenfeld and Nicolson, London.

HOOKER, D. (1952). *The Prenatal Origin of Behavior*. University of Kansas Press, Lawrence.

HUTT, C. (1972). Neuroendocrinological, behavioural and intellectual aspects of sexual differentiation in human development. In *Gender Differences: their Ontogeny and Significance* (ed. C. Ounsted and D. C. Taylor). Churchill Livingstone, Edinburgh.

——, FORREST, S. J. and RICHER, J. (1975). Cardiac arrhythmia and behaviour in autistic children. *Acta. psychiat. scand.* **51,** 361–72.

HUTT, S. J., HUTT, C., LEE, D. and OUNSTED, C. (1965). A behavioural and electroencephalographic study of autistic children. *J. psychiat. Res.* **3,** 181–197.

HUXLEY, J. (1943). *Evolutionary Ethics.* Oxford University Press, London.

IMANISHI, K. (1965). The origin of the human family. In *Japanese Monkeys* (ed. S. A. Altmann). University of Alberta Press.

ISAAC, G. (1970). The diet of early man: aspects of archaeological evidence from lower and middle Pleistocene sites in Africa. *Wld Archaeol.* **2,** (3), 278–99.

ITANI, J. and SUZUKI, A. (1967). The social unit of chimpanzees. *Primates* **8,** 355–381.

ITO, P. K. (1942). Comparative biometrical study of physique of Japanese women born and reared under different environments. *Hum. Biol.* **14,** 279–351.

JAHODA, G. (1969). *The Psychology of Superstition.* Allen Lane, Penguin Press, London.

JAMES, W. (1890). *The Principles of Psychology.* Holt, New York.

JAY, P. C. (ed.) (1968). *Primates: studies in adaptation and variability.* Holt, Rinehart and Winston, New York.

JOHANNSON, G., FRANKENHAEUSER, M. and MAGNUSSON, D. (1973). Catecholamine output in schoolchildren as related to performance and adjustment. *Scand. J. Psychol.* **14,** 20–8.

JOLLY, C. J. (1970). The seed-eaters: a new model of hominid differentiation based on a baboon analogy. *Man* **5,** (1), 5–26.

KAGAN, A. R. and LEVI, L. (1971). Health and environment—psychosocial stimuli. A review. *Rep. Lab. clin. Stress Res., Stockholm* **27.**

KANNER, L. (1943). Autistic disturbances of affective contact. *Nerv. Child.* **2,** 217–250.

—— and EISENBERG, L. (1955). Notes on the follow-up studies of autistic children. In *Psychopathology of Childhood* (ed. P. H. Hoch and J. Zubin). Grune and Stratton, New York.

KARK, E. (1956). Puberty in S. African girls: II. Social class in relation to the menarche. *S. Afr. J. Lab. clin. Med.* **2,** 84–8.

KARSH, F. J., DIERSCHKE, D. J. and KNOBIL, E. (1973). Sexual differentiation of pituitary function: apparent difference between primates and rodents. *Science, N.Y.* **179,** 484–6.

KAUFMANN, J. H. (1965). A three-year study of mating behavior in a free-ranging band of rhesus monkeys. *Ecology* **46,** 500–12.

KAWANAKA, K. and NISHIDA, T. (1974). Recent advances in the study of inter-unit-group relations and social structure of wild chimpanzees of the Mahali Mountains. *Symp. 5th Cong. Int. Primatological Soc.*, Japan Science Press.

KELLOGG, W. N. and KELLOGG, L. A. (1933). *The Ape and the Child.* McGraw–Hill, New York.

KIRITZ, S. and MOOS, R. H. (1974). Physiological effects of social environments. *Psychosom. Med.* **36**, (2), 96–114.

KOLUCHOVA, J. (1972). Severe deprivation in twins: a case study. *J. Child Psychol. Psychiat.* **13**, 107–14.

KONNER, M. J. (1972). Aspects of the developmental ethology of a foraging people. In *Ethological Studies of Child Behaviour* (ed. N. G. Blurton-Jones). Cambridge University Press.

KORTLANDT, A. (1962). Chimpanzees in the Wild. *Scient. Am.* **206**, (5), 128–38.

KORTMULDER, K. (1968). An ethological theory of the incest taboo and exogamy. *Cur. Anthrop.* **9**, (5), 437–49.

LAING, R. D. (1967). *The Politics of Experience.* Penguin, Harmondsworth.

LAWICK-GOODALL, J. VAN (1967). *My Friends the Wild Chimpanzees.* National Geographical Society, Washington.

—— (1968). The behaviour of free-living chimpanzees in the Gombe Stream Reserve. *Anim. Behav. Monog.* **1**, (3), 161–311.

LAZARUS, R. S. (1971). The concepts of stress and disease. In *Society, Stress and Disease* (ed. L. Levi). Oxford University Press, London.

LEACH, E. (1970). *Lévi-Strauss.* Fontana–Collins, London.

LENNEBERG, E. H. (1967). *The Biological Foundations of Language.* Wiley, New York.

LEVI, L. (1968). Sympatho-adrenomedullary and related biochemical reactions during experimentally induced emotional stress. In *Endocrinology and Human Behaviour* (ed. R. P. Michael). Oxford University Press, London.

—— (1972). *Stress and Distress in Response to Psychosocial Stimuli.* Pergamon Press, Oxford.

LÉVI-STRAUSS, C. (1960). The family. In *Man, Culture and Society* (ed. H. L. Shapiro). Oxford University Press, New York.

—— (1962). *La Pensée Sauvage.* Librairie Plon, Paris. (English translation: *The Savage Mind* (1966).)

—— (1964). *Le cru et le cuit.* Librairie Plon, Paris.

—— (1968). The concept of primitiveness. In *Man the Hunter* (ed. R. B. Lee and I. DeVore). Aldine, Chicago.

LEWIS, H. (1954). *Deprived Children (the Mershel Experiment). A Social and Clinical Study.* Oxford University Press, London.

LIPOWSKI, Z. J. (1971). Surfeit of attractive information inputs: A hallmark of our environment. *Behav. Sci.* **16**, 467–71.

—— (1973). Affluence, information inputs and health. *Soc. Sci. Med.* **7**, 517–29.

LJUNG, B.–O., BERGSTEN–BRUCEFORS, A. and LINDGREN, G. (1974). The secular trend in physical growth in Sweden. *Ann. Hum. Biol.* **1**, (3), 245–56.

LOIZOS, C. (1967). Play behaviour in primates: a review. In *Primate Ethology* (ed. D. Morris). Weidenfeld and Nicolson, London.

LOOMIS, A. M. (1931). A technique for observing the social behaviour of nursery school children. *Monog. Soc. Res. Child Devel.* **5**.

LORENZ, K. (1966). *On Aggression.* Methuen, London.

—— (1970). The enmity between generations. *Nobel Symposium*, **14**.

—— (1974). *Civilised Man's Eight Deadly Sins.* Methuen, London.

LUMSDEN, D. P. (1975). Towards a systems model of stress: feedback from an anthropological study of the impact of Ghana's Volta River project. In *Stress and Anxiety*, Vol. 2, pp. 191–228 (ed. I. Sarason and C. Spielberger). Hemisphere, Washington.

McBride, G. (1968). On the evolution of human language. *Soc. Sci. Inform.* **7**, (5), 81–5.

MacCulloch, M. J. and Williams, C. (1971). On the nature of infantile autism. *Acta Psychiat. Scand.* **47**, 295–314.

MacGregor, I. A., Gilles, H. M., Walters, J. H., Davies, A. H. and Pearson, F. A. (1956). Effects of heavy and repeated malarial infections on Gambian infants and children. *Br. med. J.* **2**, 686–92.

McGrew, W. C. (1972). *An Ethological Study of Children's Behavior.* Academic Press, London.

MacIntyre, A. (1970). *Marcuse.* Fontana–Collins, London

McKusick, V. A. (1964). *Human Genetics.* Prentice-Hall, Englewood Cliffs.

Mair, M. (1975). What do faces mean? *R. Anth. Inst. News.* **9**, 1–6.

Malinowski (1922). *Argonauts of the Western Pacific.* Routledge, London.

Maple, E. (1971). *Superstitions and the Superstitious.* W. H. Allen, London.

Marcuse, H. (1969). *An Essay on Liberation.* Penguin, Harmondsworth.

—— (1970). *Five Lectures: Psychoanalysis, Politics and Utopia.* Allen Lane, London.

Marshall, W. A. (1974). Interrelationships of skeletal maturation, sexual development and somatic growth in man. *Ann. Hum. Biol.* **1**, (1), 29–40.

Mason, J. W. (1968). A review of psychoendocrine research on the pituitary–adrenal cortical system. *Psychosom. Med.* **30**, (5), 576–607.

May, M. (1958). *The Ecology of Human Disease.* M. D. Publications, New York.

Mead, G. H. (1934). *Mind, Self and Society.* University of Chicago Press.

Mensh, I. N. (1972). Personal and social environmental influences in the development of gender identity. In *Gender Differences: their Ontogeny and Significance* (ed. C. Ounsted and D. C. Taylor). Churchill Livingstone, Edinburgh.

Michael, R. P. and Keverne, E. B. (1968). Pheromones in the communication of sexual status in primates. *Nature, Lond.* **218**, 746–9.

Michelson, N. (1944). Studies in physical development of Negroes. IV. Onset of puberty. *Am. J. phys. Anth.* **2**, 151–66.

Miller, N. E. (1969). Learning of visceral and glandular responses. *Science, N.Y.* **163**, 434–45.

—— and Banuazizi, A. (1968). Instrumental learning by curarized rats of a specific visceral response, intestinal or cardiac. *J. comp. Physiol. Psychol.* **65**, 1–7.

Money, J. and Erhardt, A. A. (1968). Prenatal hormonal exposure: possible effects on behaviour in man. In *Endocrinology and Human Behaviour* (ed. R. P. Michael). Oxford University Press, London.

——, Hampson, J. G. and Hampson, J. L. (1955). An examination of some basic sexual concepts. *Bull. Johns Hopkins Hosp.* **97**, 301–19.

Morris, D. (1967). *The Naked Ape.* Cape, London.

—— (1969). *The Human Zoo.* Cape, London.

Moss, H. A. (1967). Sex, age and state as determinants of mother–infant interaction. *Merrill-Palmer Q. Behav. Devel.* **13**, 19–36.

Murken, J.-D. (1973). The XYY-Syndrome and Klinefelter's Syndrome. *Topics hum. Gen.* **2**, 1–86.

Nadel, S. F. (1954). *Nupe Religion.* Routledge and Kegan Paul, London.

Napier, J. (1971). *Roots of Mankind.* Allen and Unwin, London.

Newson, J. and Newson, E. (1968a). *Four Years Old in an Urban Community.* Allen and Unwin, London.

—— —— (1968b). Some social differences in the process of childrearing. In *Penguin Social Sciences Survey 1968* (ed. J. Gould). Penguin, Harmondsworth.

NISSEN, H. W. (1931). A field study of the chimpanzee. *Comp. Psych. Mon.* **8,** (1), 1–122.

OLDMAN, S. (1973). An Observational Study of the Social Behaviour of a Class of 5–7-year-old School Children. Thesis, Bristol University.

OPIE, I. and OPIE, P. (1959). *The Language and Lore of Schoolchildren.* Clarendon Press, Oxford.

PASSMORE, R. (1968). The supply and use of energy. In *A Companion to Medical Studies* (ed. R. Passmore and J. S. Robson), Vol. 1. Blackwell, Oxford.

PATKAI, P. and FRANKENHAEUSER, M. (1964). Constancy in catecholamine excretion. *Percept. Mot. Skills* **19,** 789–90.

PATTON, R. G. and GARDNER, L. I. (1969). Short stature associated with maternal deprivation syndrome: disordered family environment as cause of so-called idiopathic hypopituitarism. In *Endocrine and Genetic Diseases of Childhood* (ed. L. I. Gardner). Saunders, Philadelphia.

PETRI, E. (1935). Untersuchungen zur Erbbedingtheit der Menarche. *Z. Morph. Anthrop.* **33,** 43–8.

PFEIFFER, J. (1969). *The Emergence of Man.* Harper and Row, New York.

PIAGET, J. (1971). *Biology and Knowledge.* Edinburgh University Press.

—— (1972). *Structuralism.* Routledge and Kegan Paul, London.

—— and INHELDER, B. (1969). *The Psychology of the Child.* Routledge and Kegan Paul, London.

PREMACK, A. J. and PREMACK, D. (1972). Teaching language to an ape. *Scient. Am.* **227,** 92–9.

PREMACK, D. (1970). The education of Sarah. *Psychol. Today* **4,** 55–8.

PRINGLE, J. W. S. (1972). A vision of man. *Biologist* **19,** (4), 223–36.

QUIATT, D. (1966). Social Dynamics of Rhesus Monkey Groups. Ph.D. thesis, University of Colorado, Boulder.

RAHE, R. H. (1972). Subjects' recent life changes and their near-future illness susceptibility. In *Advances in Psychosomatic Medicine* (ed. F. Reichsman), Vol. 8. Karger, Basel.

REYNOLDS, V. (1962). The Social Life of a Colony of Rhesus Monkeys. Ph.D. thesis, London University.

—— (1966). Open groups in hominid evolution. *Man* **1,** (4), 441–52.

—— (1967). *The Apes.* Dutton, New York.

—— (1968). Kinship and the family in monkeys, apes and man. *Man* **3,** (2), 209–23.

—— (1970). Equality. *The Listener,* **84,** (2176), 797–9.

—— and GUEST, A. (in press). An ethological study of 6–7 year old schoolchildren. *Biol. and hum. Affairs.*

—— and REYNOLDS, F. (1965). Chimpanzees in the Budongo Forest. In *Primate Behavior* (ed. I. DeVore). Holt, Rinehart and Winston, New York.

RICHARDS, M. P. M. (1974). First steps in becoming social. In *The Integration of a Child into a Social World* (ed. M. P. M. Richards), Cambridge University Press.

ROPER, M. K. (1969). A survey of the evidence for intrahuman killing in the Pleistocene. *Cur. Anthrop.* **10,** (4), 427–59.

RUMBAUGH, D. (1974). The language skills of Lana, chimpanzee. Paper delivered at *5th Congress of the International Primatological Society*, Nagoya.

RUSSELL, W. M. S. and RUSSELL, C. (1968). *Violence, Monkeys and Man*. Macmillan, London.

RUTTER, M. (1972). *Maternal Deprivation Reassessed*. Penguin, Harmondsworth.

SADE, D. (1965). Some aspects of parent–offspring and sibling relations in a group of rhesus monkeys, with a discussion of grooming. *Am. J. phys. Anth.* **23**, (1), 1–17.

SARTRE, J.-P. (1948). *Existentialism and Humanism* (trans. P. Mairet). Eyre Methuen, London.

SCHACHTER, S. (1966). The interaction of cognitive and physiological determinants of emotional state. In *Anxiety and Behavior* (ed. C. D. Spielberger). Academic Press, New York.

—— and SINGER, J. (1962). *Psychol. Rev.* **69**, 379–99.

SCHEFLEN, A. E. (1964). The significance of posture in communication systems. *Psychiatry* **27**, (4), 316–31.

—— (1965). *Stream and Structure of Communicational Behavior*. East Pennsylvania Psychiatric Institute, Commonwealth of Pennsylvania.

SELYE, H. (1971). The evaluation of the stress concept—stress and cardio-vascular disease. In *Society, Stress and Disease* (ed. L. Levi). Oxford University Press, London.

SIMMEL, G. (1955). *Conflict* (transl. K. H. Wolff). Free Press, Glencoe.

SMITH, P. K. (1974). Ethological methods. In *New Perspectives in Child Development* (ed. B. Foss). Penguin, Harmondsworth.

—— and CONNOLLY, K. (1972). Patterns of play and social interaction in preschool children. In *Ethological Studies of Child Behaviour* (ed. N. G. Blurton-Jones). Cambridge University Press.

SOUTHALL, A. W. and GUTKIND, P. C. W. (1957). *Townsmen in the Making*. East African Studies no. 9, Kampala.

SOUTHWICK, C. H. (1967). An experimental study of intragroup agonistic behavior in rhesus monkeys (*Macaca mulatta*). *Behaviour* **28**, 182–209.

SPERRY, R. W. (1971). How a developing brain gets itself properly wired for adaptive function. In *The Biopsychology of Development* (ed. E. Tobach, L. R. Aronson and E. Shaw). Academic Press, New York.

SUGIYAMA, Y. (1968). Social organization of chimpanzees in the Budongo Forest, Uganda. *Primates* **9**, 225–58.

—— (1969). Social behavior of chimpanzees in the Budongo Forest, Uganda. *Primates* **10**, 197–225.

SZALAY, F. S. (1975). Hunting-scavenging protohominids: a model for hominid origins. *Man* **10**, 420–29.

SZASZ, T. S. (1972). *The Manufacture of Madness*. Routledge and Kegan Paul, London.

TANNER, J. M. (1962). *Growth at Adolescence*. Blackwell Scientific Publications, Oxford.

—— (1973*a*). Growing Up. *Scient. Am.* **229**, 34–43.

—— (1973*b*). Physical growth and development. In *Textbook of Paediatrics* (ed. J. O. Forfar and G. C. Arneil). Churchill Livingstone, Edinburgh.

TEILHARD DE CHARDIN, P. (1959). *The Phenomenon of Man*. Collins, London.

TELEKI, G. (1973). *The Predatory Behavior of Wild Chimpanzees*. Bucknell University Press, Lewisburg.

THOMAS, A., CHESS, S. and BIRCH, H. G. (1968). *Temperament and Behavior Disorders in Childhood*. New York University Press, New York.

TIGER, L. (1969). *Men in Groups*. Random House, New York.
—— and Fox, R. (1972). *The Imperial Animal*. Secker and Warburg, London.
TIMPANARO, S. (1974). Considerations on materialism. *New Left Review* **85**, 3–22.
TINBERGEN, N. (1951). *The Study of Instinct*. Clarendon Press, Oxford.
—— (1972). Functional ethology and the human sciences. *Proc. R. Soc. Lond.* **B 182**, 385–410.
—— (1974). Ethology and stress diseases. *Science, N.Y.* **185**, 20–7.
TISSERAND-PERRIER, M. (1953). Étude comparative de certains processus de croissance chez les jumeaux. *J. Genet. Hum.* **2**, 87–102.
TOBACH, E., ARONSON, L. R. and SHAW, E. (ed.) (1971). *The Biopsychology of Development*. Academic Press, New York.
TUTIN, C. E. G. (1974). Exceptions to promiscuity in a feral chimpanzee community. Paper read at *5th Congress of the International Primatological Society*, Nagoya.

UEXKÜLL, J. von (1934). *Streifzüge durch die Umwelten von Tieren und Menschen*. Springer, Berlin. (English translation in C. H. Schiller (ed.) (1957). *Instinctive Behavior*. International University Press, New York.)

VIAUD, G. (1960). *Intelligence, its Evolution and Forms*. Hutchinson, London.
VIRGO, H. B. and WATERHOUSE, M. J. (1969). The emergence of attention structure amongst rhesus macaques. *Man* **4**, (1), 85–93.

WADDINGTON, C. H. (1960). *The Ethical Animal*. Allen and Unwin, London.
WEBER, M. (1947). *The Theory of Social and Economic Organization*. (Transl. A. M. Henderson and Talcott Parsons, from *Wirtschaft und Gesellschaft* (2nd edn. 1925).) Free Press, London.
WILLIAMS, R. J. (1956). *Biochemical Individuality*. John Wiley, New York.
WINDLE, W. F. (1971). Origin and early development of neural elements in the human brain. In *The Biopsychology of Development* (ed. E. Tobach, L. R. Aronson and E. Shaw). Academic Press, New York.
WOFINDEN, R. C. and SMALLWOOD, A. L. (1958). Annual report of the Principal School Medical Officer to City and County Education Committee, Bristol.
WOLFF, C. T., HOFER, M. A. and MASON, J. W. (1964). Relationship between psychological defenses and mean urinary 17-OHCS excretion rates. *Psychosom. Med.* **26**, 576–91 and 592–609.
WOLFF, P. H. (1969). The natural history of crying and other vocalisations in early infancy. In *Determinants of Infant Behaviour* (ed. B. M. Foss), Vol. 4. Methuen, London.
WRIGHT, R. V. S. (1972). Imitative learning of a flaked stone technology—the case of an orangutan. *Mankind* **8**, (4), 296–306.

YOUNG, J. Z. (1971). *An Introduction to the Study of Man*. Clarendon Press, Oxford.
YOUNG, R. M. (1971). Evolutionary biology and ideology: then and now. In *The Social Impact of Modern Biology* (ed. W. Fuller). Routledge and Kegan Paul, London.
—— (1974). The human limits of nature. In *The Limits of Human Nature* (ed. J. Benthall). Dutton, New York.
YOUNG, W. C., GOY, R. W. and PHOENIX, C. H. (1964). Hormones and sexual behavior. *Science, N.Y.* **143**, (3603), 212–18.

ZUCKERMAN, S. (1932). *The Social Life of Monkeys and Apes*. Kegan Paul, London.

Name Index

Subject Index